HITLER'S BLITZKRIEG CAMPAIGNS

HITLER'S BLITZKRIEG CAMPAIGNS

The Invasion and Defense of Western Europe, 1939-1940

J.E. and H.W. Kaufmann

COMBINED BOOKS
Pennsylvania

PUBLISHER'S NOTE

Combined Books, Inc., is dedicated to publishing books of distinction in history and military history. We are proud of the quality of writing and the quantity of information found in our books. Our books are manufactured with style and durability and are printed on acid-free paper. We like to think of our books as soldiers: not infantry grunts, but well dressed and well equipped avant garde. Our logo reflects our commitment to the modern and yet historic art of book-making.

We would like to hear from our readers and invite you to write to us at our offices in Pennsylvania with your reactions, queries, comments, even complaints.

We encourage all of our readers to purchase our books from their local booksellers, and we hope that you let us know of booksellers in your area that might be interested in carrying our books. If you are unable to find a book in your area, please write to us.

For information, address:
COMBINED BOOKS, INC.
151 East 10th Avenue
Conshohocken, PA 19428

ISBN 0-938289-15-2

First published in the USA in 1993 by Combined Books,Inc. and distributed in North America by Stackpole Books, Inc., 5067 Ritter Road, Mechanicsburg, PA 17055; and internationally by Greenhill Books, Lionel Leventhal Ltd., 1 Russell Gardens, London NW11 9NN

Printed in the U.S.A.

Contents

To our Parents and Cyrus

Acknowledgments

We would like to thank the following companies and individuals: N. Flayderman & Co. for use of material from Major J. Hicks book *French Military Weapons*, George R. Bradford for the use of drawings from his booklet *Armoured Vehicles*, and *Popular Science* for permission to use material from their article "Underground Fortresses Guard France from Invasion" (1936 Times Mirror Magazines, inc.).

Also, the following individuals provided much help. William Allcorn (U.S.—information on fortifications and sources), Dr. William Atwater (Director/Curator of US Army Ordnance Museum—information on armored vehicles), M. Bernard (France—information on the Abri of Zeitzerholz), M. Beckers (Belgian Army at Liege—providing plans of and helping us get permission to visit the Eben Emael), Jean Louis Burtscher and son (France—information on Ouvrage de Schoenenbourg and Rhine Defenses), Colonel Chevalier (Génie of Strasbourg—information on Maginot Line), Ulrich A. Clausen (Germany—information on Danish armor and the campaign), E. Däschele and C. Frhle (Germany - information on Germany's "Gibraltar"), Rose E.B. Coombs (Imperial War Museum), Lt. Colonel Couvin (Génie of Grenoble—information on the Maginot Line), Georges Dropsy (French—his experiences in the Maginot Line), Dale Floyd (U.S.—information on Czech military), Captain Lievin Georges (Génie of Metz—information on Maginot Line), Col. C.I. Gils (Belgium—information on Belgian defensive positions), J.R. Hackett (England—information on Danish armor), Joseph de Hasque (Belgium—information on AT ditch of Antwerp and fortifications), Mayor Raoul Heymes (France—material on Ouvrage de Hackenberg), Dr. Machiel Kiel (Netherlands—information on new Dutch defensive positions), Colonel Lemoine (Génie of Lyon—material on Maginot Line), Louis Levaux (Belgium—commander of Fort Pontisse in 1940—information on defenses of Liege), Michale Luke (U.S.—material on Norway), Georges Maistret (France—information in Ouvrage de Fermont) Geoffroy Marcel (Génie of Metz—material on Maginot Line), Y.V. Mary (France—information on Maginot Line), Raymond Mersch (French—information on Immerhof), Paul Middleton (England — information on Danish and Norwegian armor), Lt. Colonel T. Ostrowski (Polish Cavalry—his account of the Polish Campaign), Andre Paquin (French—his experiences in the Maginot Line), Günther Reiss (Switzerland—information on Swiss fortifications and Switzerland during war), Lt. Commander Charlie Robbins (documents on the Low Countries), Ronald Tarnstrom (U.S.—Orders of Battle), Colonel Thuillier (Génie of Grenoble—material on Little Maginot Line) Lt. Colonel Ph. Truttmann (French Génie and Archives—information of Maginot Line), Colonel Viennot (Génie of Metz—information on the Maginot Line), Bernard Wahl (France—Ouvrage of Schoenenbourg and Rhine Defenses), M.J. Willis (Imperial War Museum), and Steven Zaloga (U.S.—information on armor).

We would also like to thank the following organizations for their help: The Fortress Study Group, Association des Ais l'Ouvrage de Fermont et de la Ligne Maginot, Amifort (Hackenberg, Immerhof and Zeiterholz) and the Association des Amis de la Ligne Maginot d'Alsace (Schoenenbourg).

We are grateful for the assistance provided by the staff of the National Archives Photographic and German Documents Sections as well as the staff at Aberdeen Proving Ground. In addition, valuable assistance was given by the civilian personnel operating the ouvrages of Fermont, Hackenberg, Immerhof, Schoenenbourg and St. Roch as well as the Génie of the Army at Metz and Army at Lyon and the Belgian military command at Liege.

We also would thank our capable guides who included Thierry Petitgenet at Fermont and Jean Paul Houder at Hackenberg, among others. A special thanks to Stuart Mandel. Finally, we are grateful to John Cannan and Robert Pigeon for making this project possible.

Introduction

The German Blitzkrieg against Poland, Denmark, Norway, the Low Countries and France from 1939-1940 has received scant attention compared to the titanic life and death struggle which raged between Germany and the U.S.S.R. the following year. Even the small-scale North African Campaign of 1941-42 has overshadowed the events that took place in Poland, Scandinavia and Western Europe during 1939 and 1940. Yet in less than one year Adolf Hitler launched his armies in one lightning assault after another which set the stage for the remainder of the war. As if following a single well conceived plan, the German military knocked out every enemy until it was in a position from which it could destroy or dominate the last surviving nations of the continent. This was Hitler's year of Blitzkrieg.

The course of World War I had ebbed and flowed on the Western Front two decades earlier, and in 1940 no one expected that front to play a less important role. Initially, not even Hitler or the German High Command expected to achieve a quick victory in the West. Hitler began his campaign of aggression by attempting to provoke Czechoslovakia into war. However, his war plans were foiled by foolish politicians who gave in too easily to his demands; Hitler did not get his war, but received the land he wanted. One year later, in August 1939, he prepared to strike at his next target: Poland.

This time the Allies resisted, but their strategy allowed Hitler the time to destroy Poland and send his armies racing to extend offensive operations to the Western Front. Unable to launch his planned offensive in the West in 1939, he was forced to wait several months. Meanwhile, as the preparations continued, the German dictator diverted his navy and a small part of his army to the north, eliminating two Scandinavian countries and isolating a third.

Although Hitler had sought only limited objectives in the West, his eventual offensive there became one of the most decisive events of World War II. In less than two months his troops scored an almost complete victory which came close to ending the conflict. As the year-long Blitzkrieg campaigns came to an end, only Great Britain survived as the sole bastion of resistance against Hitler's victorious forces.

Traditionally, the Western Campaign has been presented as a struggle between Great Britain and Germany, with the Dutch, Belgians and French playing marginal roles. Although the Dutch never constituted a critical factor, the Belgians, who had the opportunity to play a key role, became the weak link allowing a decisive German victory. The French armed forces, however, were in fact the chief players in this drama, while the British only played a secondary role on the land. Although the British RAF was more modern and effective than the French Air Force, it contributed only a limited number of units to the Continent. British naval supremacy also had a limited effect on the campaign until the evacuation of the British forces. The French, on the other hand, allowed the opportunity given them by the heroic Polish resistance to slip through their hands as they failed to strike against Germany in a timely fashion. Be it as it may, from 1939 through 1940, the French military had actually held the key to an Allied victory or defeat.

An examination of Germany and France, and her allies, reveals a campaign which turned into the Blitzkrieg due to late planning changes, but was nonetheless hard-fought. Even though the Germans and the French were almost equally matched in numbers and types of equipment, the Allies were plagued with poor, hesitant decision-making at the highest command echelons, coupled with bad luck.

CHAPTER I

Preparations for the
Next War

World War I was a conflict unprecedented in the armies mobilized, the weapons used and the massive carnage that saw almost whole generations of nations wiped out. The Allies slugged it out for years with the Germans. Grinding offensive followed grinding offensive, and the muddy battlefields of France ran with the blood of Tommies and poilus. By 1918 the Allies effectively used massed formations of tanks which smashed through the wire obstacles, breached the enemy trenches and broke the back of the German Army. The French also deployed massed air units over the battlefield, adding more power to their assaults. It was a type of warfare that had great implications for the future.

The Treaty of Versailles returned Europe to peace, but an uneasy one for passions still remained inflamed. Members of the victorious allies, primarily France, desired Germany to pay for its aggression and saw fit to insure that it would never become a threat again. Germany fumed from its defeat and the harsh terms of Versailles.

Out of these circumstances and the turmoil of the great depression rose to power Adolph Hitler. When he took total control of Germany in 1934, he furthered the process of rearming his nation to cast off the embarrassment of Versailles and make it the dominant power in Europe.

Adolf Hitler with one of his more distinguished generals, Gerd von Rundstedt.

Though the Great War as it was known was called "the war to end all wars," shortly after its conclusion practically all of the players began preparing for the next one. In between conflicts, both sides prepared new tactical doctrines, improved and developed new weapons and equipped their armies. Of all of the nations, only Germany developed a revolutionary style of warfare that was to lead to the total defeat of once powerful nations. Ironically, the weapons the Allies used to defeat Germany in World War I were used to defeat them during the Blitzkrieg campaign.

Germany Rearmed

The Treaty of Versailles, signed in 1919, established restrictions which became the seeds of future discontent, eventually leading to the establishment of the Third Reich. Germany felt robbed of its national territory, humiliated by unreasonable war reparations and resentful for being forced to take all the blame for causing the Great War. Under the terms of the treaty, Germany was not allowed to maintain an army of more than 100,000 men, and was denied the right to own any offensive weapons such as tanks, aircraft, heavy artillery and submarines.

During the early 1920s the German Army began to rearm under the leadership of General Hans von Seeckt, who sent officers abroad to gain experience and reestablish the forbidden General Staff. Seeckt emphasized training that created quality soldiers, a policy which remained in place until reversed in the 1930s when the emphasis shifted from quality to quantity.

In 1922 the Weimar government scored a great coup for the army with the Russo-German Pact. This agreement allowed the Germans to develop and train their men with weapons restricted by the treaty, such as tanks and aircraft. The German Army operated a center for gas warfare at Saratov, a flight center for pilots and aerial observers at Lipetsk and an armored school at Kazan in the Soviet Union. From 1922 until the summer of 1933 the German military trained and developed new techniques in this little corner of Russia and the seeds of a modern German Army germinated. In 1928 a five-year plan was proposed to increase the 10 division army to 16 divisions by 1933. It was not put into action. At this time French intelligence incorrectly concluded that the Germans had already broken the treaty and even suspected them of quadrupling their 100,000-man army. This report caused some concern since the French had difficulties in maintaining their own 100,000-man army at full strength.

Also in 1928, the Germans began to experiment with a weapon that would become the trademark of their future warfare, the tank. The first field exercises with panzer (armored) units took place in Germany in 1928, but at the time all the armored vehicles were large wood and canvas structures mounted on a tricycle-like wheel assembly pushed along by soldiers. Heinz Guderian, who later became Germany's leading tank expert, had his first experience with a tank as a result of an assignment with the Swedish Army. He then set up Germany's first tank company, although it only had dummy vehicles.

One of Hitler's masterful militaristic rallies which inflamed a nationalistic passion among Germans.

Political crisis came to Germany in 1932, with the devastating effects of the Great Depression. The National Socialist Party (Nazi) led by Adolph Hitler gained control of the German Reichstag. Although Hitler failed in his bid to unseat President Paul von Hindenburg, his private army, the SA (the Brown Shirts or Storm Detachments), with its 400,000 men remained a force to be reckoned with. General Kurt von Schleicher, Minister of Defense, was appointed Reich Chancellor and ultimately sought to crush the power of the Nazi party and the Brown Shirts with the support of General Freiherr Kurt von Hammerstein, the commander of the army, but their efforts were futile. Von Schleicher was forced out of office in January 1933 by the Nazis, and Hitler took his place. Hitler's appointment was due to Hindenburg's mistaken belief that he would also fail as chancellor. From this point on, the military, afraid of being supplanted by the SA, fell in line with the new political force of the Nazis.

Hitler handled the army very carefully and always tried to reaffirm its role as the only army of the Reich. On 30 June 1934, the "Night of the Long Knives" removed the leadership of the

Germany rearms! A military parade with armored cars in the lead.

SA, reducing it to no particular significance, while affirming the army's leadership. The new strong arm of the Nazi party, Hitler's bodyguard known as the SS, was formed into larger para-military unit with the promise that in time of war they would always be under the command of the army.

The new defense minister, General Werner von Blomberg, under the influence of the Nazis, effected some key changes giving the Nazis increased influence over the military. In February 1934, the armed forces' eagle with a swastika was adopted for military uniforms. In April, Blomberg authorized National Socialist indoctrination of the military and allowed the Gestapo (secret police) to infiltrate its ranks. Hitler took complete control of the government after Hindenberg's death on 2 August 1934 and required the military to take an oath of allegiance to him. No head of state since Frederick the Great ever held as much control over the German armed forces.

In March 1935 Hitler announced to the world that Germany would rearm. One year later, on 7 March 1936, he sent three battalions into the demilitarized Rhineland only as a bluff in defiance of the Versailles Treaty. The French hesitated, and he had his first victory. He took personal control of the *Wehrmacht* (the armed forces) in February 1938 and responsibility for directing offensive planning when he created *OKW* (Oberkommando der Wehrmacht or High Command of the Armed Forces). This created an internal conflict with the *OKH* (Oberkommando des Heeres or Army High Command) which in the past dictated military strategy. Hitler put his faith in his own military skills and intuition above all others, based largely on his military background as a corporal in the Great War.

One of Hitler first more aggressive acts was the forcible unification of Austria with Germany in February 1938, the first offensive of the German Army since 1918. Though the move took place with some embarrassing difficulties, it appeared as a triumph of German arms. Hitler then turned his sights on Czechoslovakia's Sudeten border which contained ethnic Germans. But Czechoslovakia did not appear to be an easy victim. Its Skoda works produced fine modern tanks and the country was protected by modern, though incomplete, fortifications. Still, surrounded by hostile countries, the Czechs would need foreign assistance to successfully resist German aggression. As Hitler geared up for a war to take the Sudetenland, German generals, fearful of the possible intervention of a great power, considered removing their leader. They need not have worried. At the Munich Conference, Britain and France got peace by urging the Czechs to give over territory to Germany. Hitler missed the war he wanted, but settled for aiding Francisco Franco's forces with troops and equipment during the Spanish Civil War of 1936-1939. With this combat experience and, more importantly, the development of new strategies, tactics and air and land weapons, Germany was ready for bigger game.

The Panzer Division

The greatest weapon in the Nazi arsenel was their progress in the use of tanks. Heinz Guderian developed an inovative theory for armored warfare and, though with much difficulty, convinced his superiors for the need of armored divisions. His

The Panzer I, a light tank mounting only machine guns, was one of the first tanks of the new German Army. Because of the terms of Versailles it was developed under the fiction of producing tractors.

plans, similar to British theorist B.H. Liddell, was to use a mobile force of tanks, artillery and infantry to break through enemy lines, get into rear areas and leave the forces at the front isolated. With Hitler's support, Guderian developed the panzer division, a combination of the elements needed for the role he envisioned for the force. Although Chief of the General Staff Ludwig Beck did not believe in Guderian's theories, he approved the creation of the panzer division and the first three were organized by October 1935. In 1936 three light divisions, with one tank battalion each, were formed to function in the role of cavalry. The Germans secretly developed tanks under the disguise of producing tractors in the late 1920s resulting in the design of the inexpensive Panzer I. A lightly armored tank, with two mounted machineguns and a two-man crew, it remained the mainstay of the armored force for many years. At the end of 1933 the first panzer unit went into operation and a year later received its first tanks, the new Panzer Is. In September 1939, almost one half of Germany's tanks were Panzer Is.

Mounting a 20mm gun, the Panzer II was faster and better armed than the Panzer I. It was obsolete by the 1940 campaign, however.

By 1937 a new tank went on line, which provided the panzer regiments with more muscle. Although twice the weight of the Panzer I, the Panzer II light tank came in several models and was faster and better armed. It also had twice the armor protection of the Panzer I, and a 20mm cannon with the anti-tank capacity the Panzer I lacked, though by 1939 it proved to have limited value. Almost one-third of the panzer arm consisted of Panzer II tanks when the war began. Both the Panzer I and II could not truly be considered equals to most French tanks.

In the mid-1930s production on the two types of tanks intended to replace the Panzer I and II types began, although the Germans were unable to produce these new machines in sufficient numbers in time for the war. The first of these, the Panzer III, was expected to make up 75 percent of an armored division's strength. This tank had almost as much armor as many of the French models and twice their speed. Before the

A camouflaged Panzer III. This was the first German tank with the armor and armament to take on the top of the line French tanks. It saw use in the early campaigns of World War II and North Africa.

war it was up gunned from a 37mm to a 50mm gun which made it more than a match for the majority of medium and heavy French armor that mounted 37mm and 47mm guns. It also carried an unusually large crew of five men. Few of the vehicles were in service in 1939, and by 1940 they represented only about 10 percent of all German tanks.

The Panzer IV, developed with the Panzer III, was intended to serve as the heavy tank of the panzer division and to make up 25 percent of its strength. The 75mm gun gave this tank its greatest advantage and allowed it to remain the mainstay of the German panzer force from 1941 until the end of the war. It

The mainstay of the German Army throughout World War II, the Panzer IV.

was faster, better armed and better protected than almost every type of French tank. However, too few of these tanks existed from the beginning of the war until the end of the campaign in the West, when they represented only 2 percent of Germany's armor.

This was the *Wehrmacht's* main striking arm to which may be added a significant number of Czech tanks acquired with the takeover of Czechoslovakia in 1939. The Allied armored forces basically outclassed the German panzer arm.

Although the Germans started late in the development of mechanized warfare, simply following theories and techniques developed by the French and British, the Spanish Civil War gave them an excellent testing ground for their new weapons and tactics. Tanks proved their ability to entrap enemy forces and served successfully in screening operations. Light tanks, such as the Panzer I, were found to be ineffective and were later replaced by models with more powerful guns and heavier armor. Anti-tank weapons also proved their worth. While other countries concluded that anti-tank weapons would leave tanks

When Britain and France sacrificed Czechoslovakia in 1938 to placate Hitler, Czech tanks like this Panzer 35 were used by the German Army. Allied soldiers would face such vehicles on the battlefields of Europe as a result of their leaders' refusal to stand up to the German dictator.

in supporting or defensive roles, the Germans were pioneering the offensive capabilities of both weapons.

In March 1938, the takeover of Austria gave the army a chance to test the effectiveness of panzer division's mobility. The German forces experienced a number of mechanical problems on the way to Vienna. Poor weather and road conditions served as an excuse, but within a few months the army had worked out problems which became apparent during this operation.

The resulting panzer tactics called for a rapid advance combining speed and concentration of force, with the infantry in a supporting role. Plans for armor in the offense called for the penetration of the enemy's line and the exploitation of the breakthrough by encircling and destroying the enemy. Reliance

Originally built as a German airliner, the three-engined JU-52 was used as a bomber and a troop transport during the war.

on air support and infiltration tactics for breaking through enemy lines became important factors. These new tactics resulted in lightning warfare: blitzkrieg. Relying on the use of panzer divisions and air power, blitzkrieg provided the *Wehrmacht* with victories which most French and German generals had thought unattainable. Still, by the time of the Czech Crisis, most of the German Army was still non-mechanized infantry and remained dependent on horse power.

The *Luftwaffe*

The German Air Force, the *Luftwaffe*, owed its birth to the work of General von Seeckt whose collaboration with the Soviets made it possible for German pilots to train in Soviet Russia in the 1920s. Although the number of these pilots was necessarily limited, almost every high ranking officer in the future *Luftwaffe* went through this experience.

During the 1920s the German government created Lufthansa, a national airline, and through it many pilots re-

Messerschmitt ME 109s during the war. This was the principal fighter used by the **Luftwaffe** *during the blitzkrieg campaigns.*

ceived their training. The military took the outstanding JU 52, Lufthansa's main commercial aircraft, and later converted it into a bomber. Erhard Milch took part in the development of the airline and its coordination with the military through the offices of Hermann Göring. Göring, the former World War I fighter pilot and in the 1930s a high ranking Nazi in political office, created the *Luftwaffe* in March 1935 while General Milch directed its development in the 1930s.

During the 1930s many future pilots received their basic flying skills in glider clubs throughout Germany. In 1934, a year before the creation of the *Luftwaffe*, German industry turned out its first military aircraft. In March 1936 final trials took place for several aircraft which formed the nucleus of the air force throughout World War II. They included one of the best fighters of the first years of the war, the ME 109 as well as the best known aircraft of blitzkrieg warfare, the JU 87 Stuka (Sturzkampf or dive bomber). Tests also took place on the twin-engine ME 110 fighter and the DO 17 and HE 111 medium bombers and the JU 88 which eventually became Germany's main medium bomber of the war.

A Messerschmitt 110 in flight. The 110 was meant to be a strategic fighter, but it was a flat failure when it encountered superior British planes like the Spitfire.

From 1936 until 1939 the Spanish Civil War served as a testing ground for the new air arm. The air units constituted the largest element of Germany's *Condor Legion* in Spain. Not all the conclusions drawn by German air commanders from their experiences in Spain were as valuable as those concerning ground support tactics. The *Luftwaffe* emphasized ground support operations, neglecting strategic bombing for which neither effective doctrine nor sufficient aircraft existed. The conditions in Spain made it possible for fast twin-engine medium bombers to penetrate enemy air space, causing air planners to believe that this type of bomber would be sufficient for all the needs of a future war. Thus, the development of a long

The Heinkel 111 medium bomber served successfully in the Spanish Civil War and during the blitzkrieg campaigns. It also saw action during the Battle of Britain where most German planes of its kind proved poor for strategic bombing.

range four-engine bomber force was neglected. While this did not hinder the conquest of France, it did prevent the *Luftwaffe* from defeating Great Britain. The propagandists, who as early as 1938 boasted that the *Luftwaffe* would destroy its enemies through mass bombing, did not realize that this was one operation that it could not undertake. Unfortunately, most of the nations of Western Europe believed these claims right up to the spring of 1940.

In 1936, the *Luftwaffe*, with the few aircraft it had available, covered the occupation of the Rhineland through the use of skillful deception, convincing the French that it was much larger than it actually was. This included having aircraft overfly the region more than once with different identification markings painted on for each trip. In 1938, as the army rolled into Austria, the *Luftwaffe* deployed 400 aircraft, including 160 troop carriers which landed three battalions in Vienna. After the takeover the Austrian aircraft industry was used to increase

A fast bomber that assumed several different roles during the war, the Junkers 88 was a level bomber, a dive bomber and a reconnaissance aircraft.

production of ME 109 while Austrian pilots became part of the German air arm.

One year later the air force landed assault troops in Prague during the occupation of Czechoslovakia. Although previously unnoticed, the *Luftwaffe's* airborne infantry of the new *7th Air Division* soon played a decisive role in the campaign of 1940.

In March 1938 the *Luftwaffe* comprised 2,900 first line aircraft and grew to 3,750 by August 1939. German industry, like the French, had difficulties keeping up with demand. Forty percent of the air force consisted of bombers and dive bombers and only 25 percent to 30 percent of fighter aircraft. The air defense of the Reich played a secondary role to close support operations and to the destruction of the enemy in the field and of his support facilities. A large number of aircraft had a reconnaissance mission. The last major element of German air doctrine was the element of surprise in order to gain air superiority over the battlefield. German doctrine was quite effective providing the war remained a short one, a blitzkrieg.

Part of the West Wall's continuous line of "dragons teeth" tank obstacles.

The West Wall

The Western press called a series of fortifications protecting Germany's Western frontier the Siegfried Line, but it was more correctly termed the West Wall. In 1936 Hitler's gamble paid off in the remilitarization of the Rhineland, so the army set to work on construction of a massive defensive line from Switzerland to the Netherlands. Most German generals, thinking along the same lines as their French counterparts, believed that it was imperative to defend the Reich's borders in case of war, and that offensive action must be avoided.

The Führer had no problem with this point of view because it sealed off one frontier while he would be free to expand across another; however, the work of the army was too slow, so Fritz Todt took over the task with his labor force, *Organization Todt*. In less than two years he created a line of fortifications which were quite modern in concept, based on defense in depth. Todt created a continuous anti-tank barrier of "Dragon's Teeth" and over 20,000 fortified positions. The bunker served as the main type of position, but seldom housed more than a machinegun or 37mm anti-tank gun and were not designed to accept larger weapons. Numerous bunkers were deployed in depth with interlocking fields of fire. The line consisted of belts of defenses with depths up to five kilometers and vast defensive minefields consisting mainly of anti-personnel mines covered by bunkers gave the line its real strength. The West Wall was to be divided into an army zone and an air defense zone and the latter was to include positions for anti-aircraft guns. However, little or no work was ever done on the air zone.

While the German army struck Poland in 1939, the still incomplete West Wall served as a bulwark against French reaction, although the German generals did not believe it was sufficiently manned to achieve this. The strength of the line lay primarily in the propaganda concerning it.

France During the Inter-war Period

If asked what the French Army would do in the event of war, the French commander in chief in 1914 would reply: "Attack, Attack, Attack!" This offensive spirit seems to have disappeared in 1940 and with it the *esprit de corps* of the previous war. When World War II began, France did not face a German war machine which completely outclassed its own. Thus, the usual explanation for the spectacular ease with which the Nazis triumphed over the West in 1940 has been unrealistically oversimplified.

France's reactions in World War II were influenced by her successes and failures in the previous war. In 1914, the fortifications covering the French frontier were formidable, yet with the advent of the war the troops quickly abandoned them to launch an attack on Germany, in an attempt to regain the lost territories of Alsace and Lorraine. Meanwhile the Kaiser's *Imperial Army* undertook an attack known as the Schlieffen Plan, an attack through Belgium, finding the French totally unprepared for this offensive. Following World War I, France did everything possible to keep Germany weak, insisting upon three enfeebling provisions of the Treaty of Versailles. First, the German war machine was required to observe numerous restrictions on men and weapons. Second, the Germans had to demilitarize the Rhineland and allow a 15-year Allied occupa-

German heavy gun position in the West Wall.

tion. Finally, Germany had to pay for all the damages inflicted upon the Allies, especially France. But even as the ink dried on the treaty, many top ranking French officers felt this would not be enough to stop the rebirth of the German juggernaut.

During the 1920s French military plans centered around the occupation of the Rhineland and its use as a base for an offensive action which would quickly shut down the heartland of German industrial production. When the Germans fell far behind on reparation payments in 1923, French and Belgian troops marched into the industrial center of the Ruhr causing German production to come to a halt. The Weimar Republic's economy took a rapid downward spiral.

Soon the French High Command perceived problems on the horizon, suspecting German remilitarization even before the 1920s had come to a close. Worse still, the French Army faced two new threats to its offensive designs. First was the planned early withdrawal from the Rhineland in 1930. This meant that the Germans would be able to reach the Rhine and protect their main industrial region before the French could launch an offensive. Even more devastating to offensive operations was the

French troops, or **Poilus,** *on the march. Soldiers such as these would be hard pressed during the blitzkrieg attack on their country.*

introduction of one-year conscription. Although both the French and Germans had suffered heavy casualties in the Great War, the latter were able to recover numerical losses much more quickly than the French, mainly because they had a much larger population. France, on the other hand, had lost almost a whole generation of young men. To placate a tired and war weary people, military service was reduced from 3 years to 18 months, leaving conscripts with barely enough time to learn military skills before returning to civilian life. A single year was not enough to train a soldier and prepare him for the complexities of modern warfare. Furthermore, while the government mandated a 100,000-man army, this number was never achieved since it was impossible to retain enough career soldiers. In the 1920s the military became an unattractive occupation, as some officers had to work second jobs just to make a living, and promotions were a rare event.

While the French war machine was breaking down, plans had to be made to safeguard France's borders in the future. As a result the high command and the government agreed on the need for new border fortifications. These were first intended to function as a covering screen, to allow France to mobilize and prepare an army for future offensive operations. However, after the fortifications, known as the Maginot Line, were largely completed, all plans for an offensive against Germany were considered with a great deal of skepticism.

The Maginot Line

Years of discussion and indecision within the French military and government finally led to the construction of the famous Maginot Line. The French offensive of 1914 which bogged down on the German frontier fortifications, the bloody battle of Verdun of 1916 which raged around that city's major forts and the use of trenches all along the Western Front had a profound influence on French military and government officials. As a result, they decided that fortifications were vital to France's security even though new weapons had rendered the traditional strongholds obsolete. Only the creation of counter-measures against these inventions was necessary, leaving the basic military tactics employed during World War I still valid.

A special committee, the Commission for the Defense of Territories, emerged from the minister of war's office in 1922 to propose a new defensive policy. Marshal Philippe Pétain, the hero of Verdun, suggested light defenses in depth which would create a continuous front. Marshal Joseph Joffre, on the other hand, believed that France should rely on strong fortified regions similar to those of the pre-war fortress rings. The debate continued through the mid-1920s with Joffre's supporters eventually winning out, thanks largely to the success of the Verdun forts and the ability of the French Army to break the thin continuous lines of German defenses in 1918.

In December 1925, General Guillaumat headed a new committee, the Commission for Defense of the Frontiers, which proposed plans similar to Joffre's and submitted them to the War Ministry in 1926. The minister of war, Paul Painlevé, accepted the proposals for three fortified regions in the Northeast and five smaller defense zones in the Southeast. The

Avante Poste *in the Maginot Line.*

government approved the creation of fortified regions, and the work began under Painlevé's successor, André Maginot, at the end of 1929. The plans called for creating heavily fortified regions covering vital areas; other regions would be lightly protected, if time and finances permitted. The two strongest regions were more commonly known as the Maginot Line. No major construction was ever undertaken in the third fortified region which covered the Belfort Gap and faced the Swiss border.

The Maginot Line did not consist of a solid line of defenses running along the Rhine River to the southern border of Belgium as commonly depicted on maps, but rather two fortified regions: the RF (Region Fortifeé) of Metz and the RF of the Lauter. These fortifications were originally designed to hold back the Germans while the army mobilized and prepared for offensive operations. A gap existed between the two areas known as the Sarre (Saar) Gap, through which the Germans had penetrated in the 1870 campaign of the Franco-Prussian War. Because this low lying region was considered unsuitable for the construction of massive subterranean fortifications, the

Block 5 of Rochonvillers. This was the largest of all the combat blocks of the Maginot Line Proper mounting one 135 mm howitzer and three 75mm guns. Photo by William Allcorn.

French planned to use the many ponds and marshes in conjunction with a series of dams to flood the area in the event of an enemy attack. In addition, the French Army was to use this area as a springboard for an offensive into the Rhineland with the RFs on either side securing the flanks. Thus, the planners of the Maginot Line had designed it to take part in both the defensive and offensive operations.

A series of lighter defenses ran along the Rhine River where France and Germany shared a common border. Many historians have included the Rhine defenses with the Maginot Line, although they were never truly part of it. These positions included no forts, which were the hallmark of the line, and relied heavily upon the barrier of the river. In addition, the military added the Maginot Extension later in the 1930s, to extend the Maginot Line from the vicinity of Longuyon to the town of Villy south of Sedan. This section included four modern forts which were not designed to function as effectively as those of the two RFs.

Block 3 at the small ouvrage of Rohrbach. View from the rear showing flanking embrasures for infantry weapons and a GFM cloche at the right. On the top is a machine gun turret in the eclipsed position.

Aerial view of the **ouvrage** *of Hackenberg. This shows its eastern cluster of combat blocks.*

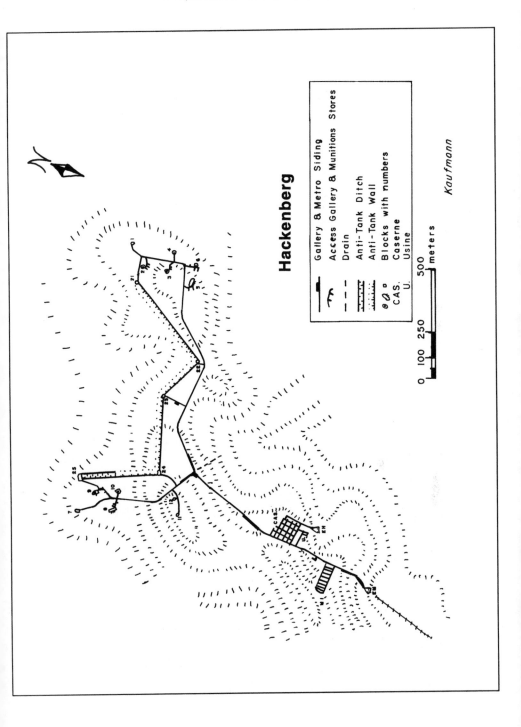

Hackenberg

Gallery & Metro Siding
Access Gallery & Munitions Stores
Drain
Anti-Tank Ditch
Anti-Tank Wall
Blocks with numbers
CAS. Caserne
U. Usine

0 100 250 500 meters

Kaufmann

Anti-tank ditch and wall of Hackenberg. This ditch linked the eastern and western cluster of the ouvrage's combat blocks.

The Maginot Line Proper included over 40 subterranean forts called ouvrages and numerous specially designed interval casemates, as well as many smaller defensive positions. The ouvrages belonged to two basic categories (although there were also sub-categories): small or petit (PO), and large or gros (GO). The PO combat blocks mounted mainly light infantry-

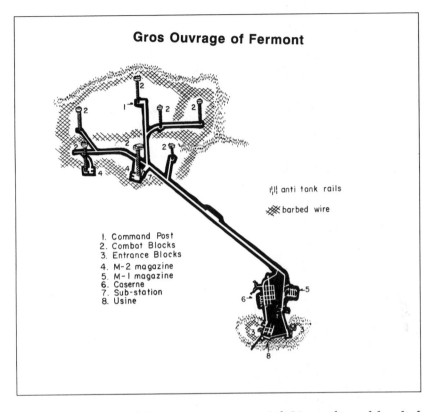

Gros Ouvrage of Fermont

I,I¦ anti tank rails

barbed wire

1. Command Post
2. Combat Blocks
3. Entrance Blocks
4. M-2 magazine
5. M-1 magazine
6. Caserne
7. Sub-station
8. Usine

type weapons and in some cases special 81mm breechloaded mortars. Some consisted of several combat blocks, although, in a few instances, they were made of a single monolithic block. The more massive GOs usually included six or more combat blocks and carried the only real artillery weapons. These larger ouvrages were also called artillery ouvrages, although the assortment of weapons they mounted included nothing more than 81mm mortars, 135mm bomb throwers (something between a mortar and a howitzer) and 75mm guns. There were no heavier caliber guns primarily because the forts were not designed for long range artillery duels, but to take an active part in close combat operations. Some of these weapons were turret-mounted while most occupied casemate positions and fired only to the flank or rear and not to the front.

No two ouvrages were identical. The GOs normally included two entrance blocks located about a kilometer behind the combat blocks, while the POs customarily used one or more of

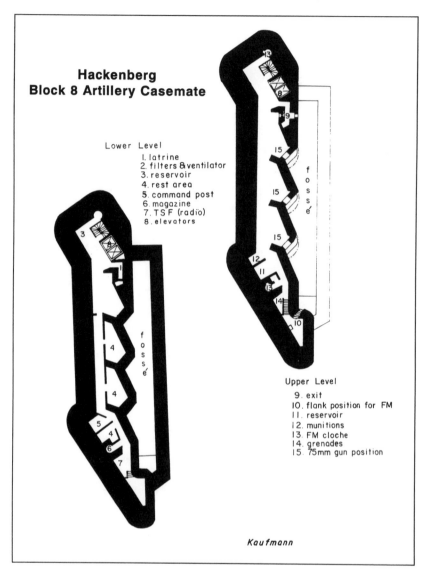

**Hackenberg
Block 8 Artillery Casemate**

Lower Level
1. latrine
2. filters & ventilator
3. reservoir
4. rest area
5. command post
6. magazine
7. TSF (radio)
8. elevators

Upper Level
9. exit
10. flank position for FM
11. reservoir
12. munitions
13. FM cloche
14. grenades
15. 75mm gun position

Kaufmann

their combat blocks as an entrance. Near the entrance blocks in the large forts lay the subterranean garrison area (caserne) as well as the main magazine (M-1) and the power plant (usine). Most of these forts maintained a garrison of 500 to 1,000 men. The facilities in the caserne could not hold the entire crew at one time, so a number of troops had to man the combat blocks, which also had some facilities. The men rotated in three shifts similar to those of a ship's crew.

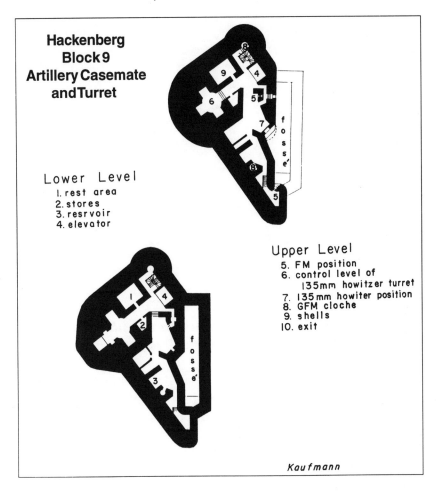

Hackenberg
Block 9
Artillery Casemate
and Turret

Lower Level
1. rest area
2. stores
3. resrvoir
4. elevator

Upper Level
5. FM position
6. control level of
    135mm howitzer turret
7. 135mm howiter position
8. GFM cloche
9. shells
10. exit

Kaufmann

A single gallery led from the support facilities to the access galleries that led to the combat blocks. In many cases a small train, known as the metro, served a fort. Special devices were designed for each of the blocks and sections of the fort, including the main gallery, for defending the interior. Filters and other special equipment protected the blocks and the caserne from poison gas and each ouvrage had all the facilities necessary to operate independently for extended periods of time.

The Maginot Line Proper consisted of a forward position near the border, including light fortifications designed to give warning and delay the enemy while the main line was several kilometers back. The enemy could not pass through the main position without destroying the ouvrages which dominated

Block 1 at the small ouvrage of Lembach. Its AT rails, which were flanked by its 47mm anti-tank gun, are still in place.

key routes. Each ouvrage could withstand bombardment from 420mm shells, and each fort had fire plans for bombarding its neighbor to drive off enemy troops. The casemates and smaller positions between the ouvrages were vulnerable and depended upon support from the nearby forts as well as the interval troops which defended the region. The Maginot Line, by World War I standards, was a major barrier and not a proper target for modern armored columns.

By 1935 most of the Maginot Line Proper was completed. The French became more defensive as they lost faith in their own ability to deal with a resurgent Germany. After the minister of war, Edouard Daladier, and General Maurice Gamelin the 62 year old chief of the General Staff visited France's defensive wall in 1934, they recommended an extension of the fortifications to close gaps and secure the left flank. As a result, the government appropriated more money to extend the fortifications and to turn the Maginot Line Proper into a solid, continuous obstacle. The politicians even authorized the creation of stronger defenses to protect the Belgian frontier, against the

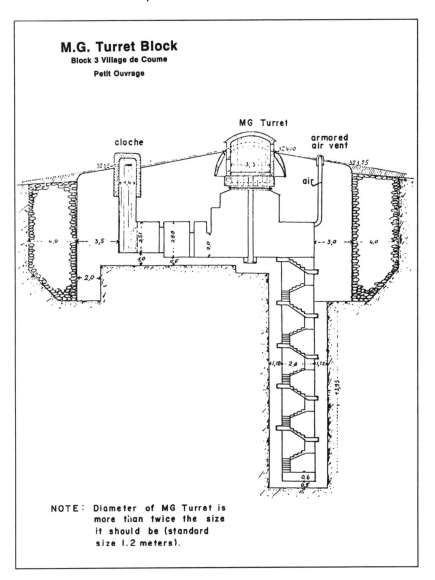

M.G. Turret Block
Block 3 Village de Coume
Petit Ouvrage

NOTE: Diameter of MG Turret is more than twice the size it should be (standard size 1.2 meters).

wishes of the army which wanted the funds to strengthen the field army.

The Commission d'Organisation des Régions Fortifiées (CORF), created in 1927, designed and oversaw the construction of the Maginot fortifications. These included plans not only for the ouvrages, but also for the casemates and smaller works until 1935. The French military never seriously attempted to complete a continuous heavily fortified line from

Artillery casemate (Block 4) and infantry casemate (Block 7) of Fermont. The three 75mm guns covered the right flank and infantry block on the right and with its 47mm anti-tank gun protected Block 4 from ground assault.

the Rhine to the North Sea, although CORF-type fortifications dotted the region, partly to placate the politicians.

Because Pétain himself had declared the region of the Ardennes impassable to a modern mechanized army, this sector of the Belgian border, with its rugged terrain, was lightly protected. Along the border with Belgium, north of this region, the French engineers converted a few old forts into POs and constructed a number of CORF works, but they erected no major works for two reasons. First, the French did not want the Belgians, who had been their allies until 1935, to feel shut out. In addition, most high ranking officers, including Pétain and Gamelin, insisted that the French Army must move into Belgium in any future war. Second, and most decisively, the low lying terrain and the close proximity of the industrial complex of Lille to the border precluded any attempt to build extensive subterranean fortifications.

Further south, along the Franco-Italian border, the French government authorized the construction of the Little Maginot Line, which included scattered sectors with ouvrages defending Alpine passes as well as a more continuous section in the

Maritime Alps which had its last fort right on the Mediterranean. The defenses of the Maritime Alps were similar to those of either of the RFs of the Maginot Line Proper. The Alpine sectors contained almost as many ouvrages as the Maginot Line Proper, but its POs were very different and mounted fewer weapons. The combat blocks of the GOs were more closely grouped by the entrance blocks. Some of the guns in casemates actually faced the direction of the enemy instead of the flanks and were protected by a heavier concrete and armor shield. With smaller garrisons and fewer combat blocks, these ouvrages still had firepower similar to those of the Maginot Line Proper, and many of their combat blocks were larger than those of the main line since they mounted combinations of artillery weapons instead of only two to three weapons of one type. Unfortunately, the French Army was not able to complete the construction of the Alpine forts because the legislature funneled most of the credits towards the northern front where it perceived the greater need.

The French Army

In the late 1920s the shrinking French field army still maintained an offensive role. At the beginning of the 1930s, the French Army continued to shrink, recruitment fell and funding declined due to the depression, though work continued on the Maginot Line.

No significant new developments took place in tactics. Most of the higher ranking officers and decision making staff were World War I veterans who seemed ready to refight the last war rather than change with the times. Nonetheless, within military circles there were dynamic thinkers who were leading the way toward modern mechanized warfare. Unfortunately, a great deal of indecision and consternation prevailing among those in power held back doctrinal development. As one government after another fell, the ever changing war ministers hindered the development of an effective military doctrine. The Superior War Council, which included France's highest ranking officers and the minister of war, and was responsible for most of the

A French armored car of a mechanized light division (DLM).

major decisions concerning military matters, was more stable though lacking inspiring leadership.

Although many critics of the period claim that the French High Command was stagnating and indecisive between the wars, this was not the case. For instance, the ideas of General Jean Estienne concerning the development of tanks, which held no favor in the early 1920s, gained popularity by the 1930s. General Maxime Weygand, the army chief of staff in the early 1930s, followed up on Colonel Joseph Doumenc's ideas from the 1920s for the formation of armored divisions. In 1930 he ordered the creation of the world's first armored division, the division légère mécanique (DLM or light mechanized division) which was ready by 1933. Weygand expected these new formations to replace the cavalry.

The first DLM was a balanced combined-arms force, and both General Weygand and General Gamelin, his deputy and future replacement, approved the conversion of cavalry divisions into DLMs. However, these new units remained subordinate to the infantry, and little changed even when the doctrine

A French Char B1 Tank.

for large combat units of 1921 was revised in 1936. The French armored division could field only half the vehicles of its enemy counterpart, the German panzer division. When the war began, the French had more tanks, but fewer armored divisions than their opponent because they allotted many armored vehicles to independent tank battalions (infantry support units) rather than armored divisions. Most French vehicles in these units were equal to, or better than, the German ones, especially the B-1's and SOMUAs.

By 1935, military threats to France were becoming increasingly serious. The Italian invasion of Abyssinia in 1935 had led the League of Nations to take ineffective actions against the aggressive state, although it was enough to irritate the Duce. As a result, a diplomatic realignment of Italy took place in 1936

The SOMUA 35 was one of the better tanks of the early war period. Mounting a high velocity 47mm gun and heavily armored, it was a match for the best German tanks.

creating another problem for the French. Mussolini's expansionist policies in the Mediterranean in the 1920s had triggered the construction of fortifications in the Alpine sectors facing Italy. When Mussolini stopped Hitler's takeover of Austria in 1934, it had seemed that Italy might act as a bulwark against Nazi aggression. However, this turned out to be a short-lived hope as Mussolini created the Axis Pact after the West condemned his aggression in Abyssinia in 1935-36. As a result, the French planners felt compelled to divert more funds to the protection of their frontier with Italy.

On 7 March 1936, Hitler took advantage of the unstable political situation in France, fostered by up-coming elections, to occupy the Rhineland. German troops advanced into the Rhineland with orders to withdraw if the French approached. The French Army was unable to respond. The DLM moved to the frontier and other units occupied the Maginot Line, but the government ordered no offensive into the Rhineland. Hitler's

The Renault R-35 mounted a 35mm gun and was run by a two-man crew.

bluff worked; the Germans tricked French intelligence into believing that their small occupation force was actually an army. French military intelligence continued to grossly overestimate the enemy until 1940, and the results proved disastrous.

In 1936, as war loomed, time was running out for the French. They increased the size of their army, extended the length of service and ordered new weapons. Unfortunately, French industry could not keep up with the demand, and the issue of tactics was still unresolved. Colonel Charles de Gaulle, supported by the politician Paul Reynaud, called for an independent mechanized striking force. Unfortunately, as in the case of Estienne, much earlier, the government and military rejected his proposals. Not before the spring of 1940 were three heavy armored divisions, divisions cuirassée de réserve, (DCRs or heavy armored divisions of the reserve) ready, with three DLMs. The role of these units turned out to be not so much offensive as defensive, which diminished their real value.

French Renault UE 31 tankettes. The Germans learned in Spain and Poland what other countries found out later, that small armored vehicles such as this one were of limited value on the battlefield.

The tactical role worked out for French armored divisions by 1939 was slightly ambiguous. The overall plan for the French Army was predicated upon defense, even during an advance, and upon waiting for the enemy to attack. French doctrine called for defense in depth, and the new mechanized units offered a great deal of flexibility for this mission. The tank units were to help break up an enemy assault and, when the time was right and the troops had gained experience, take the offensive. The armored divisions on the attack would act as a breakthrough force, then adopt a mission of exploitation. The military planners did not design the new DCRs to operate alone, but in conjunction with DLMs which had reconnaissance units and other forces to provide support.

Although the output of French industry was low, and new equipment was delivered to the military very slowly, the French Army was not totally devoid of materiel in 1939. Their artillery, a large amount dating from World War I, outnum-

French troops operating a 75mm artillery piece.

bered that of the Germans when the war began, ranging in size from large caliber railway guns to 37mm anti-tank guns and machineguns. In the 1930s the French Army ordered new 105mm guns, as well as new 47mm anti-tank guns. In the Maginot fortifications, the army engineers redesigned those blocks which were still incomplete to accept the new anti-tank gun. New machineguns began to appear, especially the very reliable automatic rifle FM 1924/29, and the military attempted to create more effective anti-aircraft weapons, one of which was the 90mm gun, an equal to the German "88."

While many of the new French tanks such as the SOMUA and Char B proved superior to the German, some had drawbacks. Larger French tanks had one-man turrets that impaired their effectiveness, since the tank commander was his own gunner and loader, unlike his German counterpart. There was also a large number of inferior light tanks which remained in use. Such weapons were no less adequate than those of the Germans, which were also employed in large numbers. Although there wasn't enough time for the military to fully

Heavy guns. These two French 340mm railway guns had a range of 44,400 meters.

modernize and obtain the updated weapons by 1939, much of the French equipment proved to be equal and even superior to the Germans, but French tactical doctrine proved to be inadequate for the new type of warfare. French tactical ideas on defense in depth, the use of armored and air units to achieve breakthroughs and mobile units for exploitation were moving along the same lines as those of the Germans. Nevertheless, French theory concerning all combat arms lagged behind the Germans; many field units remained inadequately structured and the French High Command was unwilling to remove the infantry from its dominance.

On the other hand, in the late 1930s reforms resulted in improved morale and efficiency among the troops in the active army. The government increased the number of colonial troops in 1938 to build up the army. Some of the active units serving in the Maginot Line rotated into field units of reservists to raise their morale during the winter of 1939. Reservists exhibited average skills and performance in most cases. There were two types of reserve divisions: Categories A and B. The latter contained older reservists who had only served one year of active duty and very few Regular officers, which drastically reduced their effectiveness. Unfortunately, some of the B divi-

Maryland bombers were purchased from the U.S. along with C-75 fighters to make up for the lag in production by France's aviation industry.

sions were assigned to an area opposite the Belgian Ardennes, which turned out to be the critical sector of the campaign.

The French Air Force

The French Armée de l'Air was created in the late 1920s. While France had the largest air force in the world at the end of World War I, it took the French High Command 10 years to decide to rebuild it. By the early 1930s, most of its aircraft had become obsolete, and its role remained tied to the support of the army and navy and maintaining control of French airspace

A five-seat Farman 222 heavy bomber. Though the French had such weapons in the arsenal, they were reluctant to use them in attacks against Germany for fear of retaliation.

while launching limited operations against an enemy air force. The creation of a Superior Air Council in 1929 did not change the situation immediately, and the air force was not allowed to control most of its own aircraft which were assigned to the other services.

General Victor Denain, the first chief of the air force General Staff, developed a strategic role for the Armée de l'Air and was responsible for its modernization. In 1933 he planned to equip his air arm with 1,000 new aircraft. General Bertrand Pujo, his replacement, continued his work and developed a more offensive function against the enemy air force. Pujo was fortunate to serve under the new minister of air, Pierre Cot, who insisted on an independent role for the air arm. Nevertheless, support of the army on the battlefield remained a primary concern.

Cot was responsible for dividing the Armée de l'Air into a corps of bombers and fighters and allowing reconnaissance and observation aircraft to be attached to the army. In 1938,

Hangar full of French NS-225 planes. These were representative of the large number of obsolete aircraft in the French air force early in the war.

when Guy La Chambre became air minister, the French Air Force lost its numerical superiority to the German Reich. The new chief of staff, General Joseph Vuillemin, realizing that his bomber force could not effectively support the army on the battlefield, tried to get better suited aircraft for this mission. He ordered special attack bombers, but the slow pace of French industry delayed the arrival of the first planes, which the air force received barely in time for the campaign. The French aviation industry did not succeed in producing first-line fighters in sufficient quantities either. As a result, the Armée de l'Air was not ready when the war broke out.

The primary support function of the French Air Force on the

battlefield paralleled that of the *Luftwaffe*, but its numerical disadvantage and the poor quality of its equipment became an important factor in the outcome of the campaign.

The British Factor

In 1939 the British felt committed to maintaining their obligations to France although they had tried to avoid war. Although at the time their army was no larger than tiny Belgium's, the British represented the only force which could seriously challenge German plans thanks to the Royal Navy and the Royal Air Force (RAF).

The field army the British deployed in 1939 was not the outstanding professional force they had in 1914, though it was reasonably well-prepared and the best of the Allies. The leaders of the British Army had watched their military dwindle in the 1920s. The fact that the government had no desire to pass a military conscription law made it difficult to maintain a force strong enough to stand up to Germany since troops still had to garrison the far flung outposts of the empire. The army only consisted of about half a dozen Regular divisions in the early 1930s and a Territorial Army (a national guard). The latter consisted of a poorly armed and equipped force which in the early 1930s was not considered suitable for use overseas.

The turning point for the British Army amazingly took place under the government of Neville Chamberlain. When he became prime minister in May 1937, he appointed Leslie Hore-Belisha as the secretary of war. Hore-Belisha selected Liddell Hart, a veteran of the Great War and military writer, as his adviser and was also responsible for the advancement of younger generals which included Lord Gort and Archibald Wavell. His first duties included raising the morale of the military by improving salaries and living conditions. Like the French, the British soldier was poorly paid and not well treated during the early years of the Depression. Unlike the French, however, the British had an all volunteer force and needed to make military life look inviting to get recruits. Some of the more interesting changes included recruiting professional cooks for military service. The secretary of war made signifi-

British Mark VI light tanks proved of little use when faced against better armed and armored German vehicles. During the war in France, the Mark VI served as a command and reconnaissance vehicle.

cant changes in the Territorial Army as well, raising the age limit from 25 to 28 and even 30 for those with previous service. Eligibility standards to increase the ranks of the Territorials soon even allowed the acceptance of men with false teeth! Hore-Belisha wanted four Territorial Army divisions to receive full equipment and training so they could serve with the Regular forces in the event of war.

Under this dynamic leadership were fostered the necessary changes for the reconstruction of Great Britain's military forces. Unfortunately, Hore-Belisha did not receive Prime Minister Chamberlain's full support until the Munich Crisis in the fall of 1938 revealed that his country's position was weak and the need to create a more credible military force. Even after Munich, Hore-Belisha's attempts to fill the ranks through conscription failed to get approval of Parliament. Although many volunteers poured into the Territorial units, the Regular Army still needed more men, not only to expand, but to keep its active divisions up to strength. The infantry battalion was reduced in size to under 700 men, but some improvements were made in its weapons including the introduction of the Bren gun and the Bren gun carrier. The infantry division's structure changed to one similar to that of most European armies with 9 battalions of infantry instead of 12. Before the war these divisions retained three additional machinegun battalions which Liddell Hart claimed nullified many of the advantages in reducing the number of battalions.

At the beginning of 1939, Hore-Belisha pressed for a conscription law and improvements in the Territorial Army. Like many other British and French officials, he feared an aerial campaign against Great Britain because of German propaganda, so he built up the five Territorial anti-aircraft divisions. The Parliament did not pass a conscription act until the spring of 1939 which gave the army less than half a year to receive, train and equip the new conscripts. Army planners projected the creation of a 32 division army, although they did not expect to be able to send more than 4 infantry divisions to France if war should break out with Germany. After the Germans occupied the rump of Czechoslovakia in March 1939, Chamberlain not only gave Hore-Belisha greater support, but, on his own initiative, had the Territorial Army quickly expanded. This was too little too late. Thus, when war broke out, all the British could send to the Continent was a motorized infantry force of a few divisions. Although superior in many ways to the French, Belgian and Dutch infantry divisions, the British divisions had a limited ability to stop the new German panzer divisions.

Despite the fact that important reforms took place, the mission of the army was not properly established or clarified. Liddell Hart has been accused, apparently quite rightly so, of advocating a policy of reserving British Army units for the defense of the home island and colonies, while sending only one or two armored divisions to aid the French. A number of other political and military leaders also felt that, since the British contribution of infantry divisions would be insignificant in comparison with the French, they should concern themselves with other aspects of the approaching war.

Liddell Hart's ideas will always be questionable since he later also claimed to be the father of Blitzkrieg. Although his concepts for the creation and use of armored divisions lend themselves to more modern concepts of war, his insistence on holding back most of the army for the defense of the island certainly did not indicate a true military prophet. He emphasized in his writings that the indirect approach was the only alternative to a frontal assault. In his *Defence of Britain* he indicated that there was no indirect approach possible from the North Sea to Switzerland because of the defenses of the countries involved. He also added that the British need not waste their manpower in a World War I type scenario. Though a one time supporter of armored warfare, Liddell Hart also began to downplay the importance of the tank in the 1930s. It appears that the British military, following his advice, failed to prepare effectively for any commitment. Despite his claims to the contrary, Liddell Hart's influence was not decisive, for though the British did implement many of the improvements he suggested, they sent a good portion of their military to the Continent. A larger expeditionary force may not have made much difference, but the British infantry divisions did stand up better to the Germans in 1940 than did those of their allies.

Some of the important reforms achieved within the army by the summer of 1940 according to Liddell Hart were:

1. Anti-aircraft defense of Great Britain given priority, due to fear of the *Luftwaffe*.

2. Increase in the proportion of mobile troops. Divisions received enough vehicles, mostly trucks, to make units relatively mobile, while larger armies, like the German, still had to rely heavily on horse drawn transport when the war began.

3. Creation of a mobile division in Egypt, although not completed, in response to the potential threat from Italian Libya where sizeable Italian forces already existed. After the Ethiopian War, the British had made preparations for the defense of their East African colonies, Egypt and the Sudan because an offended Italy had already joined Germany to create the Axis powers.

4. Reduction of forces in India. The threat from the

Northwest Frontier had largely dissipated while the need for British troops elsewhere made this a necessary move.

5. Army divisions reorganized:

a. Nine instead of twelve battalions.

b. Motorization of all infantry divisions.

c. Utilization of Bren carriers in each infantry battalion to eliminate the excess machinegun battalions.

7. Mobile Division split into two divisions, to create a more manageable force.

8. Field artillery batteries reorganized with 12 guns.

9. Territorial Army modernized along same lines as Regular Army including creation of mobile divisions and tank units. This was a long overdue reform which made it possible to increase the field army more quickly by allowing these reservist units to be brought up to the same standards as Regular units and shipped overseas.

It was the British who invented the tank during the Great War, so logic dictated that they become pioneers in tactics for mobile warfare. The Royal Tank Corps, an independent arm of the army since 1923, conducted exercises on Salisbury Plain in 1927 and demonstrated, among other things, that an armored force rendered infantry units moving into battle extremely vulnerable. Unfortunately armored vehicles were expensive to produce and maintain, and even though the Royal Tank Corps was an elite unit, little was done to improve this arm of the service. Actually, for a few years it faded from the scene and concentrated its activities on armored car security operations in the various parts of the empire. In 1930 the Royal Tank Corps pioneered the use of radios with tanks as a means of communication. The armor enthusiasts made little headway after this because the civilian and military leadership decided to concentrate their efforts on less glamorous elements of the army such as the infantry.

In 1933 the British Army included only 4 tank battalions and 2 regiments of armored cars while it maintained 18 regiments of horse cavalry, despite significant progress toward mechanization. The 1st Tank Brigade was formed with three of the army's tank battalions. In 1935 an additional battalion of light tanks was assigned to the brigade as a reconnaissance force. By this time, the horse cavalry began to convert to light tanks and soon the need for a Royal Tank Corps, with its medium tanks, became questionable. Fortunately, the decision to turn exclusively to light armor, designed mainly for reconnaissance, was not made.

In 1938 the Royal Tank Corps and cavalry supplied forces to create the Mobile Division. The former contributed one tank brigade of medium and light tanks, and the latter added two cavalry brigades of light tanks. The divisional troops also included battalions with motorized infantry and artillery as well as an armored car regiment. This force would evolve into an armored division and the troops mentioned became the Support Group found in British armored divisions during the war. After the Munich Crisis the Mobile Division began to replace its obsolete tanks. The rivalry between the Royal Tank Corps and cavalry ended in April 1939 when the two combined to create the Royal Armored Corps. During that year the division began to receive its first new medium tanks: the A-9, A-10 and A-13 tanks which were not extremely successful designs. The latter remained in service long enough to take part in the desert war in North Africa. Liddell Hart criticized the great number of light tanks and vehicles designed for reconnaissance, but the British still had a surplus of these when they went to war.

Like the French, the British had designed tanks mainly to support infantry formations, but their armored division was an offensive force. The best British tank, the heavily armored Matilda II, armed with a 40mm gun, was used for infantry support and proved its effectiveness in 1940 serving with a separate unit, the 1st Army Tank Brigade. While infantry supporting tank brigades received Matilda IIs, armored divisions initially were given less effective vehicles.

The Mobile Division became the 1st Armored Division which only arrived in time to become part of the last remaining British force on the Continent after Dunkirk. In 1940 a second armored division, the 7th, was formed in Egypt. The British armored troops played no significant role in the 1940 campaign in the

The first British monoplane fighter, the Hawker Hurricane was
used in great numbers in France and during the Battle of Britain.

West because their development had been held back during the
1930s.

British Air Power

The Royal Air Force, like the army, suffered during the 1920s.
Air Marshal Sir Hugh Trenchard, who served in the newly
Royal Flying Corps in World War I, guided air policy for most
of the decade, and, like many other aviators, he believed that
air power could win the next war largely on its own. As a result
he spent most of the meager funds allotted to his service on
bombers. In 1934 the RAF consisted of 67 squadrons, mostly
bombers, 25 of which served overseas. The state of Britain's air
arm alarmed Winston Churchill who warned Parliament that

The Boulton Paul Defiant's only machine guns were mounted in a rear turret. Unable to stand up to German planes, it was relegated to a nightfighter role.

the RAF would be outnumbered by the new *Luftwaffe* in 1935. Although his claims were exaggerated and the German Air Force was still in its infancy, the RAF seriously did, in fact, lack the fighter squadrons it needed. Of the 42 squadrons in Great Britain, only about a dozen consisted of fighters, many of which were rapidly approaching obsolescence.

The RAF plan to enter German territory and bomb the enemy into submission certainly was no guarantee of victory as many air theorists had claimed and in the 1930s it failed to cooperate with the army in ground support missions during maneuvers. This did not bode well for the future of any aircraft other than the bombers. Fortunately, the fear of a growing threat from the *Luftwaffe* may have led to an expansion of the fighter arm including the development of the Hurricane fighter in 1936. The number of squadrons continued to grow with fighter

A British Whitley heavy bomber in flight. The Whitley was the first British bomber to attack Berlin since World War I.

aircraft equalling almost half the number of bombers, but most of the aircraft remained obsolete. The Hawker Fury biplane served as the RAF's front line fighter aircraft in the 1930s, and was not fully replaced by Hurricanes until 1939. In September 1939 the RAF numbered 18 squadrons of Hurricanes and 9 of the more advanced Spitfires. Several squadrons included the Gloster Gladiator biplane developed in 1937, most of which were sent overseas, although a few went to France and Norway in 1940 together with some of the newer and even less successful Defiants and Blenheims. Aircraft such as the Battle proved inefficient in supporting the army. The only question that presented itself for the British command was to decide how many of the new fighter squadrons to commit to the Continent.

One of the most effective fighters of the war was the British Supermarine Spitfire. While not many were used to defend France, it proved particularly useful during the Battle of Britain.

The British Expeditionary Force

In the spring of 1939 the British government finally decided to send an expeditionary force to France in the event of war. At the same time military conscription went into effect, and the government authorized a 100 percent increase in the Territorial Army. The French military and government were told to expect a British force of four divisions within a month of mobilization. The British Expeditionary Force would also include supporting units in the form of a tank battalion, artillery and anti-aircraft regiments, numerous specialized units and other combat units. In support were two bomber reconnaissance squadrons, six army co-operation squadrons and four fighter squadrons, although most of the best aircraft would be held back. Bombers of the Advanced Air Striking Force would also be sent France. The British expected to add several Territorial divisions to this force within a few months as well as an armored division at the end of eight months. Planners selected French west coast ports as points of entry for their troops, and intended to use Rennes and St. Nazaire-Nantes as bases because they were afraid that Channel coast sites would be vulnerable to the *Luftwaffe*. The Expeditionary Force operation was known as Plan W-4 and the movement of the air elements, Plan WA-4.

Lord Gort received the appointment as commander of the British Expeditionary Force on 3 September. The first units arrived and took up their position on the French left flank as in World War I. If the Germans advanced into Belgium, the British Expeditionary Force would be where they anticipated the decisive action of the campaign to take place. The British contingent rose from a strength of four divisions in September 1939 to 13 divisions in May 1940. Combined with the French 1st and 7th Armies, the British Expeditionary Force formed the 1st Army Group, the most mobile of the Allied armies. The British commander took orders directly from General Gamelin, the designated commander in chief of Allied armies. In the event of orders which might jeopardize the British force, he was authorized to consult his government first. Lord Gort worked well with the French until the German breakthrough in May 1940 brought political considerations into play.

The Darkening Horizon

Shortly after the Munich settlement, it became increasingly obvious that the policy of appeasing Hitler was bankrupt. Hitler took over the remainder of Czechoslovakia on 15 March 1939 and then began to look towards Poland which held territory Germany had lost during World War I.

CHAPTER II

WAR!

The day of 1 September 1939 dawned with the roar of tank engines and the shrill scream of dive bombing aircraft over Poland as another world war began. France and Great Britain, no longer able to back down, declared war on Germany while the Polish Army collapsed under the onslaught of the *Wehrmacht*. The Allies found it impossible to send relief to the beleaguered Poles who resisted for about a month, allowing the world a glance at the new shape of war. Another six months passed before the Germans unleashed their forces again.

Poland Invaded

After 15 March 1939, Hitler's Reich and its satellite, Slovakia, had Poland on three sides. Except for several rivers and mostly light border fortifications, there was virtually nothing to impede the advance of German panzers on the Polish Plain. The partial mobilization of the Polish Army in the spring of 1939 did not help the situation. Even if the Soviet Union remained neutral, Polish forces had to deploy along the frontier with East Prussia, the western border with Germany and the old Czech border.

On 23 March 1939, the Poles recalled a number of reservists to the colors and formed the Krakow, Lódz, Poznan, Pomorze, and Modlin armies as well as the special Narew Group. Only four infantry divisions with two cavalry brigades and the mechanized brigade reached full strength by the end of March. The Prusy Army mobilized in June and became the last major command to organize before the war began. Just under 20 infantry divisions with 8 cavalry brigades began the process of mobilization by mid-August. Most of the remainder of Poland's reserves received orders to report to their units after a few "accidental" border raids on 26 August when Hitler called off the invasion and on 1 September when he attacked in earnest.

The Polish High Command's strategic choice was whether to deploy its forces along the long border with Germany, leaving little behind it to break up a German advance, or to pull its forces back towards Warsaw, establishing a more viable defense line on the Vistula, thus abandoning a large part of the country to the Germans. During the summer, the Poles informed the inspector general of British Overseas Forces, Sir Edmund Ironside, on an official visit to Poland at the time, that they would have to evacuate their western frontier and could not defend the Polish Corridor. In the end, however, they chose to defend their western border since to pull back would allow Hitler to take most of their country's industrial and population centers without a fight.

The Vistula constituted the most formidable obstacle in Poland since it was wide and deep, allowing maritime traffic to navigate all the way from its mouth to its junction with the San River. Douglas Wilson Johnson, a military geographer, described the Polish Plain and its river barriers in the following terms:

> (The Vistula) A majestic river of great volume, unfordable and seldom crossed by bridges, subject to terrible floods which may cover its entire valley bottom, it forms one of the most serious military obstacles in Europe....Warsaw is located on a terrace 120 feet above the level of the stream, and therefore safe from damage by floods....Military operations on the plain of Poland...encounter difficulties of considerable magnitude, especially in the winter when the roads become mired with snow and mud. (quoted from *Topography and Strategy in the War*)

He also mentioned that the area around Lodz on the Polish Plain was covered with marshes that would further impede an army's progress. Poland's roads, largely unpaved, not only turned to mud but became downright hazardous during any rainy period, let alone in winter. In the past they had plagued the march of the Napoleonic armies as well as the Russian Army in World War I. The Polish leadership was convinced that its cavalry would have an advantage over the Germans because it could negotiate the difficult terrain that would slow foot soldiers and stop mechanized units.

The Polish military leadership overestimated the defensive value of the Vistula and its tributaries. Indeed, the rivers crested in the spring and became virtually unfordable, but in the late summer, especially a very dry one like that of 1939, their water levels receded so far that fords appeared at many points, making the Polish Plain perfect tank country. Possibly the Polish High Command realized in late summer 1939 that the unusual drought had greatly reduced the effectiveness of the river barriers and felt it had no choice but to commit all its forces to the borders.

Some recent analysts have claimed that the poorly developed road system in western Poland would have slowed the German advance if the Poles had chosen to defend the Vistula instead of their western frontier. However, it seems more likely that it would have merely been a minor hindrance, unless it rained heavily. Besides, if the communications in western Poland, the economic heart of the country, were underdeveloped, one can imagine how difficult conditions were in eastern Poland which included a large part of the great Pripet Marshes. Defending the Vistula would have put Warsaw on the front line with virtually all of Poland's major cities and industrial centers on the wrong side of the barrier. Within a few months Poland would have lost the means to sustain its own armed forces even if it had succeeded in holding the Germans in check.

Though the Polish High Command had prepared for a war with Germany for several years, it had underestimated the size of the German Army and even considered it overly mechanized! Its decision to leave a minimum force on the eastern border seemed reasonable since a Russian assault combined with a German invasion would be strategically fatal in any case.

Poland's pre-war army consisted of 30 infantry divisions and 14 cavalry brigades on paper. In addition, the army included

Polish and German Tanks

W= weight in tons, Wp= Main Armament, S= Approximate Speed, C= Crew

Armored Vehicles	Total +	W.	Wp.	Spd.	C.
---Polish---					
TK.3	250	2.4	MG	29mph	2
TKS	300	2.6	MG	26mph	2
FT-17	102	6.5	MG	5mph	2
R-35	50	10.6	37mm	13mph	2
Vickers	38	7.4	47mm	22mph	3
7TP*	40	9.4	MG	20mph	3
7TP	95	9.9	37mm	23mph	3
---German---					
Panzer I	900	5.8	MG	26mph	2
Panzer II	930	9.5	20mm	25mph	3
Panzer 35t	229	10.5	37mm	25mph	4
Panzer 38t	104	7	37mm	26mph	4
Panzer III	220	15.3	37mm	25mph	5
Panzer IV	190	15	75mm	25mph	5

Note: + These are roughly the numbers of German Tanks involved which may have been about 2/3 of their tank strength.
* This was the first version of the 7TP tank and had two turrets with each mounting a machine gun. The second version had only a single turret. Totals are approximate from various sources.

several mountain brigades and a single mechanized brigade. The Poles had about 250 tanks, mainly light modified British products and a few modern French tanks as well as a fair number of old FT 17s from World War I. As the war began a second mechanized (armored) unit, the Warsaw Mechanized Brigade, began to form. The 10th Mechanized Brigade and the Warsaw Mechanized Brigade contained Vickers tanks which the Poles had re-equipped with 47mm gun turrets, as well as tankettes which included many re-equipped with 20mm guns. Two independent tank battalions had most of Poland's new 7TP tanks with 37mm guns, and a third battalion had French R-35 tanks. The army allotted more than 400 tankettes to cavalry brigades and reconnaissance units of infantry divisions, but these vehicles mounted only a machine gun and had a limited value since they were relatively obsolete in 1939. Ten armored trains, mounting 75mm guns and 100mm howitzers in turrets on armored cars, gave additional support to several armies.

During peacetime the divisions were maintained at brigade strength and gradually reached full strength after the mobilization of reserves. Apparently about a fifth of the Polish reservists never reached their units or failed to mobilize so that many units did not attain full strength. Most cavalry units had a full complement and even sent men back to form cadres for new units. Besides the reserves to fill out the active divisions, the army also included national guard units which formed 11 brigades when mobilized, but most were under strength.

The small Polish air force had a reasonable number of fighter aircraft which had been some of the best in the world during most of the 1930s but were obsolete by 1939. The bomber force included the modern twin engine P.37B Los bomber. The Polish air force had less than 40 of these operational, and a few more obsolete models which were no match for the German defenses. Amazingly, Albert Kesselring, commander of the *Luftflotte 1*, credited the Poles with having a fairly modern fighter force of almost twice its actual strength. He underestimated the value of their bomber force however, but German air superiority made it a moot point.

The German forces in 1939 consisted of 35 active divisions, similar in size to those of the Polish Army. The German forces

Polish and German Planes						
F = Fighter, B = Bomber, DB = Dive Bomber, R = Reconnaissance						
Planes	Total +	Type	Speed	Guns	Bombs	Crew
---POLISH---						
P.7	185*	F	203MPH	2xMG		1
P.11	115	F	242MPH	4xMG	1101lb.	1
P.23B	240	S/B	217MPH	3xMG	1540lb.	3
P.37B LOS	75**	B	273MPH	3xMG	5680lb.	6
---GERMAN---						
ME-109B	200	F	292MPH	3xMG		1
ME-109E	700	F	350MPH	4xMG		1
ME-110	100	F	349MPH	2x20mm 4xMG	550lb.	2
JU-87	300	DB	240MPH	3xMG	1500lb.	2
DO-17	550	R/B	263MPH	6xMG	2200lb.	3
HE-111	790	B	258MPH	1x20mm 6xMG	4410lb.	5

Note: *Only 30 of these with combat units, the remainder under repair or for training. **Only about 36 fully operational in September of 1939. German totals are approximate.

also included four motorized infantry divisions and three mountain divisions. The armored striking force consisted of 5 panzer divisions of about 320 tanks each which included the light Panzer Is and IIs and medium Panzer IIIs and IVs in small numbers. Only the *1st Panzer Division* and the *3rd Panzer Division* had a large proportion of medium tanks (the *3rd* was reinforced with a *Panzer Lehr Battalion* of Panzer IIIs and IVs). Added to the panzer units were 4 light divisions of which the *1st Light* and the *3rd Light Divisions* had about 220 tanks and 150 tanks respectively. Of those tanks, over 100 of the *1st Light* and 60 of the *3rd Light Division*'s tanks were Czech medium tanks. These Czech tanks were compatible to the Panzer IIIs and proved a valuable asset. Except for their awkward estab-

1939
The Wehrkreis

**The Military District System used by
the Home Army for recruitment,
replacement and rehabilitation of
men from corresponding Corps.**

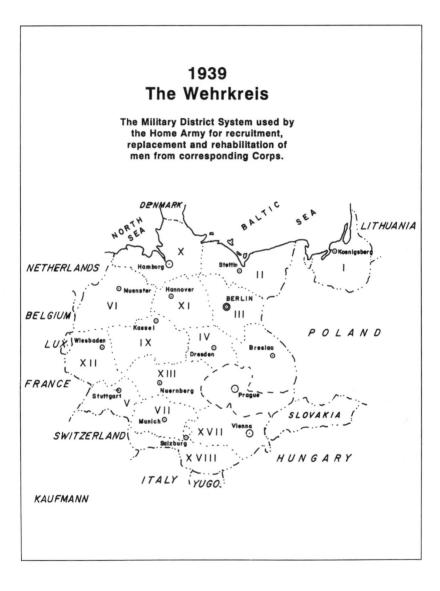

KAUFMANN

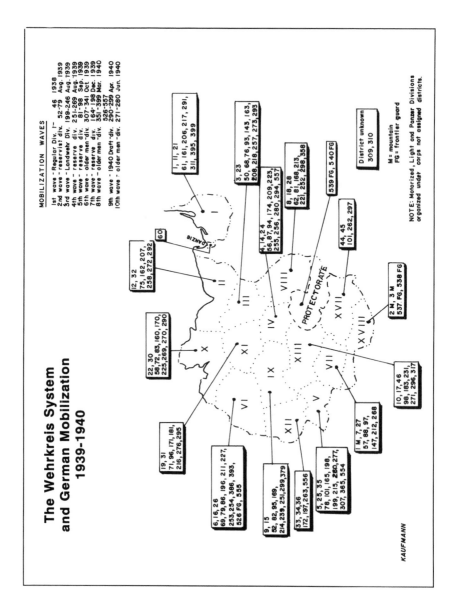

The Wehrkreis System and German Mobilization 1939-1940

MOBILIZATION WAVES

1st wave – Regular Div.	1 – 46	1938
2nd wave – reservisit div.	52-79	Aug. 1939
3rd wave – Landwehr Div.	199-246	Aug. 1939
4th wave – reserve div.	251-269	Aug. 1939
5th wave – reserve div.	81 – 98	Sep. 1939
6th wave – older man-div.	307-341	Oct. 1939
7th wave – reserve div.	164-198	Dec. 1939
8th wave – older man-div.	351-399	Mar. 1940
	526-557	
9th wave – 1940 Draft div.	290-299	Apr. 1940
10th wave – older men-div.	271-280	Jun. 1940

NOTE: Motorized, Light and Panzer Divisions organized under corps not assigned districts.

M = mountain
FG = frontier guard

District unknown
309, 310

1, 11, 21
61, 161, 206, 217, 291, 311, 395, 399

3, 23
50, 68, 76, 93, 143, 163, 208, 218, 257, 273, 293

8, 18, 28
62, 81, 168, 213, 221, 252, 298, 358

539 FG, 540 FG

4, 14, 24
56, 87, 94, 174, 209, 223, 255, 256, 280, 294, 557

44, 45
101, 262, 297

2 M, 3 M
537 FG, 538 FG

60

12, 32
75, 162, 207, 258, 272, 292

22, 30
58, 72, 83, 160, 170, 225, 269, 270, 290

10, 17, 46
98, 183, 231, 271, 296, 317

19, 31
71, 96, 171, 181, 216, 276, 295

1 M, 7, 27
57, 88, 97, 147, 212, 268

6, 16, 26
69, 79, 86, 196, 211, 227, 253, 254, 386, 393, 526 FG, 555

9, 15
52, 82, 95, 169, 214, 239, 251, 299, 379

33, 34, 36
172, 197, 263, 556

5, 25, 35
78, 101, 165, 198, 199, 215, 260, 277, 307, 365, 554

KAUFMANN

72

lishment, the two light divisions had almost as much power as an armored division, while the other two light divisions comprised less than a hundred light tanks each.

Mobilization more than doubled the number of infantry divisions, but war with Poland meant that the German Army must also defend its Western Front since the Poles had an alliance with the British and French, and Prime Minister Chamberlain had finally abandoned his appeasement policy. He was determined that the Allies would honor their commitment to the "faraway country" of Poland.

At the end of April, Hitler abrogated the Polish-German Non-Aggression Pact signed in 1934 and then announced that the problem of the international city of Danzig must be settled. He had already intimidated Lithuania into surrendering the Memel district and hoped to do the same with the Poles. As the diplomats talked, the Poles began to maneuver their forces in expectation of the worst, but full mobilization did not occur for fear of triggering a violent German response.

A month before tearing up his Polish treaty, Hitler ordered the *OKW* to prepare plans for the conquest and destruction of Poland: Case White. During the summer, tensions mounted in the East. General Ironside met Marshal Edward Rydz-Smigly, the commander in chief and president of Poland, who expressed his belief that the Danzig question was nothing more than a pretext for a war. No matter what the British government promised, Ironside refused to believe that the Allies could offer any serious help to Poland in the event of war. Then on 23 August the world received the announcement that Germany had concluded a non-aggression pact with the Soviet Union. Poland's fate was sealed.

Case White, the German invasion of Poland, was set for late August. The German Army moved up to its planned assembly areas in East Prussia, Pomerania, Silesia and Slovakia. The original German plan called for the army's active divisions to undertake the operation, but by August Germany mobilized, and numerous reserve units found themselves involved in the operation. The *Wehrmacht* poised to attack before mid-August, but just as Germany signed the pact with Soviet Russia the British signed their own agreement with Poland on 25 August, the eve of Hitler's proposed invasion. The Führer balked when

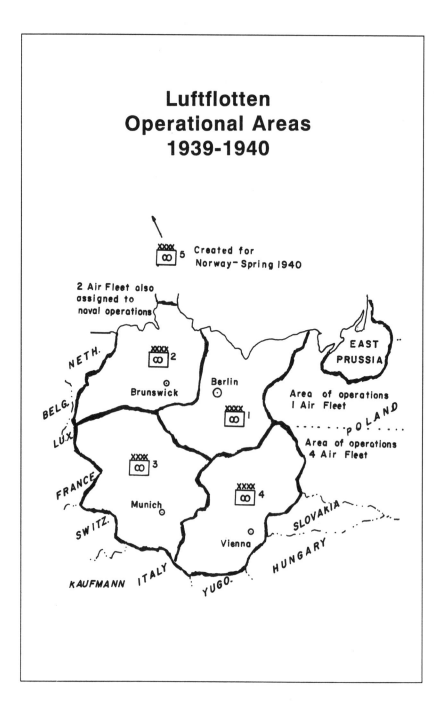

Luftflotten Operational Areas 1939-1940

he realized that the Allies would back Poland and that Mussolini would not enter the war without German weapons and munitions to make up for deficiencies in his own armed forces. He postponed the opening of the campaign, and messengers rushed out to the front line units with the cancellation orders. Some units did not get the word and began to engage the Poles on 26 August until they received the recall. These border incursions put the Poles on alert. Hitler reopened negotiations and sent his final ultimatum to the Poles demanding Danzig and the Polish Corridor linking Germany to East Prussia. The Poles, still remembering the humiliation of 18th century partitions, opted to fight.

The Germans, in keeping with diplomatic formalities, staged an incident where supposed Polish troops attacked a German radio station to provide them with a pretext for war. On 1 September 1939, the German Army opened hostilities assisted by elements of the navy and the *Luftwaffe*. However, the panzer tactics they used in this campaign were not those for which the Germans later became renowned. With the exception of the *XVI Panzer Corps*, the Germans did not mass their panzer divisions into armored corps to create breakthroughs and make deep penetrations before enveloping enemy forces. The overall general strategy called for an advance of the two army groups from the north and south to encircle the Polish Army west of the Vistula to trap the Polish Army. This strategy was later associated with blitzkrieg, but only one panzer corps led the offensive, whereas several served as a spearhead in future campaigns.

Two German army groups took up position on the Polish frontier in a semicircle running from the puppet state of Slovakia to East Prussia. General Fedor von Bock's *Army Group North* included two armies. One was *3rd Army* with 8 infantry divisions and a panzer division in East Prussia. The other, *4th Army*, in Pomerania, had seven infantry divisions, the main striking force of *3rd* and *10th Panzer Divisions* and two motorized divisions which were to cross the Polish Corridor, and a Frontier Corps holding the East Wall.

General Gerd von Rundstedt's *Army Group South* contained the bulk of the main forces grouped in three armies. In Silesia was *10th Army* with the main strike force of *XVI Corps' 1st* and

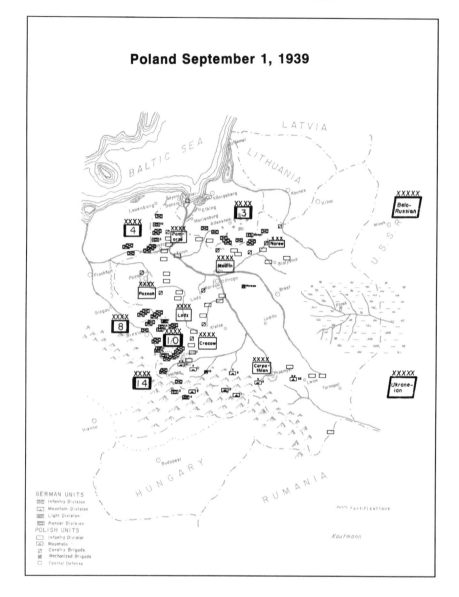

Poland September 1, 1939

GERMAN UNITS
- Infantry Division
- Mountain Division
- Light Division
- Panzer Division

POLISH UNITS
- Infantry Division
- Mountain
- Cavalry Brigade
- Mechanized Brigade
- Coastal Defense

Fortifications

Kaufmann

3rd Panzer Divisions and two infantry divisions; *XV Corps* with *2nd* and *3rd Light Divisions*; and *XIV Corps* with *1st Light Division* and two motorized divisions, as well as two other corps totaling four infantry divisions. On *10th Army*'s left flank was *8th Army* with four infantry divisions and *Frontier Guard* units. In the Carpathians of Slovakia on Rundstedt's right was *14th Army* with two panzer divisions, a light division and 5 infantry divisions plus three mountain divisions.

The above placements left three armies of 22 divisions, mostly reserve units, on the Western Front should France and Britain martial their forces to attack German. Only 14 divisions were in reserve.

Against the vast array of German forces the Poles deployed six armies and readied new ones. The Modlin Army and Narew Group only had seven infantry divisions and four cavalry brigades to guard the border with East Prussia. The Pomorze Army guarded the Polish Corridor with five infantry divisions and a cavalry brigade. The Poznan Army defended the bulge in the western border with four infantry divisions and two cavalry brigades. The Lodz and Cracow Armies covered most of the Silesian frontier with eight infantry divisions, three cavalry brigades and the 10th Mechanized (armored) Brigade. The Kaparty Army included a mountain division and two mountain brigades plus an infantry division along the southern border.

The battleship *Schleswig-Holstein* stopped at Danzig for an "official visit" with a special assault detachment of marines at Memel who remained concealed until the fateful day. After arriving, the Germans carried out diplomatic courtesies while accusing the Polish military garrison of leveling its guns on the *Schleswig-Holstein*. On 1 September 1939, shortly after 0400, the ship fired the opening shots of the war against the Polish fortifications at Westerplatte. The *Luftwaffe* joined in later. A special SS Home Guard unit of youths, took part in the fighting while a special unit known as the *Eberhard Brigade,* made up of two regiments of German Danzigers, crossed over from East Prussia. The contest went on for about a week. The Germans took heavy casualties and additional destroyers entered the fray in order to help reduce the Polish positions. Other German naval units opened fire on the Polish defenses at Hela and

On 1 September at 0300, the German battleship Schleswig-Hol-stein *fired its guns while at Danzig. It was the signal for the German invasion of Poland and the beginning of World War II.*

Gdynia. The German *207th Infantry Division*, a third wave unit of older reservists, moved across the German-Pomeranian border and began ground operations against the Polish coastal positions. During the fighting the Poles lost the destroyer *Wicher* and a minelayer to dive bombers in the defense of Hel, but, reportedly, not before engaging two German destroyers and heavily damaging one. Poland's most modern armed force was its small navy, consisting of 4 relatively new British and French built destroyers and 5 submarines of Dutch and French origin, several other vessels such as minelayers and 16 gunboats on the Vistula River. The small Polish fleet could do nothing to repel the much larger German Navy, and only the smaller vessels remained behind to aid in the defenses of Polish naval fortresses while others escaped to Great Britain to fight again or to Sweden and internment.

After early morning reconnaissance flights on 1 September, the *Luftwaffe* dispatched bombers from General Albert Kesselring's *1st Luftflotte* over northern Poland and General Löhr's *4th Luftflotte* which carried out operations against southern Poland. Hermann Göring, commander of the *Luftwaffe*, planned Operation Seaside to open the first day of the war, using every bomber unit of Kesselring's air armada in an aerial assault on Warsaw. However, most of his air units remained fogged in at their bases in the morning, and returning reconnaissance aircraft reported heavy cloud cover over the Polish capital. Reluctantly, Göring canceled the mission and the air units received new assignments. By the time they took off, much of the element of surprise had been lost. The bombers joined Löhr's group hitting major installations at Krakow, Radom, Lublin and several other key airfields.

The two luftflotten deployed about 1,500 aircraft, including only 210 fighters, against the Polish air force of approximately 750 aircraft of which almost 300 were fighters and only two-thirds of those were combat-ready. The best Polish fighter, the P.11 fighters, engaged the superior German ME-109 and ME-110 fighters with some success in the days that followed and Polish pilots made up for their lack of numbers and obsolete planes with skill, courage and dedication. The Polish air force was not destroyed on the first day, but with no replacement aircraft, it grew weaker daily.

The German claim that the early strikes virtually wiped out the Polish air force on the first day of the war, and that the *Luftwaffe* had swept all opposition from the skies over Poland, was generally accepted. In actuality the Poles had withdrawn their aircraft to secret airfields days before the invasion, leaving only relatively useless aircraft on the targeted airfields. Most of Poland's first line aircraft survived, even though the Germans outnumbered and outclassed these as well.

The *Luftwaffe* struck hard at key Polish military installations, as well as communications centers. At the same time, it delivered tactical ground support to the advancing infantry and panzer divisions helping to create breakthroughs. In one case dive bombers broke up the advance of a Polish cavalry brigade on the first day. In some cases bridges became key targets not for destruction, but for protection with smaller bombs and machine guns being used in an attempt to prevent Polish units from carrying out demolition missions.

The real weapons of blitzkrieg were the German aircraft; more specifically the JU-87 Stuka dive bomber. This infamous plane dived out of the sky like a vulture, creating terror among those in the target area below as it screamed down and cut loose its 550 pound (250 kg) bomb that impacted with a devas-

Spotting a target, a Stuka divebomber goes in for the kill (left). Reaching an almost 90 degree dive, the plane drops its deadly load (right).

tating explosion. Even though slow moving and lightly armed, JU-87s demonstrated their ability to shoot down the best Polish fighters.

By the end of the campaign, the Polish flyers had shot down over a hundred German aircraft while losing fewer of their own to the Germans in air-to-air combat. Many of the Polish pilots escaped to fight again, but against more equal odds. The remnants of the Polish Air Force flew on to Rumania after 18 September.

As the panzers roared across the border, and German aircraft began shooting up Polish airfields on the first day of the invasion, another secret force had already moved into position. These were the *Abwehr's* (military intelligence) Brandenburg units of ethnic Germans who spoke fluent Polish. Some of these men had sought employment in Poland where they could protect factories and mines from sabotage until German troops arrived. Apparently, they achieved great success, but little information is available on them. Several sources report that another Brandenburg formation was assigned the capture of the Jablonka tunnel when the invasion began, but their premature attempt on 26 August led to the destruction of the tunnel by the Poles. The Germans also engaged a ruse in which special troops, concealed on a freight train attempted to seize a key bridge over the Vistula at Dirschau. The Poles managed to divert the train, and *Luftwaffe* bombers failed to destroy the wires running to the demolition charges planted on the bridge. The Poles successfully detonated the structure as well as another important bridge over the river further south at Graudenz. But, these Polish successes failed to significantly delay the Germans who quickly bridged the river after cutting through the Polish Corridor.

The *4th Army* of *Army Group North*, with nine infantry divisions plus the *3rd* and *10th Panzer* divisions, launched its attack against the Polish Pomorze Army which defended the corridor with five infantry divisions and a cavalry brigade. In a relatively hopeless position this Polish Army found itself reeling back from the corridor as the German *4th Army* struck it from the west, and two divisions of the German *3rd Army* attacked from East Prussia. Some Polish units like the Pomorska Cavalry Brigade attempted to check the German advance, and, initially, had some success. General Guderian, commander of the *XIX Army Corps* (motorized), cut through the fog of battle and personally directed elements of his *3rd Panzer Division* against the Polish defenses on the Brahe River. The division commander was at army group headquarters so Guderian took over and pushed a motorcycle battalion across a bridge the Poles had tried to burn. As the Germans quickly overwhelmed the defenders, the tanks raced across the bridge making the Polish situation on the Brahe hopeless. Instead of letting the division settle down in a state of confusion short of its objective, Guderian had pushed it right through the light opposition of a Polish bicycle company at the crossing, and by evening the division reached its assigned objective. This helped create the breach which soon brought about a general collapse

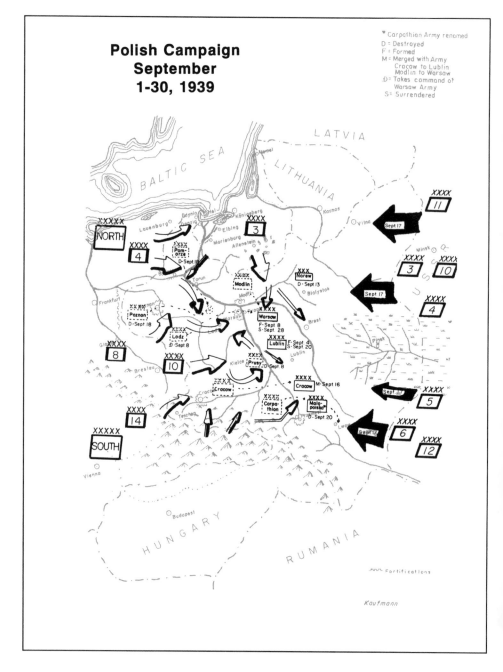

Polish Campaign
September
1-30, 1939

* Carpathian Army renamed
D = Destroyed
F = Formed
M = Merged with Army
    Cracow to Lublin
    Modlin to Warsaw
Đ = Takes command of
    Warsaw Army
S = Surrendered

Kaufmann

~~~ Fortifications

of the Poles in the corridor, but not before Guderian found himself shocked to see his troops in a state of panic when they heard that Polish cavalry was advancing. Guderian once again took charge and guided his *2nd Motorized Division* back into action.

In some cases the Poles succeeded in stopping the light German tanks, but Guderian would not let a minor setback deter his corps from completing its mission. The *3rd Panzer Division* included an additional battalion equipped with the newer Panzer III and Panzer IV medium tanks which contributed significantly to the German success in the corridor. The Poles were virtually helpless against these medium tanks.

The 18th Lancer Regiment of the Pomorska Cavalry Brigade, while covering the retreat of the infantry from the corridor, launched the first cavalry charge of World War II at Krojanty on 1 September 1939. This brief success caused the before mentioned stir among Guderian's troops. The horsemen literally cut down an unprepared German infantry unit with their sabers, but soon they encountered German armored cars and the cavalry regiment shattered under a hail of bullets as it attempted to seek cover (this one incident inspired the legend of Polish cavalrymen attempting to charge tanks with sabers and lances). At the end of the first day, the Poles had briefly checked the Germans in the corridor, but only after heavy losses. Night brought some relief to the Poles, but they could not sustain such an effort another day.

Meanwhile, four infantry divisions of the *3rd Army* led by the ad hoc *Kampf Panzer Division* struck south from East Prussia hitting two infantry divisions of the Polish Modlin Army. Their drive south met stiff resistance at the fortifications of Mlawa on 1 September. On 2 September the panzer division shifted eastward and led a drive through a more weakly held area. The remainder of the *3rd Army*'s units, consisting of older reservists, held the frontier and attempted to repel the Polish Podlaska Cavalry Brigade from the Narew Group which galloped into East Prussia raising havoc on the second night of the invasion. The raid only served to give a boost to Polish morale.

The *207th Division* and smaller units of the *4th Army* advanced against the Polish coastal defenses and remained engaged there until the end of the campaign. On 3 September the

4th Army crossed the corridor to link up with the *3rd Army* as the shattered Polish Pomorze Army began to fall back from the Corridor, and the Modlin Army withdrew southward from its strong, but flanked, position at Mlawa.

Army Group South of General von Rundstedt included the *8th*, *10th* and *14th Armies*. The *14th Army* deployed 10 divisions and 2 panzer divisions, the *2nd* and the *5th*, in Silesia, Moravia and Slovakia. The Polish Krakow Army had only about five divisions, a cavalry brigade and the 10th Mechanized Brigade to meet the *14th Army*'s assault. The Carpathian Mountains of the Slovakian border aided in the defense, but out of this sector came the *2nd Panzer Division* with infantry and mountain units threatening Krakow from the south. In the opening days of the campaign the panzers and supporting troops engaged the Polish 10th Mechanized Brigade, and after several attempts finally drove it back while other Polish and German mountain units fought in the Carpathians.

The bulk of *14th Army*'s divisions, led by *5th Panzer Division*, came out of Silesia and drove steadily eastward towards the Vistula River and Krakow. The *14th Army* acted as the southern pincer which pushed forward to meet the *10th Army* and isolate the Polish Krakow Army before beginning the advance north.

The *10th German Army*, with 13 divisions plus the *1st* and *4th Panzer Divisions*, delivered the main blow. The *8th Army* and its six divisions on its left took part in the drive against the Polish Lodz and Prusy Armies. Those two Polish armies had about nine divisions between the border and the Vistula. Even if the Poles held the flanking thrusts of the *14th* and *3rd* armies (*Army Group North*), the *8th* and *10th* armies formed an irresistible force plunging forward towards the Vistula and Warsaw.

The Polish Poznan Army with four divisions and two cavalry brigades occupying the western bulge of the Polish frontier faced nothing but German frontier forces behind the East Wall while the two German army groups threatened both of its flanks by the end of the first day. No aid came from the Allies on the first day, but by 2 September France prepared to make its declaration of war while the British entertained peace overtures from the Italians. The British demanded that German troops pull back from Poland before any discussions were carried on. When the deadline set by the Allied ultimatums expired on 3 September, both the British and the French declared war on Germany.

In the first days of the campaign, *Army Group South* found the Polish resistance fierce enough to prevent it from encircling those units west of Krakow while Polish troops attempted to hold the line of the Warta River. By 5 September Rundstedt's troops pushed back the Polish forces from the Carpathians as well as eastward towards Krakow and Kielce. By 6 September the Polish front in the southeast began to collapse as many units attempted to rally at Kielce and Radom, and German mountain troops moved to isolate the Polish fortress of Przemysl in the south. The advancing German columns, having no time to round up prisoners, bypassed thousands of Polish troops. Some German infantry divisions in the first couple of weeks made advances of up to 15 miles (25 kilometers) a day on foot. This sometimes created problems because these divisions relied on horse-operated supply units and the further they moved away from the railhead, the more difficult it became to maintain services.

In the north, the German *3rd Army* advanced on Warsaw while the remnants of the Pomorze and the Poznan Armies faced encirclement. By 5 September these armies fell back towards the Vistula as the Modlin Army faced the *3rd Army* reinforced with *4th Army*'s panzer divisions only to be driven back on Warsaw. The first German units reached the suburbs of the capital briefly on 6 September. The *4th Panzer Division* of *10th Army* approached the capital from the south. It had penetrated further than any other armored unit up to this point despite being held up by an entrenched cavalry brigade on the first day of the campaign suffering a number of tank casualties from a small Polish tank unit. On 8 September the *4th Panzer Division* attempted to break into Warsaw, but the Poles had prepared the capital with new gun positions. The German unit lost about 60 vehicles to the Polish gunners and withdrew to await the arrival of the infantry and began a siege of the city.

Warsaw held on while the Polish field armies struggled to avoid encirclement. General Juliusz K. Rommel, isolated from the Lodz Army which he commanded, took charge of the creation of the Warsaw Army and the defense of the city. Marshal Rydz-Smigly and his staff could do little to coordinate

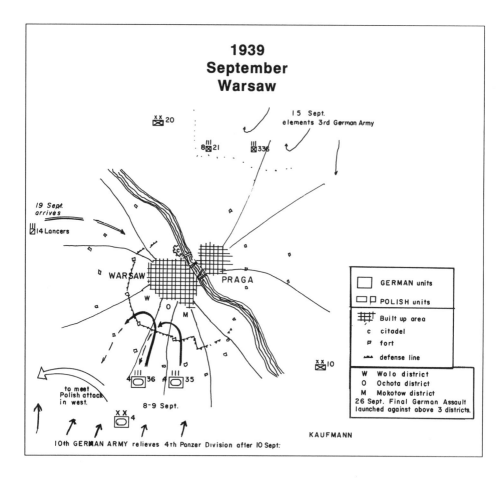

the defense of Poland after the first few days since the *Luftwaffe* had virtually destroyed the Polish lines of communication. He made preparations to move the government from Warsaw.

General Tadeusz Kutrzeb, commanding the Poznan Army, launched his divisions against the *30th Division* of the German *8th Army* beginning the battle of the Bzura River on 9 September an offensive action Rydz-Smigly had refused a few days earlier. The German advance on Warsaw was slowed as the German *8th Army* pulled back to meet this attack. After several days of fighting, about a dozen divisions of three Polish armies were isolated at Kutno to the west of Warsaw. The *Luftwaffe* unleashed its full force on the trapped units as German troops tightened the encirclement and began a methodical destruction of those Polish forces. Some Polish units, after their southward breakout attempts failed, moved toward the east in an attempt to reach Warsaw. On the way, they encountered the German *10th Army*, which had destroyed a large Polish force at Radom on 11 September, and soon after had the capital under siege. One of these units was General Abraham's Cavalry Brigade, organized from the remnants of two cavalry brigades. In their breakout attempt on 17 September they engaged the German *4th Panzer Division* in the Kampinos Forest and with two Polish infantry divisions broke through to Warsaw. After the battle the entrapped Polish armies rapidly disintegrated and were completely destroyed by 21 September.

By 17 September only small pockets of resistance existed throughout the northern part of the country. The Russians then advanced across Poland's largely undefended eastern borders causing the Polish situation to become totally hopeless.

The Krakow Army remained the only major Polish field force, and, after retreating from the fierce battles in the southeast, it took up positions in the region between Lublin and Lwow. To the south of it was the remnants of the Malopolska Army which was formed at the end of the first week of the invasion. The Malopolska Army had attempted to hold the Dunajec River line and was forced to retreat to the San River and the fortress of Przemysl on 7 September. By 12 September it had suffered heavy losses. Rydz-Smigly, with most of the government, departed Warsaw during the second week of the war and moved southeast towards Rumania. Allied aid was not forthcoming, and no shuttling of Allied bombers across Germany to Poland took place since most Polish airfields soon became vulnerable to ground assault. Allied fear of German retaliation precluded any early air strikes against targets in Germany.

With the Soviet invasion the Polish commander in chief ordered the retreat of all his forces east of the Vistula to Hungary and Rumania. The Malopolska Army began to fall apart as Soviet troops quickly moved on Lwow. With the Germans advancing on its other front, the escape route to Rumania and Hungary was closing for the Krakow Army to the north. Polish armored forces of the Warsaw Mechanized Brigade and the 1st Light Tank Company spearheaded the

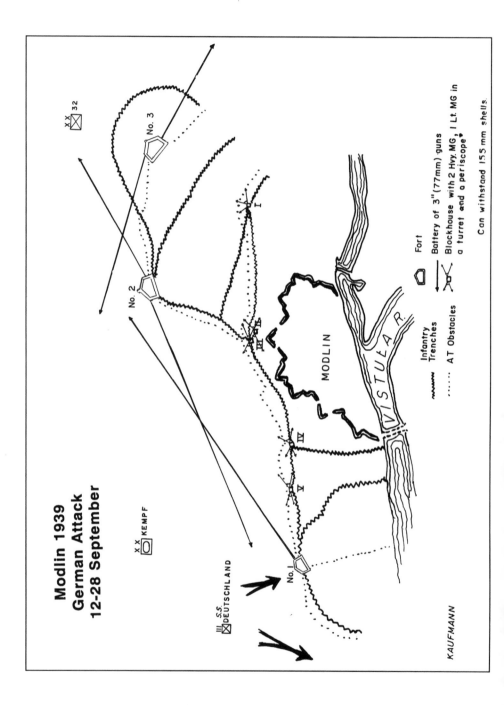

Modlin 1939
German Attack
12-28 September

XX 32

No. 3

No. 2

No. 1

MODLIN

VISTULA R.

KEMPF XX

III S.S. DEUTSCHLAND

KAUFMANN

Fort

Battery of 3"(77mm) guns

Blockhouse with 2 Hvy.MG, I Lt. MG in a turret and a periscope*

Infantry Trenches

AT Obstacles

*Can withstand 155 mm shells.

southward advance of the Krakow Army with about a hundred tanks. Soon after successfully engaging the *4th Light Division*, the *2nd Panzer Division* arrived. The Polish tanks, outnumbered four to one fought a three-day battle which ended with the surrender of the Krakow Army on 20 September.

General Guderian's *XIX Corps* advance on Brest-Litovsk served to cut off Polish units retreating eastward. His units found themselves on the Russian side of the demarcation line after 17 September and had to make preparations to pull back. All German units in eastern Poland had to disengage and prepare to move back to their side of the line with some minor clashes taking place with the Russians.

On 16 September the Germans began a major effort to bomb Warsaw into submission. Before the air assault began in earnest, the bombers dropped leaflets over the capital warning the population to evacuate their city. When the actual air assault began on 25 September, the bombers dropped high explosive bombs and JU-52 transports unloaded incendiaries to add to the devastation. The fierce bombings and artillery bombardments continued until General Juliusz Rommel, commander of the Warsaw Army, surrendered the city on 27 September with its 140,000 Polish troops. Not all the Polish soldiers surrendered—some removed their uniforms and fell in with the civilian population to fight another day. Throughout Poland the same thing occurred as the nucleus for what became occupied Europe's largest underground army began to form.

The fortress city of Modlin, to the north of Warsaw, surrendered the next day. Though Polish positions at Danzig had fallen in the first week of the war, other coastal positions held out longer. Gdynia fell on 14 September and then the assault on Hela began. By 24 September the German Navy brought up its other old battleship, the *Schlesien*, which added its guns to the naval bombardment. On 1 October Rear Admiral J. Unrug, commander of Polish coastal defense units, had the dubious honor of surrendering Hela and ending the resistance of the last Polish port. A small Polish force at Kock, east of Warsaw, fought the final battle of the campaign which ended with its surrender on 3 October. Some Polish units continued to roam through the country and resist as partisan formations while many units, including the 10th Mechanized Brigade and the

21st Tank Battalion, escaped into Hungary and Rumania respectively. The latter unit, equipped with French R-35 tanks never had an opportunity to engage the enemy.

Throughout the campaign, Polish troops scored minor successes. Polish cavalry units did not launch effective charges directly against armored units, but they conducted some mounted sweeps against infantry and also moved into positions from which they could assault tanks, but they attacked mostly on foot. They developed techniques for attacking and destroying German armored vehicles which included forcing open hatches with lances or swords and tossing in grenades. The Polish anti-tank gunners found that their weapons could take out German light tanks and became very proficient using them. In the one month of combat the Poles destroyed 217 tanks including 45 mediums. By the fifth day of the campaign, a Polish light tank battalion successfully knocked out over 30 armored vehicles of the two panzer divisions with only a loss of 2 of their own tanks. This proved how effective Polish anti-tank gunners could be and demonstrated what the Polish Army might have done if it had been modernized.

The Germans succeeded because they maintained a distinct advantage in men, weapons and tanks while the *Luftwaffe* provided successful tactical ground support operations. Contrary to popular opinion, German infantry did not perform well in Poland, and in numerous cases the only reason they succeeded was because they kept repeating their attacks.

The Germans learned important lessons from the Polish campaign. The *OKH* usually allotted a single panzer division to spearhead the drives of each army's advance. Because they proved rather ineffective, the light divisions were sent back to Germany for reorganization as the campaign drew to a close. A panzer regiment was added to each light division later in the fall to convert the four of them into panzer divisions. The supporting motorized divisions turned out to be too large and awkward, so the army decided to remove one motorized infantry regiment from each division after the campaign. This move also made expansion of the number of motorized units possible.

The *OKH* also discovered the effectiveness of their 88mm anti-aircraft gun as an artillery piece in actual combat. Although designed as an anti-aircraft weapon, it received a new

German Armor Losses in Poland	
674 tanks were lost or damaged of which a third, according to German sources, were totally destroyed including:	
Type of Tank	**Quantity**
Panzer I	89
Panzer II	78
Parzer 35t(Czech Tanks)	6
Panzer III	26
Panzer IV	19

According to historian Bryan Perrett, about another third of the damaged tanks were not worth repairing, especially the Panzer Is and IIs, and should also be added to the losses making the total number of tanks taken out of service over 400. The Poles also claimed destroying 319 armored cars. Historians Steve Zaloga and Victor Madej pointed out that over 5,500 motorcycles were destroyed mostly as a result of scouting operations. This accounts for a large number of German casualties but did not seem to deter the Germans in their continued use.

ground support role for the close support of combat units. Lighter *Luftwaffe* anti-aircraft units also achieved some success in containing a breakout during the encirclement of Radom until army units arrived. Anti-aircraft units had to train and prepare to function in a dual role after this campaign.

The German High Command was concerned about a possible Allied offensive in the West during the attack against Poland and had serious reservations about advancing too far into the eastern part of the country. The Polish road and rail system was in no condition to accommodate the rapid move-

Polish Campaign Statistics					
The Polish Campaign began on 1 September 1939 and ended early in October 1939 as the last units crossed the border into neutral territory or surrendered to the German or Soviet occupying forces.					
Country	KIA	WIA	POW	Interned*	MIA
Poland	66,300	133,700	787,000*	85,000	
Germany	16,000	32,000	32,000		5,000
Soviet Union	737	1,862			
Note: *587,000 Taken by Germans, 200,000 taken by Russians. Interned = number of Polish troops taken in by Neutral countries.					

ment of units disengaging to return to the West. This may have affected mechanized units more than others because it resulted in extensive wear and tear on vehicles. As for the infantry units, it meant that they would have had to move great distances on foot to reach railheads from where they could be transported out. There was no quick way to extract troops from Poland and send them to the West in the fall of 1939.

Both Germans and Allies benefited from the campaign by discovering the most effective type of tactical moves and the most efficient use of their new equipment. Unfortunately, the Germans seem to have profited from this lesson to a much greater extent than the Allies. General Gamelin claimed that he could easily cut off the rapidly advancing panzers and isolate them. He might have been successful if the Germans had refought the Polish Campaign in the West.

War on the Western Front

On 1 September 1939 Hitler, donning his new simple military uniform, took the rostrum to address the Reichstag in the Kroll Opera House in Berlin. The building functioned as the meeting center for the legislative body after the Nazis burned down the Reichstag building in February 1933. Here, the German representatives voted away their law making powers to the German chancellor, Adolph Hitler, with the Enabling Act, a month after the fire. Appropriately, Hitler addressed his powerless parlia-

French Order of Battle - Air Force			
September 1939			
Army	1st Air Army	2nd Air Army	5th Air Army
HQ & Commander Sector	Paris General Mouchard Northeast Front	Aix en Provence General Houdemon Southeast Front	Algeria General Bouscat
Forces	15 Fighter Groups 15 Bomber Groups 11 Recon Groups 31 Obsv. Groups	5 Fighter Groups 4 Bomber Groups 1 Recon Groups 5 Obsv. Groups	3 Fighter Groups 11 Bomber Groups 1 Recon Groups 9 Obsv. Groups

19 of 23 Fighter Groups were modern aircraft (12 of MS 406, 4 of Curtiss 75, 3 of Potez 631)

After October 1939 the 1st Air Army divided into sectors corresponding to Army Groups of Northeast Front.

Organizational Changes	Northern Zone of Air Operations (ZOAN) General de la Vigerie Covered 1st Army Group	Eastern Zone of Air Operations (ZOAE) General Pennès Covered 2nd Army Group	Southern Zone of Air Operations (ZOAS) General Odic Covered 3rd Army Group

ment informing it that Polish forces had violated the sacred territory of the Reich and that he had begun to take the appropriate retaliatory steps. "Bomb will be met by bomb," he threatened while proclaiming how deligently he had sought a peaceful solution.

The streets of Berlin remained calm with no rejoicing for most of the citizenry did not look forward to a war. In Paris and London the reaction was virtually the same. Not only did the horrors of the Great War still haunt the citizens of each country, but the new weapons of terror seen in action during the Spanish Civil War struck many with a feeling of dread.

On 1 September the news media flashed to the world a report that the British had begun to mobilize, and on 2 September the headlines announced that France was preparing to mobilize some of its 8,000,000 men on call. The French Army was portrayed as a force ready to seriously challenge Germany and possibly rescue Poland. The next day French news sources proclaimed that Paris was "Stripped and Ready for War" and reported a mass evacuation of the frontier and the city of

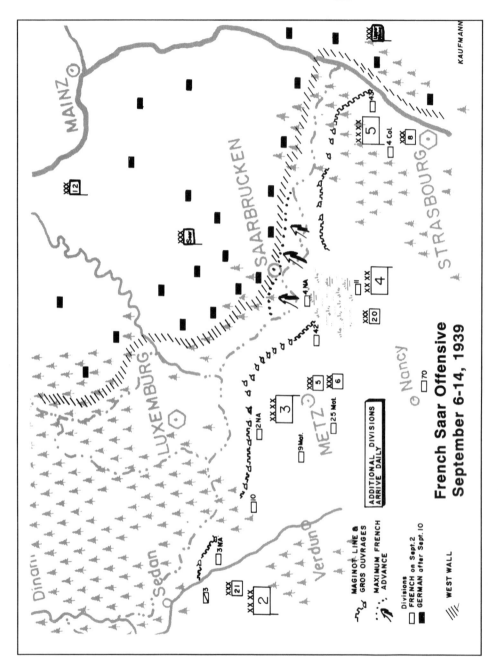

KAUFMANN

**French Saar Offensive
September 6-14, 1939**

ADDITIONAL DIVISIONS
ARRIVE DAILY

MAGINOT LINE &
GROS OUVRAGES

MAXIMUM FRENCH
ADVANCE

Divisions
☐ FRENCH on Sept.2
■ GERMAN after Sept.10

///// WEST WALL

Strasbourg. On 5 September, the first news reports asserted erroneously that the French offensive against the West Wall had begun. The French authorities issued War Communique No. 1 which stated: "Operations have begun by combined land, sea and air forces." That evening War Communique No. 2 claimed: "Contacts are being made progressively on our frontiers. French naval forces have gone to the positions assigned to them. Our air forces are making the necessary reconnaissances." In reality, the French had undertaken no offensive action on their eastern border.

On 4 September the new chief of the Imperial General Staff, General Edmund Ironside, met with his French counterpart, General Maurice Gamelin, at the latter's headquarters in the fortress of Vincennes, just outside Paris. Gamelin, who also served as commander of all Allied forces in France, informed his British guest that he intended to squeeze out three German salients between the French border and the West Wall by 17 September. He would next begin "experiments" against the German fortified line, but he would advance no further. He also assured Ironside that the Germans had too small a force to launch an attack in the West, but expressed the hope that they would.

Only about a week before the war, Gamelin informed his government that France could not hope to launch a major offensive for another two years. Back in July, Lord Gort, then chief of the Imperial General Staff, received a notification from Gamelin that France needed much more time to prepare. Apparently there was no room on Gamelin's agenda for the promise of a major offensive made to Poland. As a matter of honor, he launched a token advance a few days after mobilization: Gamelin's Saar offensive. On 7 September French units advanced mainly out of the Sarre Gap between the RFs of Metz and La Lauter of the Maginot Line moving towards the German industrial center at Saarbrücken. The French units lumbered forward into one of the most heavily defended sectors of the still incomplete Siegfried Line, and penetrated less than 6 miles (10 kilometers).

On the night of 8/9 September the first of the Maginot forts opened fire on German territory. The gros ouvrage of Hochwald aimed a rapid fire barrage from several of its guns against the German village of Schweigen as a unit of Moroccan Tirailleurs advanced on it. The Hochwald was one of the few ouvrages located close enough to encompass German territory within the range of its 75mm guns. During this first action one older model of 75mm gun had difficulty maintaining the rapid fire and soon bolts burst from the mounting flying through the chamber like shrapnel, but fortunately didn't cause any injuries. The gunners did not detect problems before the war because there had never been live firings from the fort; they had practiced with other weapons in training camps. At the time the war broke out the forts of the Maginot Line still needed time to work out equipment problems.

The attitude of Gamelin and the Allies contributed to their lack of success. As the offensive began, Gamelin quickly concluded that the Polish position was rapidly becoming hopeless. The French commander had no intention of forcing the Germans' hand and this provided him with an excuse to shy away from committing additional divisions and support. On 12 September at Abbeville, Gamelin informed the Allied Supreme War Council that the situation in Poland did not justify further Allied efforts in the Saar. Although at this meeting Prime Minister Chamberlain declared the Polish situation hopeless, and requested the French to cease supportive actions, he did not necessarily agree with the termination of the Saar offensive. After the meeting, on 16 September, General Ironside noted that Gamelin had abandoned the initiative and had decided to settle in and wait for a German counterattack between the fortified lines. Gamelin also anticipated a large scale invasion of Belgium and the Netherlands on or about 15 October in repetition of Germany's 1914 maneuver. On 21 September he officially called off the Saar operation, but did not make this decision public. To help downplay all the optimistic and exaggerated reports of French success on German soil, the news media were informed on the previous day that German forces were massing near Aachen. The implication was obvious; the threat to the Low Countries meant a possible repetition of 1914 and French armies must not be caught striking out towards the Rhine while the Germans outflanked them. Newspaper reports that Belgium and the Netherlands broke dikes to flood lands near their German borders added weight to the threat, but at the time neither country believed a German invasion was imminent. The media soon noted that the buildup at Aachen was a false report.

Nothing of any significance actually occurred on the Saar front during the remainder of September. The French armies quietly and secretly slipped away, withdrawing back to pre-invasion positions by 4 October to await the expected German offensive.

The Germans attacked the small French covering force left behind in its territory on 16 October. By 17 October the Germans, with new formations returning from the Polish Front, completed an offensive which recaptured their lost territory. At the end of the day on 16 October the press claimed that the Germans now occupied the first town on French soil, the village of Apach, and that they would not advance much further. The armies on both sides began to settle in, awaiting further developments as a new phase of the war began. The Germans called it Sitzkrieg, the French La Drôle de Guerre, the British the Bore War and their American cousins the Phony War.

Thus the Allies had lost a golden opportunity to strike at the small, heavily outnumbered, mixed force of German Regular and poorly trained reservist divisions defending the Western Front in the first days of the Polish campaign. Even many high ranking German officers believed that a determined Allied offensive might have carried the French through the West Wall and up to the barrier of the Rhine in only a couple of weeks, well before the Germans could have brought back formations from the East.

Although many historians blamed the lack of French aggressiveness on the defensive "Maginot Mentality," the facts do not seem to bear them out. A major offensive towards the Rhine would not have required the French to abandon their primary defensive position, the Maginot Line, which the French High Command admittedly was reluctant to give up. A large part of the Maginot Line proper would have remained part of the main defenses even if French units had reached the Rhine. Most of the heavy defenses of the RF of Metz faced the borders of neutral Belgium and Luxembourg, and an offensive through the Saar towards the Rhine would still have left major sections

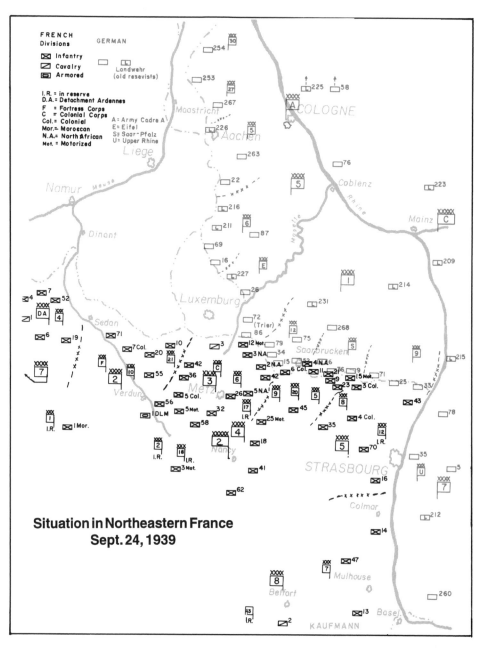

Situation in Northeastern France
Sept. 24, 1939

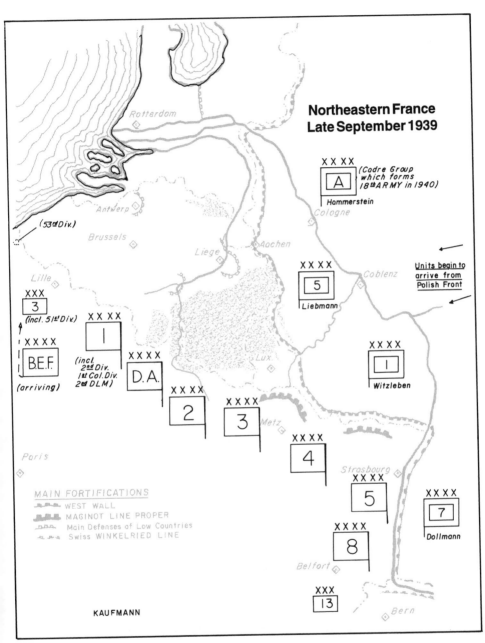

Northeastern France
Late September 1939

XXXX
A   (Cadre Group
      which forms
      18ᵗʰARMY in 1940)
Hammerstein

Units begin to
arrive from
Polish Front

(53ᵈDiv.)

XXXX
5
Liebmann

XXX
3
(incl. 51ˢᵗDiv.)

XXXX
1
(incl.
2ⁿᵈ Div.
1ˢᵗ Col.Div.
2ⁿᵈ DLM)

XXXX
B.E.F.
(arriving)

XXXX
D.A.

XXXX
1
Witzleben

XXXX
2

XXXX
3

Metz

XXXX
4

XXXX
5

Strasbourg

XXXX
7
Dollmann

XXXX
8

Belfort

XXX
13

Bern

MAIN FORTIFICATIONS
WEST WALL
MAGINOT LINE PROPER
Main Defenses of Low Countries
Swiss WINKELRIED LINE

Paris

KAUFMANN

of both regions defending each flank. This was indeed one of the original offensive roles of the Maginot Line.

The fact that the French undertook no serious offensive after the collapse of Poland became imminent was not only due to General Gamelin's lack of confidence in his army's capabilities, but also to their fear of German retaliation. General Gamelin had informed Prime Minister Daladier, back on 1 September, that the only way the Allies could relieve the pressure on Poland was to advance through Belgium. The Belgian king would not cooperate, and had actually deployed troops along the French border when he began mobilization. Did this become only an excuse for a lack of aggressiveness or was the general actually serious about an offensive? His suggestion that the French advance into Belgium did not mean that he wanted to cross over the Belgian-German border, since that would have involved either breaching the West Wall defenses in front of the German city of Aachen, or advancing through the rough terrain of the Ardennes into equally difficult terrain on the German side of the border. Most apparently, his suggestion to occupy Belgium was only to shorten defensive lines and create advanced air bases. The facts demonstrate that the French High Command incorrectly believed that its army could not move forward without more training and equipment and that a major setback in the field would not only shatter the morale of the French troops, but would also encourage the Germans to attack. As a result, Gamelin became deeply involved with mobilization, training and equipping the army at a time when he should have engaged the enemy more vigorously if only to boost the morale of his troops and give them combat experience.

Air Offensive

One of best ways for the Allies to strike Germany early in the war was with their large air fleets. After the invasion of Poland, the Allies, mainly the French, were reluctant to launch an air offensive for fear of German retaliation. General Joseph Vuillemin, the commander of the Armée de l'Air, had visited Germany in August 1938, and the Germans skillfully convinced him during his inspection of aircraft factories that they were expanding an already formidable air force. With only a year to rebuild, Vuillemin did not feel the Allies would be ready to engage the *Luftwaffe* in offensive actions for several more months. He expressed the belief that French fighters would be able to defend the homeland, but he placed no confidence in the obsolete aircraft that made up most of the French bomber force that might take part in offensive operations. He believed that when the German offensive began, his bombers would be able to operate only at night and that the British must handle daylight operations. The RAF prepared for this role with new aircraft which soon proved totally inadequate for the task. The French air commander, his government and the British government did not want to provoke Germany in the air before the Germans began offensive action.

Vuillemin planned to use his fighter force to protect the interior of France, while Gamelin insisted those aircraft cover the army zones near the frontier to protect mobilization. Early in the war the fighters of the French Armée de l'Air engaged in combat over the front with little success. The *Luftwaffe* remained grounded in the West during the first days of the war, and the anti-aircraft gun crews were ordered to withhold fire on Allied aircraft. Those orders changed after the French Saar offensive began. On 8 September French aircraft began observation and reconnaissance missions under the protection of fighters while some fighters actually attacked the Saarbrücken aerodrome. The Germans easily drove back or destroyed most French aircraft on reconnaissance missions. By the end of September Vuillemin called off most observation missions because of heavy losses, and he concentrated his efforts on defending the interior while the Armée de l'Air received more modern aircraft during the winter. For the remainder of the year, French aircraft engaged in limited reconnaissance and leaflet dropping missions with the British.

British inter-war theory postulated that the bomber would always get through and although this belief became the centerpiece of the development of the RAF, it also caused the British to dread the consequences of air attacks as they watched the growth of the *Luftwaffe*. The fear of terror bombing witnessed in the Spanish Civil War was magnified by the conviction that it was only a small foretaste of the havoc a bomber offensive could now wreak.

Bombing and the use of poison gas caused a great deal of concern in Great Britain. When the war began, all major participants, including Germany, renounced the use of poison gas, declaring that they would observe the Geneva Convention and would also avoid bombing population centers. Throughout Great Britain, the fear of gas persisted anyway, and the populace continued to carry gas masks.

Shortly after the British government declared war on Germany on 3 September, about mid-day, the air raid sirens wailed and the population of London scurried for cover. The drone of German aircraft over the skies of London did not materialize because the alert had been triggered by a British aircraft returning from France. Another false alarm occurred a few days later in Paris.

The British began their air war on the night of 3/4 September when 10 Whitley bombers dropped almost 5,500,000 propaganda leaflets over northern Germany. The next day, the RAF undertook its first serious operation. Fifteen Blenheims flew to Wilhelmshaven and fourteen Wellington bombers were sent against Brunsbüttel at the entrance to the Kiel Canal. For a loss of seven aircraft, the British succeeded in hitting the pocket battleship *Admiral Scheer* with a few bombs which failed to explode, and damaging the cruiser *Emden* at Wilhelmshaven. One of their aircraft flew off course and bombed a Danish town in error. Although the British hit a few military targets, mostly naval, the majority of the air action was devoted to littering Germany with propaganda leaflets from Whitleys on 22 more night missions before Christmas (Air Marshall Arthur Harris later commented that the RAF effort provided the Germans with enough toilet paper to last the war). At the end of September, General Ironside bitterly commented that the RAF and the British government failed to effectively employ the Bomber Command, and that, due to its poor condition, the Germans would annihilate the French air force just as quickly as they had eliminated the Polish air fleet.

Meanwhile, Winston Churchill, a cabinet member and First Lord of the Admiralty as of 2 September, endorsed an aggressive operation, Operation Royal Marine, a plan to launch mines into the Rhine River from French territory and hopefully obstruct river traffic necessary to the German war industry. But French Prime Minister Daladier, worried about retaliation, would not allow the activation of the plan until the German offensive actually began.

These feeble attempts at agression failed to achieve anything. Although the British thought the mining of the Rhine and the bombing of the Ruhr early in the war might disrupt the German war effort, events later proved them wrong. The RAF's bomber force was too small to cause great damage and the effect of floating naval mines down the Rhine, when finally released the next year, turned out to be a disappointment. On the air and on the ground, the Allies were not prepared to act.

French troops on their way to the front. After Poland fell, the Allies had to wait several months for major action against their foe.

CHAPTER III

Sitzkrieg in the West

The so-called Phony War supposedly began in October, with the conclusion of the Polish campaign as the Germans settled down on the Western Front after recapturing the territory in the Saar. Actually the first acts of a Sitzkrieg had taken place earlier. The first reports of strange activity had come from Switzerland on 8 September when a small article reported that

French troops manning an anti-aircraft gun.

French and German soldiers were removing their uniforms and diving into the Rhine for a casual swim. Whether true or not, the news from Switzerland claimed that at the same time German troops along the Rhine were displaying huge placards written in French. These signs proclaimed in large print that the Germans had orders not to shoot at the French unless they fired first, and that Germany had no reason to make war on the French.

Gamelin's Strategy

With the successful conclusion of the Polish campaign, the German *Wehrmacht* established its reputation as the most modern and effective armed force on the Continent. Their blitzkrieg was believed to have been a result of the overwhelming superiority of the *Luftwaffe* and the panzers. The Allies studied that victory and many analysts and writers concluded that what happened in Poland could not happen in the West. After all, the Germans had surrounded Poland on three sides, and the Poles had depended on cavalry rather than tanks. Furthermore, the Allies knew that the Polish border was only thinly defended, and that the Poles had had no heavy border fortifications. Surely the West was better prepared, with the Maginot Line covering the entire frontier with Germany.

If the Allies took the offensive, how would they defeat Germany? The whole of western Germany was defended by the West Wall from Switzerland to the North Sea. How were the Allied armies to breach these positions any better than they expected the Germans to take on their own? Would the British naval blockade bring victory or could the Allied air forces bomb them into submission?

Even though the Germans did not have a vastly superior air force, they had no more tanks than the Allied armies and most certainly had no field army greatly superior to that of the Allies, but both France and Great Britain were convinced that they did. Worse still, Germany's Axis partner, Italy, also had a significant military force which always remained in the back of the minds of Allied planners. The Allies felt their armies needed months or even years to prepare to fight their powerful

French signal troops in the field.

adversaries, their air forces needed possibly the same amount of time, while their navies were ready to do their job.

During the Phony War the Allies continued to make plans while the troops underwent additional training, constructed new positions and waited for the Germans to make the next move. General Gamelin and his commander of the Northeast Front, General Georges, had concerns about what they considered their vulnerable flanks when the war began. One of their worries was the possiblility of a Germans move through Switzerland. Considering the fact that the mountainous terrain was on the French side of the border, and that Switzerland had its own defenses, this was a rather unfounded concern. No force, however fast moving, could overwhelm Switzerland and storm through the rugged terrain of the Franco-Swiss border before French forces could seal off all approaches. Another concern was the Ardennes, the rugged region on the border of Belgium and Luxembourg. General Georges fretted about a thrust through the Ardennes and initially deployed a number of mobile units to counter such a move.

At the end of September Gamelin actually devised a reasonable strategy for thwarting a German offensive. His plan was to thin out the defensive front, using reservists, and create a considerable reserve of Regular infantry units and armor for counterattacks. These designs contained serious flaws. Gamelin stated positively that he could cut off any German armored thrusts, probably thinking in terms of the events in Poland, where single German panzer divisions led breakthroughs followed by infantry divisions. But he may never have considered an armored phalanx of several panzer divisions leading a breakthrough. Even if he had prepared for a large scale penetration, if the *Luftwaffe* took aerial dominance, it still might have proved impossible to move the reserves forward to launch a coordinated counterattack.

Knowledge of the potential of German air power came from General Paul Armengaud of the Armée de l'Air who witnessed the collapse of Poland as a military observer. In early October he reported to Gamelin, warning him of the German tactics. He emphasized the German use of the *Luftwaffe* in conjunction with the advancing panzer forces which had led to the destruction of the Polish armies and insisted this combination could crack any lightly held defensive line, cripple communications and break up the movement of reserves. This seemed to indicate that whatever strategy Gamelin chose would fail unless he denied the Germans control of the air. Some historians claim Gamelin ignored Armengaud, but this does not appear correct. In fact, soon after this interview, both Gamelin and Daladier insisted that the British send more fighter squadrons as Armengaud recommended. The British, reluctant to strip their island of protection, had already held back some squadrons earmarked for duty on the Continent because the French had not made enough airfields available for them.

General Gamelin considered General Georges and General Gaston Billotte to be two of his best officers and gave them the most important assignments in the defense of France. Georges commanded the Northeast Front while Billotte was assigned to the Southeastern Front. The latter held great importance for the commander in chief since before the war Gamelin had wanted an offensive launched through the Alps against the northwestern industrial region of a pro-German Italy in the event of war with that country. His idea to hold the Germans with the Maginot Line while attacking through the Alps had several flaws, but also demonstrated that he could not be accused of a "Maginot mentality." Understanding that both German and Italian industrial centers lay close to the French border, he chose to strike only at Italy concluding that the Italian armed forces would have less staying power. It is amazing that he advocated his army fight its way through an obstacle like the Alps, but this would explain his belief that the Germans could swiftly overrun the western part of Switzerland and reach France. Perhaps his ideas were still being shaped by the Great War in which infantry had dominated the field of battle.

When Gamelin realized that Italy would not enter the war, he recalled Billotte from the Alpine frontier and assigned him to a new army group on Georges' Northeast Front in late September. Billotte took command of the 1st Army Group while General Prételat's armies, including those that had taken part in the Saar offensive, took the designation of 2nd Army Group. On Gamelin's orders, he prepared for an advance into Belgium with the key mechanized units of the reserve echelon in the lead. To further complicate matters, at the beginning of November Gamelin created 3rd Army Group under General Antoine Besson along the Rhine and Swiss border. This shortened the front of General Prételat's 2nd Army Group, but it tied down more units as reserves were needed for two army groups instead of one.

A month after General Besson left his command of the Southeast Front, that front's only army, the 6th Army, moved to the Northeast Front to form the reserve. The 7th Army, which had previously constituted the front's reserve reinforced the 1st Army Group. Gamelin had stripped the Southeast Front, but after September he had no doubt that the German offensive would take place on the Belgian plains and prepared to meet them there with his best formations and commanders. The few remaining units of the Southeast Front became the Alpine Army under General René Olry. Of all the major French commands, only Olry's would cover itself in glory.

A British Hurricane refuels on a French airfield.

The British Expeditionary Force
Moves Up

The arrival of the British Expeditionary Force (BEF) proffered some relief to the French position. The advance parties departed from Portsmouth on 4 September, and the big troop convoys, escorted by the Royal Navy, embarked at Southampton and west coast ports on 9 September, arriving at Cherbourg in Normandy and Nantes and St. Nazaire up the Loire River. While troops arrived in northwestern France beyond the normal effective range of the *Luftwaffe*, the Channel ports from Le Havre to Dunkirk were opened to supply ships. The first two divisions moved up to a sector near the old World War I battlefields around Arras, and, by 27 September, over 152,000 men had safely crossed the Channel. Unlike German and French units, British ones relied extensively on vehicles rather than horses and over 21,000 vehicles accompanied the expeditionary force, albeit not all were designed for military service since the government commandeered many from civilian sources. By mid-October Lord Gort deployed two corps of four

British M.G. Bunker in Flanders

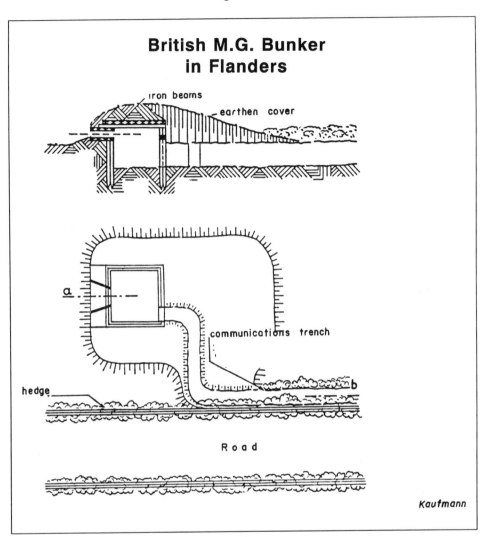

Kaufmann

Regular divisions: the I Corps under General John Dill with the 1st and 2nd Divisions and the II Corps under General Alan Brooke with the 3rd and 4th Divisions. The expeditionary force took up its position between the French 1st and 7th Armies of General Billotte's 1st Army Group. The French 7th Army began to move into position on the left flank of the BEF during October. Lord Gort's troops came under French command, and he carried out orders as instructed by Gamelin and later Georges.

On 7 October, just as the divisions of the II Corps began to settle in, Lord Gort escorted General Ironside on an inspection tour of the British sector. Ironside found that it included an industrial region where thousands of people crossed the border daily on their way to and from work. He noted that no concealment was possible and that the existing French anti-tank ditch following the border was covered at every turn by a blockhouse equipped with machine guns, anti-tank weapons and a periscope in the roof which afforded excellent observation. The defenses had heavy barbed wire protection and even anti-tank rail obstacles appeared in some places. The whole area reminded him of Flanders in World War I.

The region, according to Ironside, was virtually waterlogged. This presented a special problem because the weapons positions could not be dug deep enough and the men had to build breastworks above ground level. The choice of sites was rather surprising, especially since it was not dictated by necessity, as in World War I, and there was no reason to put troops in such miserable positions to defend a small slice of territory.

The I Corps occupied a low lying area dotted with numerous farms and typical farmland vegetation and included many streams and ditches. On his inspection Ironside noticed that here the soldiers occupied well concealed positions. On the other hand, he found the II Corps on more exposed terrain, but at a higher elevation where it occupied a trench system reminiscent of the Great War.

General Bernard Montgomery, commander of the 3rd Division since August 1939, found the British field army unprepared for its mission. He criticized Hore-Belisha for telling Parliament that the army sent to France in 1939 had been equipped "...in the finest possible manner." The army's communications systems as well as the transportation vehicles were inadequate and his division left a trail of broken down vehicles across France as it moved into position in October. Montgomery, apparently unable to appreciate the fact that the British were the most mobile of the Allied forces, made sure that his division's transportation services operated adequately. He also took steps to arm his troops properly. While British infantry divisions had Boys anti-tank rifles which Montgomery knew could not stop German armor, he obtained French weapons of a larger caliber for his infantry brigades to replace the inadequate ones.

Some historians as well as British general officers present at the time have pointed out that if Hitler had begun his offensive in October or early November, he might have met with success for the British were simply not ready for it. In the first weeks of October the overall British position and defenses, especially their left flank, were weak and exposed. The quality of the troops in the expeditionary force was questionable since many reservists, who needed more training in order to function properly, filled out the ranks of its four Regular divisions. Soldiers were late in arriving too. Though the 5th Division arrived before the end of the year (its 15th Brigade would later be sent to Norway for the campaign there), none of the Territorial Army divisions crossed over to France until early 1940 and even then they still lacked sufficient training.

As winter set in the British troops continued to dig in along the frontier while securing a line of communications with their main bases in Western France. In November a dozen companies of Royal Engineers from the Territorial divisions with auxiliary units and a special Excavation Company (with trench digging equipment) arrived in France to handle the major construction work on the defensive position. Brigadier A. Minnis commanded a special construction unit consisting of five field companies and a field park company (serving as a headquarters and service company, it included mobile workshops) of the Royal Engineers known as Force X. This unit operated in the sector of the BEF, constructing five standard types of bunkers based on French designs, in order to give depth to the already existing front. On this sector, the French had already dug an anti-tank ditch, erected some obstacles with blockhouses at key points and placed the bunkers at intervals of about 1,000 yards (900 meters). Although the engineers accomplished their objective, the British soldiers never had a chance to use their handiwork.

During November 1939 Hore-Belisha inspected the BEF, and on his return to London he criticized Lord Gort's troops for not preparing their defensive positions properly. He actually spent little time looking at their work, although he seemed dissatisfied with Force X, the special unit he had created. General Ironside investigated the situation which resulted in a rift between the upper echelon of the army and their civilian director. It culminated in Hore-Belisha's resignation in January 1940 .

As Gort settled into his position in France, serious problems became evident. Gort's headquarters command system became widely scattered at Arras and thus reduced its effectiveness as his staff began to mushroom in size. Furthermore Gort's precautions for his troops appeared effective only for trench warfare, and not air attack.

The British political leadership was no more inspiring than the lackluster top military brass. Chamberlain's exhortations to Parliament and the public barely motivated anyone. One member of Parliament, Harold Nicolson, remembered that Chamberlain's speeches put many to sleep, and that the Prime Minister "...might have been the Secretary of a firm of undertakers...." The one man who had the ability to fire the spirit of the public was Winston Churchill. Nicolson remembered that his speeches on paper were nothing compared to the way the great orator read them. But Churchill was on a leash, and the inspired leadership he could offer as prime minister came only when the Allies were teetering on the verge of disaster.

The British units conducted training exercises at divisional level between the end of October 1939 and April 1940. Montgomery began to demonstrate his outstanding leadership capabilities and impressed his corps commander, General Alan Brooke. His division became the best of the expeditionary force with three major divisional exercises that set a standard and prepared the 3rd Division not only for the movement forward into Belgium, but also an orderly retreat. A winter visit to one of his battalions, rotated into the Maginot Line for combat experience, left him with no confidence at all in the ability of the French to fight. Even though he underestimated the French, his conclusions led to redoubled efforts to prepare his division for the worst.

The harsh, cold winter did not help Allied preparations, nor did the boredom of inaction improve troop morale. At the suggestion of the French early in the war, some British units, eventually reaching division strength, moved into interval positions of the Maginot Line, not just to gain experience, but also to have troops on an active front. This contributed a partial relief from the drudgery of an inactive front. Nine brigades, at least one from each of the five Regular Army divisions, rotated individually up to the Boulay sector of the Maginot Line, in the RF of Metz, during the winter of 1939-40. Each brigade served under a French infantry division and when one finished its time on the line after about 15 days another brigade came to relieve it.

The 1st Battalion of the Black Watch reported for duty on the Maginot Line front in March 1940. It was followed in April by the remainder of the 51st Highland Division of the Territorial Army. The division took up a position between the French 2nd and 42nd Divisions in front of Hackenberg, one of the two largest ouvrages of the Maginot Line. The division pushed its men up to the line of contact near the border and occupied old French positions. These consisted of small log cabins which the French had thrown up all along the forward line to shelter their troops in advanced posts. When the weather began to improve, the British troops created dugout positions to replace the cabins while they destroyed a number of positions the French had erected because the division did not have enough troops to man them all. The 51st Division remained in position on the front until two weeks after the German offensive began and actually repelled some large enemy combat patrols early in May.

The expeditionary force received the first Territorial division in January 1940, the 48th South Midland Division. In February the 50th Northumbrian and the 51st Highland Division arrived, followed in April by the 42nd East Lancashire and 44th Home Counties Divisions. Sir Ronald F. Adam formed the III Corps with a couple of these new divisions. Because the newer formations lacked experience, Gort allowed the exchange of some Regular and Territorial units between divisions.

A large number of troops engaged in the construction of rear area bases and established lines of communication during the winter. This included the creation of 59 new landing fields for the RAF as well as 100 miles of railroads. In April three Territorial divisions, which still had not completed their training, came to France to work on the lines of communication: the 12th Eastern, 23rd Northumbrian and 46th North Midland and West Riding Divisions.

Allied Plans

The Allies prepared plans in anticipation of the German invasion of the Low Countries, assuming that Belgium and Luxembourg would be attacked. General Gamelin's first plan was known as the Escaut Maneuver or Plan E, which called for the occupation of the Escaut (Schelde) River line in Belgium and the defense of Antwerp and Ghent, thus extending the Allied front. His plan left out most of Belgium, largely as a result of Leopold III's refusal to cooperate with the Allies. (In 1939 the Belgian Army, which began mobilizing in September, deployed its troops along the French border to prevent Allied intervention.) Since Gamelin felt the Allies could do little offensively, he believed this plan was within the capabilities of his forces since it only required the army to advance a short distance to take up a defensive position. However, British General Ironside and French General Georges were against the move. The former appeared to be even more entrenched in World War I methodology than Gamelin while the latter, one of France's best military leaders, seemed afraid to take any action. Both were against giving up the position they had prepared on the Belgian border for an advance.

The three generals met at Gamelin's headquarters at Vincennes on 6 October. Gamelin, having analyzed the outcome of the Polish campaign, made the following observations:

1. German success came as a result of the actions of their fast and powerful armored formations which, with their close air support, could make deep penetrating thrusts.

2. The French plan consisted of:

a. Allowing the Germans to attack the fortified positions and counterattack after inflicting heavy casualties.

b. Holding on to all fortified positions if the Germans

King Leopold III of Belgium. His stubborn refusal to allow French and British armed forces into his country after war broke out caused tremendous difficulties for Allied planners.

penetrated through gaps and counterattack when the attackers out distanced their supporting logistical units.

c. Preparing as many positions as possible with anti-tank weapons, and creating a system of defense in depth.

3. The German assault divisions were as far back from the frontier as 100 miles (160 kilometers), waiting for the moment to attack. The main thrust might be through:

a. Switzerland or Italy in the south or

b. Belgium and possibly the Netherlands in the north. Gamelin believed that the main effort probably would be directed through Liege, as in 1914, and not through Luxembourg and the Belgian Ardennes because the terrain would hinder the deployment of tanks. Amazingly, while he ruled out the Ardennes, he considered the Jura Mountains on the Swiss bor-

The Belgian Gates during the Phony War. This tank obstacle was an important part of the Belgian defensive line.

der as a possible invasion site, although he was rather firm in his conclusion that the Allies would fight the decisive battle on the plains of northern Belgium.

At the meeting, Gamelin also insisted that the British must send more fighter support, not only because the *Luftwaffe* ran the risk of wearing down the French air force, but also because every available fighter squadron was necessary to help prevent the Germans from dominating the air and possibly the battlefield. General Vuillemin, the commander of La Armée de l'Air, had already divided his 1st Air Army on the Northeast Front into zones of operation corresponding to the army groups of the region in order to give each air support. He established a third zone when the 3rd Army Group was created, and this new sector came under the 3rd Air Army. While Gamelin called for planes, he overlooked one significant weakness: France was desperately short of anti-aircraft weapons. Each ground army handled its own anti-aircraft units, while the air force had only five anti-aircraft regiments which made the task of air defense more difficult for the air commander.

The Allies continued to plan on Belgium being included in their defensive scheme. The Belgian Army was partially modernized and included about a dozen tanks in each of its army's 20 divisions. The defenses of Belgium had never been linked to those of the French. The old fortress rings of Antwerp, Namur and Liege were revitalized. Since Liege was near the German border, and back towards a point south of Liege. This line contained the only four modern forts built in Belgium. In some ways they were similar to those of the Maginot Line, except the two large forts of Battice and Eben Emael also had turrets mounting 120mm guns as well as those with 75mm guns. The main line of defenses included Liege as well as fortified positions on the Albert line of defense unless allowed to enter Belgium before an invasion. In late October, Colonel Blake, the British military attache to Belgium, informed General Ironside that the Belgians had completed a defensive line from Antwerp to Wavre and were still working on an anti-tank obstacle linking Wavre to Namur. The construction crew completed 300 meters of steel anti-tank obstacles (Belgian gates) daily. Still, King Leopold III of Belgium continued to insist that he would not give the Germans an excuse to invade by letting the Allies violate his neutrality, and that he did not believe any invasion would take place during the winter.

On 20 October General Gamelin informed the British that the Germans could deploy up to 130 divisions on the Western Front by the spring of 1940. He added that he would move troops from southern France and the Alps and create another 10 divisions. The British government had already authorized expanding the army, but Ironside noted that only 100 infantry tanks could be produced for the infantry divisions by June 1940. A dozen of these divisions would require about 450 of these tanks between them. Because of faulty intelligence which kept inflating the enemy's strength, the Allies remained convinced that their prospects of matching the Germans were poor.

Several serious questions remained unresolved between September and October on the employment of the RAF. The Armée de l'Air was incapable of launching any type of bombing missions, and still awaited new aircraft to provide ground support for the army. Though British military chiefs and politicians disagreed on whether or not to bomb Germany, by November General Ironside found the RAF lacked the means to carry out the operation. He also argued the RAF's plans for supporting the ground forces and interdicting an enemy advance were intolerable. For example, assuming German units would obligingly move along targeted transportation lines at the time of the attack, the RAF intended to bomb pre-selected transportation points at prearranged times to slow a German advance!

On 17 November 1939, Gamelin adopted a new plan which seemed far more adventurous than his previous attitude would have led one to expect. Some theorists believe that this new plan, called Plan D or the Dyle Maneuver, involved great risk, although the objectives appeared quite realistic. It required that when the Germans attacked, the 1st French Army Group would advance deep into northern Belgium and occupy a line running from Antwerp to Namur, along the Dyle River, with its three most mobile armies: the French 1st and 7th with the BEF sandwiched between them. Gamelin expected the Belgian Army to delay the Germans on the Meuse River and Albert Canal and then fall back on the Dyle Line. He never considered rushing the Allied armies to the Belgian main line of defense along the Albert Canal and at Liege, knowing that the troops would not be able to reach these positions in time to deploy properly if they did not enter Belgium before the enemy. (During secret negotiations led by British Admiral Sir Roger Keyes, of Zeebrugge fame, the Belgians agreed to complete a continuous anti-tank barrier which would seal the Gembloux Gap and link the Dyle River positions with Namur on the Meuse, transforming the Dyle Position into a solid line. Unfortunately, the Belgians never finished this project.) As the three armies began their long march, Gamelin planned for the 2nd and 9th French Armies to advance a shorter distance into southern Belgium, use its rugged terrain to delay the Germans, and then fall back to assume positions along the Meuse. Neither of these two armies was extremely powerful, but no major encounter was anticipated in there, especially in and around the "impassable" Ardennes.

All of these plans were complicated by a 1939 special arrangement which required the placement of all three army

With gas masks on, these French troops pass time during the Phony War with practice drill against gas attack.

groups facing Germany under the command of the Northeast Front. By the end of 1939, Gamelin found himself unable to direct all Allied operations from Vincennes, so, with the permission of Prime Minister Daladier, he made Georges commander in chief of the Northeast Front and had him set up a new headquarters in January 1940. At the same time, General Joseph Doumenc became commander of GHQ Land Forces. This arrangement complicated the situation between Vincennes, which De Gaulle described as more like a monastery than a general's headquarters, and the new headquarters of Doumenc at Montry and Georges at La Ferté-sous-Jouarre. Gamelin had no radio communication and the telephone system was not heavily used. His new subordinate commanders had to travel many miles back and forth between headquarters to contact the commander in chief and to contact service sections which had been split between these posts. When the campaign began, Gamelin remained secluded in his headquarters without a radio link to the outside world, and was seldom kept up to date on the developments on the front. Thus, he became isolated from the commands doing the fighting, but retained the power to intervene even though his decisions were based on outdated information. Another snag was Belgian neutrality. Despite British success in opening a channel to the Belgian military hierarchy, the king obstinately continued to refuse to allow the Allies to advance into his country before a German attack.

In March 1940, Gamelin added a Dutch option to his plan: the Breda maneuver. This plan proposed sending the French 7th Army into the Netherlands to help the Dutch in the event the Germans invaded. Georges, who disagreed with both Plan E and D, was totally opposed to this proposal because the Allies would greatly overextend themselves and virtually end up committing almost all of the 1st Army Group's reserves. Thus, Plan D was hindered not only by Belgian lack of cooperation, but also by a lack of enthusiasm on the part of the commander of the Northeast Front. This left most decisions in the hands of Georges, who attempted to carry out Plan D with the planned movement into the Netherlands, as instructed. By the time the commander in chief realized the magnitude of the disaster and attempted to take action, he only compounded the problems.

While the Allied leadership had adopted a more agressive plan, Ironside began to show some anxiety about Gamelin's refusal to launch any real offensive action soon, possibly not for years. He was convinced that Gamelin believed Hitler had to launch an offensive on the Western Front or face defeat, not just from military inactivity, but because of "explosive" internal German problems. This, Gamelin believed, conceded Hitler the option to decide how to conduct the ground war.

The Allies Wait

As La Drôle de Guerre continued and the French and British made their preparations, a propaganda war took place between the French and Germans. Most incidents took place along the Rhine where the river hindered active combat patrols. The Germans made their first friendly overtures along the Rhine in September when they waved placards proclaiming peaceful intentions. Then, French soldiers were bombarded with appeals for peace from loudspeaker broadcasts to message carrying balloons. Troops all along the front were occasionally

Snow covers Maginot fortifications as both the Allies and the Germans wait out the Phony War.

subjected to aircraft dropping leaflets. At least in one instance French troops were serenaded by a German Army band playing popular music. Perhaps the most effective attention getters were the long banners unfurled across the Rhine: "Why do you fight?" and "We Germans want nothing from France." Other messages proclaimed: "The British will fight to the last drop of French blood," "This is an imperialist war for the British," and, of course, an all-time favorite ploy, "What is happening to your wives back home, where the British are stationed in your villages?"

The French military began to take more positive action on the Rhine in October when orders arrived to begin the destruction of the bridges across the Rhine. In the previous month French troops had established barricades at the approaches to the bridges on their side of the river and soon the bridges began to fall into the Rhine. One major railroad bridge north of Strasbourg was not demolished properly and fell into the river in such a way that troops could still cross it. The defenders of Strasbourg were faced with a more serious problem when they

Chenillette Renault UE 31s on parade. These vehicles were used for reconnaissance and utility purposes.

delayed the destruction of the two bridges to Kehl until they received orders to blow them up on 14 May 1940 after the German offensive in the West had begun!

In the fall, some of the forts of the Maginot Line began to test their guns, in most cases for the very first time. Some ouvrages such as Hochwald and Schoenenbourg had the opportunity to fire their 75mm guns in September. The ouvrage of Bréhain practiced firing its guns on 3 October while on 21 October Latriremont created quite a stir among the population of a nearby village when it began firing its casemented 75mm guns with practice ammunition. The townspeople, realizing that the fort's guns were firing toward the Belgian border, thought that German troops were advancing from Belgium.

The winter turned unusually severe across the Continent

The Maginot fortifications seen here during the idle period known as the Phony War. British officers and press correspondents toured these facilities and firing demonstrations were staged for their benefit.

from occupied Poland to Scotland. Along some parts of the Allied front, the ground was frozen hard below the surface making it impossible to improve positions, while in other places the trenches filled with mud. Sleet formed on trails and roads creating hazards for both soldiers and vehicles. Even under these conditions Hitler still contemplated a winter offensive while the Allies were lulled into a sense of false security.

From the beginning of the fall until the beginning of the campaign in May 1940, the French and their ally not only continued to improve defenses, but also built new blockhouses. The severe winter slowed the progress on these tasks, but the

French erected several hundred additional bunkers of various styles in preparation for the German invasion.

During the winter, several of the Maginot forts received visits from important British leaders including King George, Winston Churchill, General Ironside and several others, including members of the British Parliament and news reporters. Most of the visitors found the ouvrages impressive, but few had the opportunity to see them in action. Many of the larger forts along the Maginot Line received visitors and those who had the opportunity to visit Hochwald witnessed gun crews in action because there were German troops within range. After years of secrecy, some correspondents received permission to visit the forts which staged firing displays to encourage favorable press coverage. Many British officers visiting the Maginot Line were impressed by the fortifications, even though they later chose to criticize their value. These British officers, Montgomery among them, also came across some French Category B reservist units and found them wanting, commenting especially on their slovenly, unprofessional appearance and their low morale. They leapt to the conclusion that the whole French Army was the same and later blamed the whole 1940 debacle on the supposed sloppiness and disheartened condition of the French troops.

Not all French troops avoided the exchange fire with the Germans. During the bitter winter the fort of Four à Chaux fired 80 rounds of 75mm ammunition into the nearby German village of Northwiler where observers had identified a group of German combat engineers.

Some fortress troops exchanged places with field troops during the winter to help bolster morale. In March 1940, as winter came to a close, the garrisons of the ouvrages of Hochwald and Schoenenbourg acquired old 120mm artillery pieces which they installed on the surface of their forts so that they could strike back at German positions with these longer range weapons.

In organizing for war, the Allies began to experience manpower difficulties. The French Army mobilized so many men for war that industrial output was slowed, causing Paul Reynaud, the French finance minister and a powerful voice in Daladier's cabinet, to complain to the British during a visit to

London in November 1939. He argued that the French had called up 1 out of 8 men while the British had only tapped 1 out of 40. As a result the British did not severely reduce industrial production, while the French suffered from the drain on manpower. By December, the French government even authorized a partial demobilization of older reservists to help alleviate the problem.

Some additional manpower arrived on the Western Front from Poland. Almost 85,000 Polish servicemen had escaped to the Baltic States, Rumania and Hungary after September 1939. Although only 500 of more than 14,000 men reached the West from the Baltic states, almost 47,000 made their way through the Balkans to France, including most of the 9,000-man Polish Air Force. Most of the Polish servicemen had escaped from internment camps in the host countries with the help of the local populations. The French set up a training camp for the Polish soldiers in Brittany where volunteers from Polish communities in the West came to join them as well. By the end of the spring of 1940, the French formed the 1st and 2nd Polish Divisions which moved into position with the 2nd Army Group. The 3rd and 4th Polish Divisions, still in the process of being formed, arrived on the Western Front piecemeal as it was collapsing. The same happened to the newly reformed 10th Polish Mechanized Brigade which had escaped from Poland largely intact. In addition to the army, the Armée de l'Air used Polish veterans to create four additional squadrons. Only one had completed its training near Lyon and received its aircraft in time for the campaign.

The Poles were by no means the only foreign element in the French Army. A number of Czechs, who had fled to France after the German occupation of their country, found themselves incorporated into the French Foreign Legion before the war began. The French spent the next eight months organizing the 1st Czechoslovakian Division which went into action as German forces moved into Southern France.

More serious problems plagued the Allies when certain vital weapons, such as anti-tank guns and more importantly tanks, were in short supply. In addition, the army reorganized the French tank force, which appeared to be just as formidable as the Maginot Line on paper. Indeed, the army created three

Munitions entrance to a Maginot ouvrage. Note the painted crenels and trees above the entrance.

heavy armored divisions, the DCRs, based on lessons learned from the German blitzkrieg against Poland, but many tanks still remained with infantry support battalions. Although the light and heavy armored divisions in 1940 constituted a greater proportion of the total tank force, they needed time to train. The British proposed adding their own tank division of about 300 tanks to the French armored force. The problem was that the Mobile Division was being reequipped as the 1st Armored Division, and General Ironside could only inform the French that they should not expect it to arrive before March of 1940. It was not ready until after the campaign began and, by then, it was too late to have any effect. In spite of all the problems, the morale of the troops in the French armored divisions stayed high because they possessed medium and heavy tanks of relatively good design. However, the new armored divisions needed more time to train and familiarize troops with equipment and refine tactical doctrine. The army scheduled maneuvers for the late spring of 1940 to improve tactics and identify deficiencies, but before they could be completed, the Germans struck and the new divisions went forward largely unprepared and without a defined mission.

During the Phony War, Allied production continued to lag behind the requirements of both the French and British military. The British government pressed the Americans for more material help. One signficant improvement was the production of more modern aircraft for L'Armée de l'Air, but by the spring of 1940 it was a case of too little, too late.

During the long months of inactivity other problems appeared among both French and British troops. Boredom did not help troop morale, and the added chore of constructing additional defenses caused even more discontent. The French troops grumbled that the cooks were adding something to the food to dampen their sexual drive while many wives became unhappy about the long periods of separation and the ready availability of brothels. For the British, one of the major problems was venereal disease. General Montgomery, in an attempt to control the problem, instructed his troops to use brothels and contraceptives instead of risking problems with unregulated women. This gave rise to so much discontent that Lord Gort almost relieved the general of his command. But these were only symptoms of the greater problems.

Repeatedly during the Phony War, the French alerted their troops to prepare to advance into Belgium, and later in the spring the 3rd DLC (cavalry division), assigned to advance into Luxembourg, also went on alert. Each time the troops had to pull back. The two most serious alerts took place in November 1939 and January 1940. In the first case the Low Countries witnessed a German build up, but the Allies still could not convince the Belgian king to let their troops enter his country. General Robert van Overstraeten, the king's military adviser, replaced the chief of staff for removing border barriers to allow the French to enter Belgium on 14 January. One French cavalry unit crossed the border, but returned after Overstraeten made it clear that the king did not want the Allies in his country before a German invasion. General Gamelin and General Ironside had no choice but to await further developments. The only really disappointed parties were the Allies as the waiting continued. The winter of 1939-40 became one of discontent for the

A captured Nazi banner is a small token of French success during the Phony War.

Allies as well as the Germans, from private, to general, to politician.

German Plans and Preparations

The planning for the German operation in the West, known as Case Yellow (Fall Gelb), was initiated over a month after the war began. At the outbreak of the war, Hitler directed the army to take no offensive action in the West, and assigned the *Luftwaffe* the mission of preventing enemy aircraft from violating Reich territory. After the Allies declared war, Hitler, who was in direct charge of overall strategy, ordered the navy and air force to attack Allied countries only as an act of retaliation.

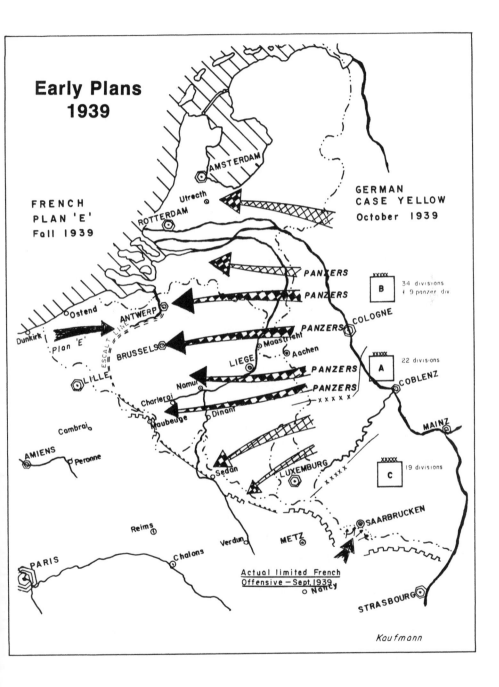

Early Plans 1939

FRENCH
PLAN 'E'
Fall 1939

GERMAN
CASE YELLOW
October 1939

AMSTERDAM

Utrecht

ROTTERDAM

PANZERS

PANZERS

B 34 divisions + 9 panzer div.

Ostend

ANTWERP COLOGNE

Dunkirk

Plan 'E'

BRUSSELS PANZERS

Maastricht

LIEGE Aachen

PANZERS

A 22 divisions

LILLE

Namur PANZERS

Charleroi COBLENZ

Maubeuge Dinant x x x x x

Cambrai

MAINZ

AMIENS Peronne

Sedan C 19 divisions

LUXEMBURG x x x x x

SAARBRUCKEN

Reims

METZ

Verdun

PARIS Chalons

Actual limited French
Offensive — Sept. 1939
Nancy

STRASBOURG

Kaufmann

ESCAULT LINE

By 25 September, he gave permission for air and naval units to operate against the enemy at sea, but allowed only air reconnaissance operations across the French border. This uncharacteristic lack of belligerence stemmed from a desire to avoid provoking the Allies until the *Wehrmacht* could move into position in the West, and this had to wait until the defeat of Poland. In addition, Germany made peace overtures. Apparently, other peace initiatives were underway including one by the U.S. ambassador to Great Britain, Joseph Kennedy, who wanted the British to abandon hostilities. To this day, the British government has maintained the secrecy of documents which may well reveal that political intrigue for peace ran deep and that secret arrangements between highly placed British and German personalities culminated in the mysterious flight of Hitler's deputy, Rudolf Hess, to England in 1941. (See John Costello's *Ten Days to Destiny* for further details on this subject.)

Under the mantle of a Phony War, Hitler vigorously planned for the offensive in the West. On 27 September Hitler held a conference with General Franz Halder, the army chief of staff. Halder noted in his diary some of the conclusions drawn at this meeting including:

1. The quality of French troops would improve in six months, thus the Allies had time on their side.

2. The arrival of British troops would lessen the emotional division between the Allies concerning the British not doing their part. (This was one of the favorite topics of German propagandists to convince the French soldiers they were the tools of the British.)

3. The *Wehrmacht* had not completed its armament program, although the Polish experience had brought benefits including improved anti-tank capabilities.

4. The *Luftwaffe* and the panzer force, considered to be the key to success in the East, would have to attempt to achieve the same type of victory in the West.

5. The Allies lacked anti-aircraft defenses, but that situation would improve during the winter. Hitler concluded the Allies had not helped the Poles during September due to a lack of anti-aircraft weapons.

These conditions made it essential for the Germans to plan an attack on the West immediately before they lost their advantages.

The conference also exposed some problems which precluded the Führer's demands. Guderian reported that about 20 percent of the losses from the Polish campaign could be quickly replaced, but German industry could not replace all the tank losses before winter began. At the same time, the *Luftwaffe* could not adequately equip itself with new types of aircraft and replacements before the spring of 1940, even if Hitler felt the offensive could not wait that long. Since the Allies had not violated Belgium's neutrality, the Germans assumed that the Belgians would shift their divisions from the French to the German frontier. Halder also noted that if peace could not be made with Chamberlain, then Hitler's goal was *"to bring England to its knees; to destroy France."*

At another conference with Hitler two days later, General von Brauchitsch, commander in chief of the army, tried to explain to him that the techniques used in the Polish campaign would not suffice in the West. The dictator did not want to hear this from his generals. Von Brauchitsch was too weak in character to take on the Führer, so the army had to put up with Hitler's demands.

The Führer's Directive No. 6 of 9 October 1939 stated that if the Allies did not want to end the war, he was prepared to put German troops on the attack as soon as possible with an offensive through Belgium and, possibly, Holland in order to gain as much territory as possible. The Low Countries and Northern France would then serve as a base of operations for the air and naval war against Great Britain. The directive concluded with a request for Hitler's military leaders to submit the plans for the operation as soon as possible. In early October, the generals prepared Case Yellow. This operational plan called for a main thrust launched by *Army Group B* in the north against the Netherlands and Belgium. This army group would replicate a modified Schlieffen Plan, and advance through the main line of Belgian defenses, while elements of the new *7th Air* (Airborne) *Division* landed near the Albert Canal and secured such key objectives as Fort Eben Emael. In addition, the plan committed the panzer divisions to this part of the operation. *Army Group A* was assigned the mission of advancing through

Southern Belgium and the Ardennes in support of *Army Group B* while *Army Group C*, composed of only infantry divisions, held the Franco-German frontier in a largely static role.

In the first part of October, Hitler amended his previous command by dropping the Netherlands from the campaign, hoping that he could directly influence the Dutch. His directive specifically called for a limited victory which must eliminate a large Allied force and secure a significant amount of territory. Hitler and the General Staff did not anticipate as easy a victory as that which had been won in Poland and, like the Allies, they seemed to think in terms of World War I operations.

At a conference on 10 October, Hitler insisted that everything possible be mobilized and that the generals must speed up the troop transfers from the East. He insisted that the offensive would quickly topple Belgium and that the army must attack at different points along the front to tie down the enemy and allow the German commanders freedom to maneuver. Tanks were ordered to avoid cities and industrial areas where they would get bogged down, as had happened in Poland. The fact that success depended on the *Luftwaffe* was emphasized and if Göring could not make it ready, the German Army could not undertake an offensive. Hitler's goal remained the annihilation of the French Army and its troops since he believed the population of France could not absorb or tolerate heavy losses, a philosophy shared by his opponent, General Gamelin. Finally, Hitler informed his generals that Italy would not join the foray unless Germany attacked.

There was another meeting on 16 October between Hitler and Brauchitsch. This time, the Führer emphasized that the British would not come to the peace table unless they suffered defeat in battle, and the Germans must strike at their expeditionary force as soon as possible. He set the date of the offensive between 15 and 20 November.

Hitler's Directive No. 7 of 18 October ordered the *Wehrmacht* to immediately occupy Luxembourg and attempt to disrupt an Allied advance if the French marched into Belgium; his new orders also permitted more aggressive action by the *Luftwaffe* and the navy at sea. Other meetings followed, and Hitler demanded changes in the *OKH* (Army High Command) plan at the end of October.

During 3 November General Halder noted in his diary that the German divisions in the West needed more time to prepare and train for an offensive, and many units still remained under strength and under equipped. He also noted that the Army High Command did not feel that the offensive ordered by *OKW* would achieve success under the present circumstances and that *Army Group A* was convinced that the French would launch a counteroffensive from the Maginot Line soon, although he did not agree.

A critical conference took place with Hitler and his generals on 5 November. What made this meeting at Berlin so important was that Brauchitsch and Halder, as well as their staff, believed that the offensive must be postponed from the designated date of 12 November to avert disaster since the army was not ready. They even believed that their own infantry, about 90 percent of the army, was not up to standards and needed more time to prepare and train, especially after their performance in Poland which they considered anything but outstanding. Most certainly his generals were of a similar mind as the Allies; the French generals had similar feelings about their own infantry, and, like the Germans, they were concerned with the condition of their reservists. At the conference with Von Brauchitsch, Hitler ranted and raved, claiming that he faced a conspiracy of defeatism from his generals. After the meeting concluded Von Brauchitsch returned to the *OKH* headquarters complex at Zossen visibly shaken.

Several important generals had considered overthrowing their Führer in the fall of 1938 when he ordered them to prepare for an invasion of Czechoslovakia. In 1939 there were still some generals conspiring against him. General Curt von Hammerstein, recalled to the colors when the war began, commanded *Army Detachment A* which held the northern part of the West Wall, opposite the Low Countries, in September. Historian Telford Taylor wrote that he had his own plan about Germany's future. During the few weeks he commanded that unit, he unsuccessfully attempted to lure Hitler to his headquarters to assassinate him. Halder, Von Brauchitsch's chief of staff, joined a larger conspiracy in October and November and positioned panzer divisions in the vicinity of Berlin in preparation for a coup. Halder even began to carry a pistol in his pocket. When

Von Brauchitsch returned to headquarters, he told Halder that Hitler had discovered a plot at Zossen (the Führer had actually said that his generals' defeatist attitude was a conspiracy). Halder panicked and destroyed all the papers relating to the planned coup and withdrew his active support. Without Halder, there was no one else in the army who would lead a coup.

Within a few days, poor weather saved the situation for the Germany Army. Meteorologists succeeded where Hitler's generals had failed; the invasion was postponed until the next year when Germany would be ready. But there was still conflict between Hitler and his generals. *OKH*, in failing to conform with Hitler's wishes, drew the Führer's wrath and, as a result, was considerably weakened. Heinz Guderian attempted to explain to Hitler the unhappiness the senior officers of the army shared with him concerning the situation. Although Hitler approved of the sincerity of the founder of Germany's panzer force, he informed him that he had no senior army officers he trusted or had any confidence in. Hence, it was only logical that he would bypass their authority when his decisions were challenged.

Hitler issued his Directive No. 8 on 20 November. The code name for attack was "Danzig," and "Augsburg" was the word to delay the offensive. The invasion of the Netherlands was reinstated in the plan though the army commanders were to avoid attacks against cities in the Low Countries. Hitler hoped to launch the offensive in the winter, but because of bad weather he had to cancel it 28 times between November 1939 and May 1940. While the army officers waited for the code word "Danzig," the German soldiers maintained an almost peaceful and friendly coexistence with the French on the border.

Meanwhile, the chief of staff of *Army Group A*, General Erich von Manstein, prepared his own plan for an offensive as he believed the current one would only lead to a partial success. Instead of the main assault taking the form of a charge through the Low countries, he advocated a strong blow be delivered in northern France to cut off Allied forces advancing into Belgium. General Gerd von Rundstedt, his commanding officer, agreed and the new plan was submitted to the *OKH* during the winter. For weeks, no one paid attention to the proposal.

Then Case Yellow fell into jeopardy through an interesting

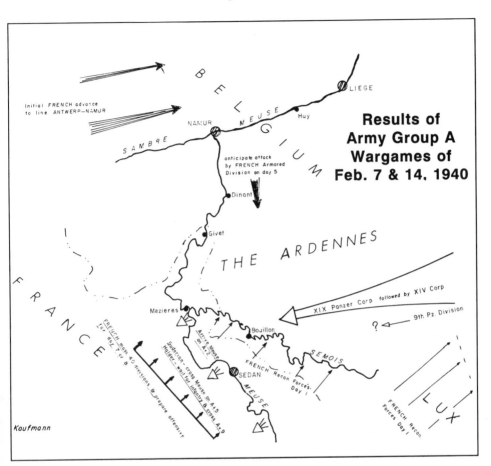

Results of Army Group A Wargames of Feb. 7 & 14, 1940

turn of chance. In early January, Major Helmut Reinberger flew in a small aircraft out of Münster for Cologne for an important meeting concerning the invasion. Though it was against established security policy Reinberger was travelling with a copy of the operational plans for the airborne units in Case Yellow. The aircraft went off course in poor weather and when the engine cut off, the pilot made a forced landing in Mechelen, Belgium. The major attempted to burn the documents, but Belgian soldiers arrived in time to put out the fire. As the documents were not completely destroyed, the Allies were alerted by the Belgians to the German plans. Hitler now feared that the Allies knew his intentions, although he did not know how much they had actually discovered. Fortunately for the Germans, the

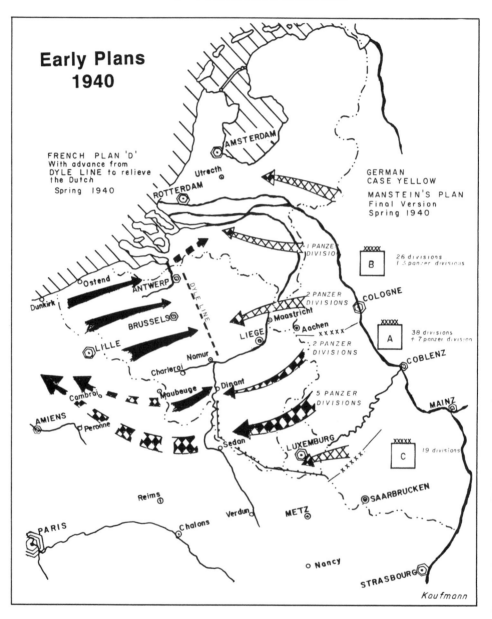

**Early Plans
1940**

FRENCH PLAN 'D'
With advance from
DYLE LINE to relieve
the Dutch
Spring 1940

AMSTERDAM

Utrecth

ROTTERDAM

GERMAN
CASE YELLOW

MANSTEIN'S PLAN
Final Version
Spring 1940

Ostend

Dunkirk

ANTWERP

DYLE LINE

BRUSSELS

LILLE

Charleroi

Namur

Cambrai

Maubeuge

Dinant

AMIENS

Peronne

Sedan

PARIS

Reims

Chalons

Verdun

METZ

Nancy

1 PANZER
DIVISIO

2 PANZER
DIVISIONS

COLOGNE

Maastricht

LIEGE

Aachen

2 PANZER
DIVISIONS

5 PANZER
DIVISIONS

COBLENZ

MAINZ

LUXEMBURG

SAARBRUCKEN

STRASBOURG

B   26 divisions
     1 3 panzer divisions

A   38 divisions
     + 7 panzer division

C   19 divisions

Kaufmann

Allies were not positive the documents were not just part of a clever ruse.

Soon after the Mechelen incident, Hitler had what would become a momentous meeting with Manstein. The general convinced Hitler to adopt his plan for an attack in northern

France and a modified form was adopted which became known as "sickle cut." In February the High Command tested the plan with war games at *Army Group A*'s headquarters, and determined that it offered a good chance for success. Manstein was rewarded with reassignment as commander of an army corps.

Manstein's plan assigned most of the panzer divisions to *Army Group A*, which would launch the main thrust. *Army Group B*, reduced in strength, was to continue with its original attack with the objective of diverting the enemy. In the meantime, the armored force of *Army Group A* would secretly and swiftly advance through the Ardennes. If all went well, the panzer spearheads of *Army Group A* would break out of the Ardennes, and cross the Meuse between Dinant and Sedan, and drive to the sea through the rear of the British and French forces. The anticipated victory would cut off and destroy a major portion of the Allied army to bring about the complete collapse of France.

The Allies ignored many warnings of impending invasion including copies of the German plans for an operation through the Ardennes. In addition, reconnaissance and intelligence agents warned them of the German armored buildup opposite Southern Belgium. However, since they were also cognizant of the Schlieffen Plan, they refused to consider the possibility that the Germans might change their schemes, even after the Mechelen incident. They thought, instead, that the Manstein plan might be a trick. Furthermore, the Dutch military attaché to Berlin was told by a member of German military intelligence each time the codeword "Danzig" was to be given. The attack was canceled so many times that the Dutch ended up ignoring the warning when the operation actually took place. Evidently, the Allies did not suffer from a lack of intelligence information but rather from an inability to evaluate and use it properly.

As the spring thaw began, patrolling activity increased on both sides along the front. At the end of March the friendly war along the Rhine came to an end. French defenders reported German patrols had paddled across the Rhine and been driven back in the vicinity of Marckolsheim. In April, when the Scandinavia campaign began, things calmed down on the Western Front, and a number of senior officers decided to go home on leave. Blitzkrieg seemed to have been forgotten.

CHAPTER IV

Norway Diversion

While both sides prepared for the eventual clash on the Western Front, a new war erupted in the East in November 1939 when the Soviet Union launched its Winter War against Finland to solve a territorial dispute and allow the military to flex its muscles. As the Soviet offensive against the Mannerheim Line ground to a halt early in December, other Red Army divisions, which had penetrated Finnish territory further to the north, found themselves cut off later in the month and on the verge of destruction.

The feeble League of Nations authorized its members to intervene on behalf of Finland as the year drew to a close. Ironically, the Anglo-French Alliance saw an excellent opportunity to seize the initiative against Germany as a result of the Russian aggression. First Lord of the Admiralty Winston Churchill had tried to convince Prime Minister Chamberlain of the importance of cutting the Swedish iron ore supply to Germany. Cabinet minister Paul Reynaud also wanted Prime Minister Daladier to take action for the same reason. Now the Finnish Winter War provided an excuse for action. To aid Finland, an Allied expeditionary force would have to occupy at least the town of Narvik in northern Norway and secure the railway running through Sweden to Finland. This would not only impede the shipping of Swedish iron ore from Gälivare through Narvik to Germany, but also close down the rail line to the Gulf of Bothnia. The possibility of Allied troops actually

A Heinkel 111 armed with torpedoes takes off for operations during the winter 1939-1940. The **Luftwaffe** *played an important part in the campaign for Norway, supplying ground forces and attacking enemy troops and ships.*

fighting the U.S.S.R. seemed rather remote since most of the units would be involved in holding open the supply lines, but at least one division might have to confront Soviet troops.

Although sympathy ran high for Finland, the Allies could only prepare an expeditionary force of less than a half dozen divisions—a mere drop in the bucket against the huge Soviet forces. In fact, Winston Churchill estimated an initial deployment of 5,000 British and 7,000 French troops in Scandinavia. Eventually, he thought, the Allies might send an additional light British armored battalion and a Territorial division as well as three French light divisions. Of course, the Scandinavian nations would be in a very precarious situation if Allied intervention forced the U.S.S.R. and Nazi Germany to become fighting allies.

Like the Allies, the Germans had designs for Scandinavia, especially Norway. In October 1939, the German Navy, under Admiral Raeder, toyed with the idea of acquiring bases in

Norway, especially at Trondheim and Narvik, to help expand naval operations against the British. The planners did not consider the operation feasible at the time, and Hitler lacked enthusiasm for it. The Germans later became concerned about Swedish timber shipped through Norway to Great Britain for use in coal mines, and Hitler considered the possibility of blocking neutral trade with the British as an economic blockade.

However, keeping Norway neutral was in the best interest of Germany for the moment, since merchant ships sailing along the deep channels of its southern coastline, known as the Leads, were protected from Allied interception. The Leads also weighed heavily on the minds of German naval leaders who wanted to obtain northern bases allowing an open exit to the Atlantic. They feared that the Allies wanted, as they actually did, to close the Leads either by mining or occupation of the coastline.

On 12 December, visiting Norwegian Fascist party leader Vidkun Quisling succeeded in convincing Hitler of the necessity of occupying Norway. Quisling explained that the Norwegian government had decided not to resist an Allied landing. If this should happen, neutral Sweden might be induced to cut off iron ore shipments to Germany as an Allied occupation would eliminate the winter transportation route through Narvik and on down along the Norwegian coast. Quisling was a man who the Nazis felt was worth listening to. Alfred Rosenberg, the German foreign affairs expert, prepared a memorandum early in December in which he underscored the importance of Quisling as a German ally. He pointed out that there were 15,000 members in his National Unity Party, a Norwegian Fascist organization and his followers made up 10 percent of the population. Still, the majority of Norwegians and Swedes were anti-German in their attitude. A plan was suggested calling for a select group of Norwegians to train in Germany and assist a future German occupation by acting as a fifth column.

In the meantime, Hitler was becoming increasingly irritated by his neighbors to the north. The Winter War produced one minor problem for Germany in the form of a joint Swedish-Finnish minefield laid in the Aaland Sea. This interfered with

German merchant shipping and resulted in some losses to patrol boats causing the Germans to lodge diplomatic protests. In a report of 8 December 1939, Raeder insisted that Denmark must cease sending foodstuffs to Great Britain. He also added Germany would have to occupy Norway to intercept the very active Swedish and Norwegian trade with Britain, and to achieve success in the economic war against the island nation.

During a conference that took place on 30 December 1939, Hitler, Keitel and Raeder came to a final decision for an invasion of Norway since if British troops occupied the country, they would probably encounter no real resistance from the Norwegians or the Swedes. Hitler had already directed that invasion preparations be made after his meeting with Quisling on 12 December though the seriousness of German intentions at this point might be open to speculation. Others disagreed with the wisdom of the operation. On 1 January 1940 army Chief of Staff Franz Halder noted in his diary that Sweden and Norway remained strictly neutral during the Winter War and that Quisling had no followers. He also commented that Norwegian neutrality was in Germany's interest, unless England threatened that status.

What finally nudged the Germans to open a northern campaign was the intrusion of the British destroyer *Cossack* in neutral Norwegian waters in pursuit of the German supply ship *Altmark* in mid-February. The *Altmark* supplied the pocket battleship *Graf Spee* during its short raiding career and had taken on Allied prisoners. The supply ship was en route to Germany when British destroyers attempted to intercept her. Hoping to work her way home on the final leg of the trip, the *Altmark* stayed in neutral Norwegian waters. The Norwegians searched the *Altmark* and claimed that the ship carried no weapons or prisoners, a response that dissatisfied Captain Philip Vian of the six destroyer flotilla pursuing the German vessel. Vian dispatched one of his ships, the *Cossack* to follow the ship right under the noses of the Norwegians until it was able to board her. With the cry "The Navy's here!" his men then liberated 299 prisoners and also discovered weapons which demonstrated *Altmark*'s violation of Norwegian neutrality. The German propaganda machine condemned the crew of the *Cossack* as "criminals" and "law breakers." Hitler assumed that the

Allies would then occupy Norway at the earliest opportunity and decided to act quickly.

On 19 February 1940, Hitler demanded that planning for Operation Weser, the invasion of Norway, be pushed forward. General Jodl, in charge of *OKW's* Operations Section convinced the Führer that a corps commander should take charge of the operation. General Nikolaus von Falkenhorst, veteran of World War I experiences in Finland, was selected to take Norway with his *XXI Corps* and his staff began making plans in Berlin.

On 21 February General Halder, chief of staff for *OKH*, devoted his attention to the planned invasion of Norway. He wrote that Von Falkenhorst and his *XXI Corps* were placed directly under *OKW* to avert command problems with the *Luftwaffe*. The troops assigned to this operation were the *7th Air Division* (Parachute) and the *22nd Air Landing Division* with a regiment of the *1st Mountain Division* and two other divisions. The *11th Rifle Brigade*, with tanks, was also included. Halder's attention did not return to Norway until just before the invasion since *OKW* had removed *OKH* from the picture.

Falkenhorst and his staff examined the earlier plan prepared for *OKW* by navy Captain Theodor Krancke and his staff in February. The Krancke Plan divided Norway into several regions and selected certain objectives which would allow German forces to occupy small sectors that controlled most of Norway's population and economic resources. They were:

1. The Oslo Fjord in the Southeast.

2. A coastal strip in Southern Norway. The German objectives would be Kristiansand, Arendal and Stavanger.

3. Bergen and its surroundings in Southwest Norway.

4. Trondheim and Central Norway.

5. Narvik and Northern Norway as well as the rail line into Sweden.

6. Tromsö with its two airfields and Finnmark. It was considered too far removed to be a key to securing Norway.

Krancke's staff also calculated that half of the 16 Norwegian regiments would be eliminated by a swift takeover of the positions indicated in sectors 2 through 5 listed above. If successful, the Germans would quickly eliminate most of the Norwegian Army's heavy weapons and airfields.

Earlier planning and post-campaign propaganda revealed that German merchant ships carried troops into Norwegian ports before the invasion began. This trick had not been proposed in the Krancke Plan or the final plan of the *XXI Corps*. Krancke had recommended that warships carry the troops instead of the merchant ships playing "Trojan horses" since the invasion troops required speedy transportation and security which only the warships could afford in such a high risk operation.

Falkenhorst and Jodl decided that it was important to keep the operation independent from Case Yellow. As a result the two airborne divisions, the *7th Air Division* and the *22nd Air Landing Division*, were removed since they had higher priority assignments against the Low Countries. The few paratroop battalions assigned to Exercise Weser came from the *7th Air Division*.

The *OKW* and *XXI Corps* staffs also decided against using Quisling's forces since they doubted their ability to make a significant contribution. As would happen later in the West, the fifth column became a propaganda tool and remained largely a mythical force. The planners also decided that diplomatic pressure would not be enough to control Denmark and that nation had to be physically occupied.

Finally, Hitler decided on 3 March that Exercise Weser must take place before Case Yellow. Planning did not progress as smoothly as anticipated. Herman Göring was incensed that army and navy staffs had laid out the operation without any significant input from *Luftwaffe*, and early in March he refused to put his men under the command of the army. On 4 March the *X Air Corps* received command of the air units for Exercise Weser. The commander in chiefs of the three services met on 5 March and decided to allot stronger forces for the landing at Narvik and to station naval units at Norwegian ports during the campaign. The army would deploy six infantry divisions and a few platoons of tanks, including the special pre-war experimental heavy multi-turret Neubaufahrzeuge V tanks, some of which mounted 105mm guns. On 7 March Hitler

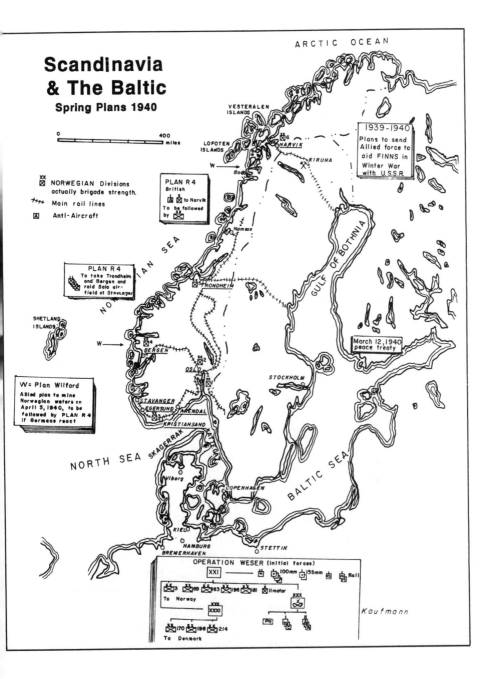

Scandinavia & The Baltic

Spring Plans 1940

ARCTIC OCEAN

```
0                    400
|_____| miles
```

XX
NORWEGIAN Divisions actually brigade strength.

+++ Main rail lines

A Anti-Aircraft

1939-1940
Plans to send Allied force to aid FINNS in Winter War with U.S.S.R.

PLAN R 4
British
A | to Narvik
To be followed by

PLAN R 4
To take Trondheim and Bergen and raid Sola airfield at Stavanger

VESTERALEN ISLANDS

LOFOTEN ISLANDS

NARVIK

KIRUNA

Bodø

Namsos

TRONDHEIM

GULF OF BOTHNIA

SHETLAND ISLANDS

NORWEGIAN SEA

W →

BERGEN

OSLO

STOCKHOLM

March 12,1940 peace treaty

W= Plan Wilford
Allied plan to mine Norwegian waters on April 5, 1940, to be followed by PLAN R 4 if Germans react.

STAVANGER
EGERSUND ARENDAL
KRISTIANSAND

NORTH SEA SKAGERRAK

Viborg

COPENHAGEN

BALTIC SEA

KIEL

HAMBURG
BREMERHAVEN

STETTIN

OPERATION WESER (initial forces)

XXI ——— 100mm 155mm Rail

3 69 163 196 181 Ilmotor
To Norway

XXX
XXXI

170 198 214
To Denmark

Kaufmann

approved the assignment of the following units to the operation:

Weser North, the Invasion of Norway: *3rd Mountain, 69th, 163rd, 196th* and *181st Infantry Divisions* and the *11th Motorized Rifle Brigade.*

Weser South, the Occupation of Denmark: *170th, 198th* and *214th Infantry Divisions.*

The Allies planned to land their expeditionary force in Norway by mid-March, but by then the Finns, under heavy pressure from the Russian offensive, negotiated a peace and the pretext for an Allied landing in Scandinavia evaporated. Prime Minister Daladier fell from power as a result of his failure to take timely action, even though the Allies continued to plan for a landing.

At this point the Allies had to devise new plans. Wilfred, the first plan, called for creating two minefields in Norwegian waters, one north of Bodo and the other between Alesund and Bergen to block German ore shipments and also provoke a German reaction: a German landing in Norway in response. The Allies then planned to respond quickly with Plan R-4 with their forces immediately taking over Narvik. The British also insisted that the French allow the activation of Operation Royal Marine, floating mines down the Rhine.

Plan R-4 projected one brigade landing immediately at Narvik with an anti-aircraft battery attached. Meanwhile, five battalions would land at Trondheim and Bergen and also carry out the raid on the airfield at Stavanger, as mentioned earlier. It appeared as though the Allied mission was doomed to fail. The British, if not the French, underestimated the ability of the Germans to move large formations into Norway quickly. Furthermore, the Allies had not counted on the Germans transporting troops by air to rapidly build up the strength of the initial assault force. And worst of all, while the Allies thought in terms of battalions, the Germans planned to use divisions.

The Norwegians ended up a mere pawn of Allies and Germans alike in this operation. The Allies hoped for some local support, while the Germans counted on none and intended to use the *Luftwaffe* to break the morale of the Norwegians. German pre-war propaganda, especially films, already partially instilled fear in Germany's opponents.

A Matter of Days and Hours

Admiral Raeder urged Hitler to begin the operation before the Arctic nights became much shorter. He insisted that by mid-April the nights would be too short to mask the movement of his invasion fleet from Allied eyes. Hitler decided to begin the invasion on 7 April 1940. While waiting for Exercise Weser to begin, the navy's surface units and U-boat fleet remained largely tied down, waiting to carry out their mission in the invasion while the naval war against the British suffered.

At the same time, the Allies moved forward with their operational plan and set the date of Operation Wilfred for 5 April giving them a slight edge over the Germans. Then the problems began. The French government refused to allow Operation Royal Marine to take place on the Rhine. Daladier, then Minister of War, still fearing German retaliation, wanted to wait until the quality of the Armée de l'Air improved before taking active measures against the Germans on the Western Front. Churchill informed the French that Operation Wilfred would begin anyway, but the date was moved back to 8 April a day after the Germans were to begin their own attack on Norway. British Bomber Command sent patrols in the first week of April over the German North Sea ports in search of ships preparing for an invasion of Norway, but the Blenheims which attacked several naval targets failed to do any significant damage. On 6 April the Norwegian government realized the imminent danger and Foreign Minister Halvdan Koht publicly reiterated Norway's desire to remain neutral, but added that the Norwegians would fight if threatened. He also tried to deter Allied intervention by pointing out that Norway shipped more ore to the Allies than to Germany. On the same day, German officials also issued a statement declaring that Germany had been carefully watching Allied attempts to open a Scandinavian front. They also added that "If Norway seeks to preserve its neutrality by halting iron ore shipments from Narvik to both Germany and Britain, it will thereby sacrifice its neutrality by bowing to British pressure." The Germans also made it clear that they considered that Allied mine laying operations had put an end to Norway's neutrality. Of course, many ships of the German invasion fleet had already begun departing from their ports well before these declarations.

Early on the morning of 8 April four British destroyers laid a minefield near Bodo at the entrance to the fjord leading into Narvik. In London, on the same day, the government informed the press that three minefields had been laid in Norwegian waters and that they would not interfere with Norwegian shipping. The British also stated that they took this action in reprisal for Germany's "brutal and illegal campaign against shipping of all nations." After formally receiving this information, Norway presented a protest, upon which its diplomats in London were made privy to the fact that a German invasion fleet was detected moving north. On the same day, the Polish submarine *Orzel* sank the German troop ship *Rio de Janeiro* off the coast of southern Norway. According to news reports the vessel carried 500 German soldiers of which about 300 drowned. The survivors insisted that they had come to protect Norway from the Allies. The Norwegians and the Danes were also notified of Germany's plans by the anti-Nazi official of the German military intelligence agency, the *Abwehr*, who passed on information through the Netherlands.

The Allies raced forward, preparing to send their battalions across the North Sea. As they detected German naval movements, Churchill decided to rush forward some of the cruisers of the Home Fleet which were to carry a battalion of troops each. Three battalions of infantry remained behind with their supplies dumped at Rosyth and others were still aboard ship as the cruisers raced to meet the enemy on 8 April. Meanwhile, advanced formations of German divisions had already begun moving by sea towards their Norwegian objectives. The *Luftwaffe's X Air Corps* committed a thousand aircraft to the operation which included 500 troop transports and supply aircraft and another 500 bombers and fighters. Allied aircraft operating from Great Britain would have to fly at extreme ranges to intercept them and only one aircraft carrier was in the area. The German troops reached Norway first.

The German Invasion Force

The German Navy fully committed itself to Exercise Weser. Ten groups were organized for the naval operation:

Group 1 for Narvik—Battle Cruisers *Scharnhorst* and *Gneisenau* and 10 destroyers with 2,000 troops of the *3rd Mountain Division.*

Group 2 for Trondheim—Cruiser *Hipper* and 4 destroyers with 1,700 troops from the *3rd Mountain Division.*

Group 3 for Bergen—Cruisers *Köln* and *Königsberg*, service ships *Bremse* and *Karl Peters*, 8 torpedo boats with 1,900 troops of the *69th Infantry Division.*

Group 4 for Kristiansand and Arendal—Cruiser *Karlsruhe*, service ship *Tsingtau*, 10 torpedo boats and 1,100 troops of the *163rd Infantry Division.*

Group 5 for Oslo—Cruisers *Blücher, Lützow* and *Emden*, three torpedo boats, 8 minesweepers with 2,000 troops from the *163rd Infantry Division.*

Group 6 for Egersund—Four minesweepers with 150 troops from the *69th Infantry Division.*

Group 7 for Korsör and Nyborg (Denmark)—1,990 troops from the *198th Infantry Division.*

Group 8 for Copenhagen—1,000 troops from the *198th Infantry Division.*

Group 9 for Middelfart—400 troops from the *198th Infantry Division.*

Group 10 for Esbjerg—supply mission.

Group 11 for Tyborön—supply mission.

Groups earmarked for Denmark received the old battleship *Schleswig-Holstein* as an escort to support the landing at Korsör.

Tanker and *Export Echelon* carried the supplies necessary to maintain the operation.

Tanker Echelon—Eight ships (two for Narvik, one for Trondheim and the remainder for ports in the south. Carrying fuel.

Export Echelon—Seven ships (three for Narvik, three for

German submariners on their way out to sea. U-boats were an important element in the German campaign against Norway.

Trondheim and one for Stavanger). Carrying military equipment and supplies.

Eight transport echelons for troops and supplies.

1st Sea Transport Echelon for Oslo, Kristiansand, Stavanger,and Bergen with 15 ships for invasion day.

2nd Sea Transport Echelon for Oslo on third day with 11 ships.

3rd Sea Transport Echelon for Oslo on seventh day with 13 ships; *4th, 5th, 6th, 7th* and *8th Sea Transport* echelons to use ships returning from first three echelons.

In addition, 28 submarines were to be deployed off the coast of Norway. Most of the German invasion units departed German ports on Sunday 7 April.

Successful Landings

The German invasion of Norway was the first major combined air-land-sea effort in history. Considering all the problems between the leadership of the three services, the operation was remarkably successful. The key to victory was getting troops ashore in large numbers and winning control of the air to dominate the sea lanes. The Germans accomplished both of these objectives, although they failed to win control of the sea despite the initial success of their surface fleet.

On the first day of the invasion, 9 April, the weather was far from perfect and, in some areas, the advancing naval units found the coast shrouded in fog. The cold spring morning cleared to reveal the ragged, mountainous, partially snow covered coastline with the deep fjords leading to the ports. Most of the major harbors were defended by gun batteries dominating the entrances to the fjords in which they were located. Naval units delivered a regiment of the *3rd Mountain Division* to Narvik where they overwhelmed the Norwegian defenders. A Quisling commander of the Narvik garrison helped the Germans take the town. At Bergen and Trondheim the navy slipped past protecting forts and batteries to deliver troops in spite of some naval losses. Along the south coast, all units landed safely.

The only significant failure was the bold attempt to sail up the fjord to Oslo. German naval units destroyed a small patrol boat late in the evening of 8 April and forced their way into Oslofjord. As the German ships moved up the fjord on the 9th, the Norwegians finally received permission to engage the Germans. A patrol boat sank a German torpedo boat and damaged another, before it was destroyed.

The invasion fleet, which included the cruiser *Blücher* and pocket battleship *Lützow*, both carrying troops, attempted to pass the obsolete fortress of Oskarsborg. Its guns, Krupp cannon from the turn of the century, were slow in reloading but remained quite deadly. The *Blücher* suffered heavy damage before it passed by and then suffered two torpedoes from an outdated shore position on an island. The ship was destroyed with the loss of up to 1,000 men. The damaged *Lützow* and the remaining ships retreated southward. Plans quickly changed,

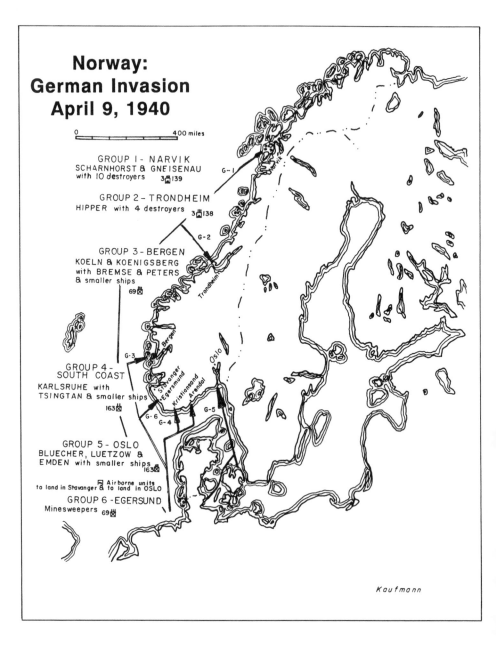

Norway: German Invasion April 9, 1940

0 ——————— 400 miles

GROUP 1 - NARVIK
SCHARNHORST & GNEISENAU
with 10 destroyers   3⚓139

GROUP 2 - TRONDHEIM
HIPPER with 4 destroyers   3⚓138

GROUP 3 - BERGEN
KOELN & KOENIGSBERG
with BREMSE & PETERS
& smaller ships
69🏰

GROUP 4 -
SOUTH COAST
KARLSRUHE with
TSINGTAN & smaller ships
163🏰

GROUP 5 - OSLO
BLUECHER, LUETZOW &
EMDEN with smaller ships
163🏰

🏴 Airborne units
to land in Stavanger & to land in OSLO

GROUP 6 - EGERSUND
Minesweepers 69🏰

G-1
G-2
G-3
G-4
G-5
G-6

Narvik
Trondheim
Bergen
Oslo
Stavanger
Egersund
Kristiansand
Arendal

Kaufmann

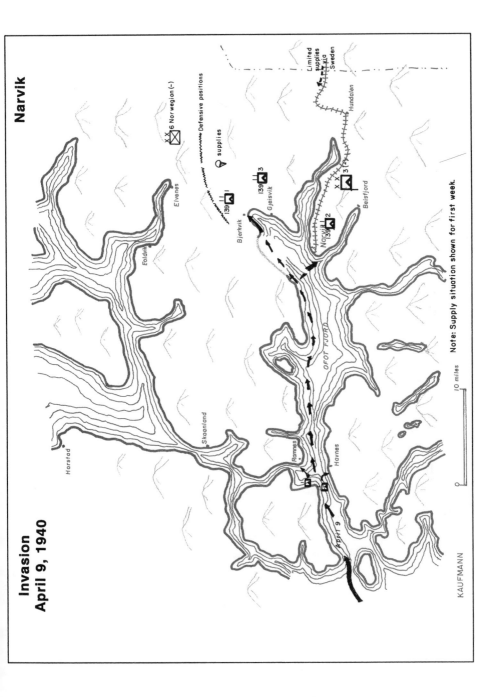

Narvik

Invasion
April 9, 1940

Note: Supply situation shown for first week.

KAUFMANN

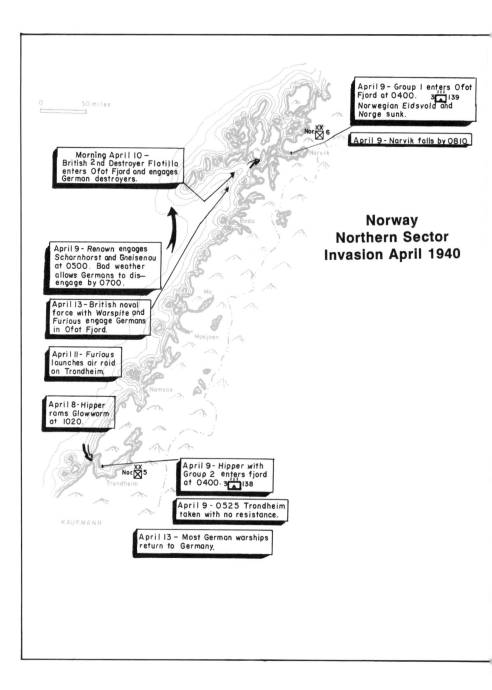

April 9- Group I enters Ofot Fjord at 0400. 3◻139 Norwegian *Eidsvold* and *Norge* sunk.

April 9- Narvik falls by 0810

Nor.⊠6

Narvik

Morning April 10 – British 2nd Destroyer Flotilla enters Ofot Fjord and engages German destroyers.

**Norway
Northern Sector
Invasion April 1940**

Bodo

April 9- *Renown* engages *Schornhorst* and *Gneisenau* at 0500. Bad weather allows Germans to dis— engage by 0700.

Mo

April 13- British naval force with *Warspite* and *Furious* engage Germans in Ofot Fjord.

Mosjoen

April 11- *Furious* launches air raid on Trondheim.

Namsos

April 8-*Hipper* rams *Glowworm* at 1020.

Nor.⊠5

Trondheim

April 9- *Hipper* with Group 2 enters fjord at 0400. 3◻138

April 9- 0525 Trondheim taken with no resistance.

KAUFMANN

April 13 – Most German warships return to Germany.

0   50 miles

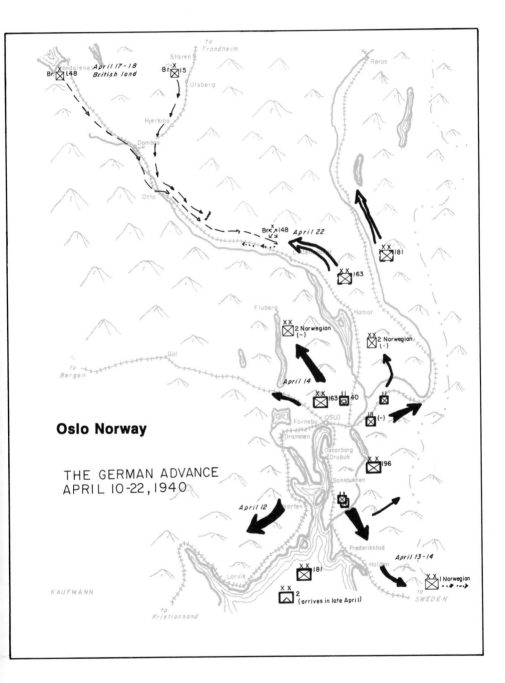

Oslo Norway

THE GERMAN ADVANCE
APRIL 10-22, 1940

and German troops landed along the fjord to secure the approaches to Oslo.

Earlier in the day two companies of paratroopers from the *1st Battalion* of the *1st Parachute Regiment* aborted their mission to land at Oslo's Fornebu airfield because of morning fog. The *2nd Battalion* of the *324th Infantry Regiment, 163rd Division* transported in JU-52s, continued on although the paratroopers had not secured the airfield for them. A squadron of eight ME-110 twin engine, long range fighters was already over Fornebu to give air support to the landing. The pilots apparently had been unaware that the attack had been called off and the ME-110s tangled with Gladiator fighters of the Norwegian Air Force. Below on the airfield were a dozen more modern American Curtiss fighters still in shipping crates. Both sides lost a few aircraft, but the Norwegians had to find another place to land since the airfield was under attack. The ME 110s, running out of fuel, shot up the active Norwegian defenses of the airfield and began to land just as some of the JU-52s with the *2nd Battalion* did the same. After landing, the fighters' machine guns went into action on the ground against the Norwegian defenders and forced them to give up. Even though the naval force had already been turned back, elements of the air-landed German battalion clung to the airport. They reported their success and within a few hours reinforcements, including the paratroopers and additional troops of the *324th*, arrived. After noon the regimental band assembled at the airfield and the troops went into formation and boldly marched, as if on a victorious parade, into Oslo. The move successfully intimidated the local defenders and population of Oslo, resulting in the fall of the city. The Norwegian king and his government fled while Norwegian troops under the leadership of General Ruge covered his retreat.

German paratroopers of the *3rd Company, 1st Battalion* of the *1st Parachute Regiment* also took part in the capture of Sola airfield. Like the other companies of the battalion flying to Oslo, they ran into heavy cloud cover, but continued on. They also met resistance from ground defenses at the target, but successfully jumped and, with the aid of a couple of ME-110 fighters, finally secured the airfield making possible the landing of a couple infantry battalions. Both Oslo and Stavanger-

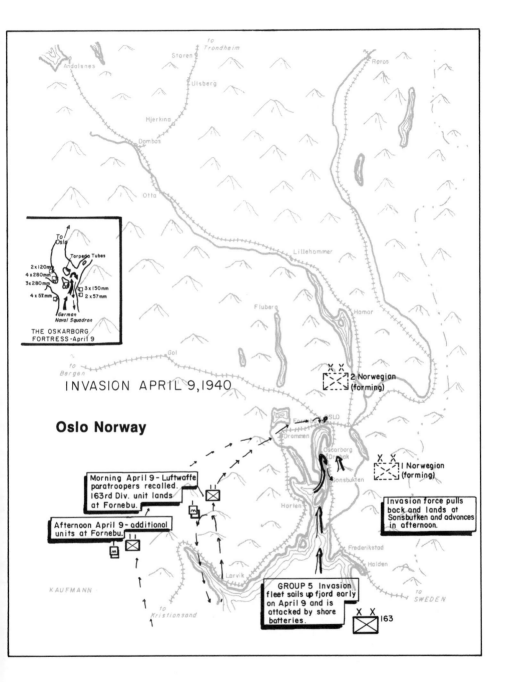

THE OSKARBORG FORTRESS-April 9

To Oslo

Torpedo Tubes

2 x 120mm
4 x 280mm
3 x 280mm
4 x 57mm

3 x 150mm
2 x 57mm

German Naval Squadron

INVASION APRIL 9, 1940

Oslo Norway

2 Norwegian (forming)

1 Norwegian (forming)

Morning April 9 - Luftwaffe paratroopers recalled. 163rd Div. unit lands at Fornebu.

Afternoon April 9 - additional units at Fornebu.

Invasion force pulls back and lands at Sonsbutken and advances in afternoon.

GROUP 5 Invasion fleet sails up fjord early on April 9 and is attacked by shore batteries.

163

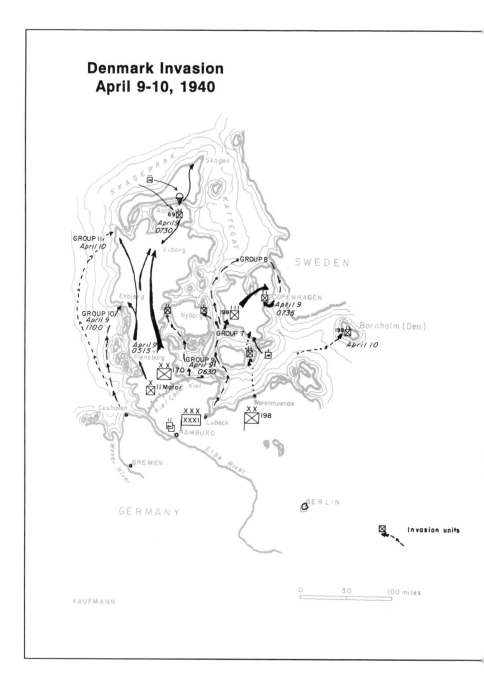

Denmark Invasion
April 9-10, 1940

Sola turned out to be high risk operations successfully realized by a handful of men. Both objectives were crucial to the German campaign.

The German X *Air Corps* flew in bombers and twin engine fighters on long range missions suppressing the Norwegian defenses, seizing control of the air and demoralizing civilians and soldiers alike. *Luftwaffe* transport units became vital in flying in supplies and troops to make up for the delay and loss of several supply ships. These missions did not always succeed, as was the case in the far north at Narvik, when a few days later transports carrying a mountain battery landed on a frozen lake and sank through the ice.

The quick fall of Denmark shortened the lines of communication and allowed improved air support. The German Navy began to suffer heavy losses after the first day, especially at Narvik. While the Germans rushed in regiments, and the *Luftwaffe* continued to dominate the air, the Allies landed with their few battalions and the British RAF had to operate at extreme range to provide support. The Norwegian divisions attempted to mobilize on the second day, but these brigade-size units seldom reached full strength. On 10 April the Germans were driving back and eliminating the 1st and 2nd Norwegian Divisions.

Allied troops only slowly began to arrive. The original plan called for a strong Allied force to seize Narvik, but as that command was set in motion the British War Cabinet started having second thoughts. The rapidly unfolding events in Norway made it necessary for the Allies to change their plans to recapture Trondheim. Churchill, one of the most influential members of the group, gave the operation his full support. Fortunately for him the failure of the mission fell upon Prime Minister Chamberlain. The 15th Brigade received orders to detach itself from the 5th Division and the BEF, and by 15 April moved back for shipment to the Norwegian theater. Other units, including the 24th Guards Brigade, had already departed from the naval base at Scapa Flow, but they left much of their equipment behind. Churchill described it as the beginning of a "ramshackle campaign." With the splitting of the so called Rupert Force originally destined for Narvik, the Allies weakened their hand. In addition, the weather in April brought

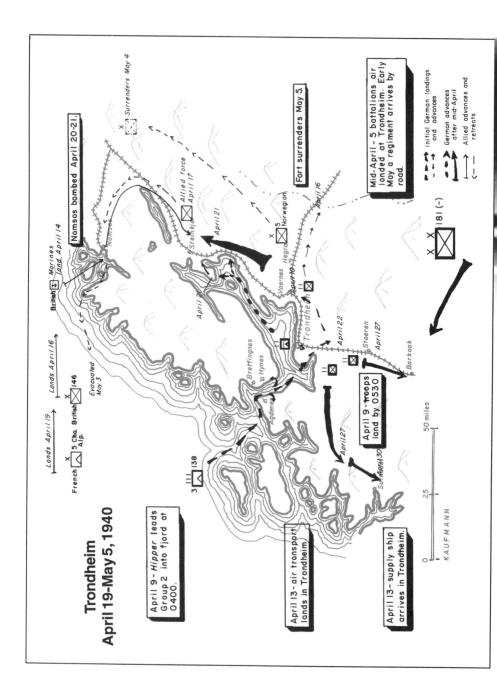

Trondheim
April 19-May 5, 1940

April 9 - *Hipper* leads Group 2 into fjord at 0400.

April 13 - air transport lands in Trondheim.

April 13 - supply ship arrives in Trondheim.

April 9 - troops land by 0530.

Mid-April - 5 battalions air landed at Trondheim. Early May a regiment arrives by road.

Fort surrenders May 5.

Namsos bombed April 20-21.

British Marines land April 14

Lands April 19

Lands April 16

Evacuated May 3

French 5 Cha. British Alp.

146

138

Allied force April 17

Steinkjer

April 21

April 2

Surrenders May 4

Verdal

Sunnan

Vaernes

April 10

Hegra

5 Norwegion

April 16

Trondheim

April 22

Stoeren April 27

Berkaak

Breifflingnes

Hynes

Orgdenes

April 27

Sult April 30

181 (-)

Initial German landings and advances

German advances after mid-April

Allied advances and retreats

0   25   50 miles

KAUFMANN

162

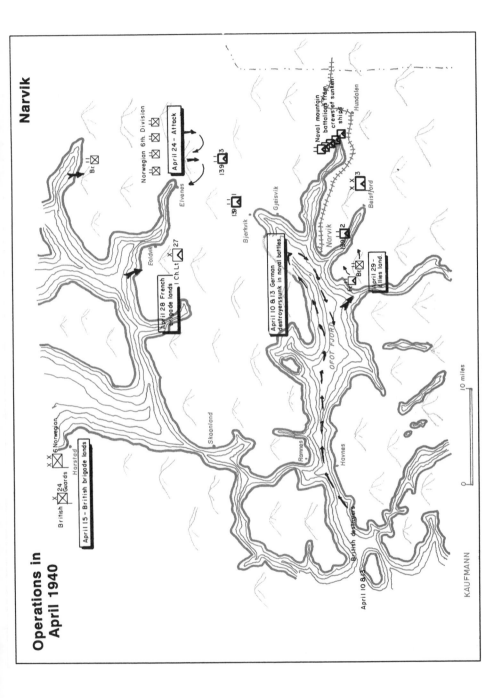

Operations in
April 1940

Narvik

Norwegian 6th. Division

April 24 - Attack

Elvenes

Foldvik

April 28 French
brigade lands

1 Ch.Lt. 27

Bjerkvik

Gjeisvik

Naval mountain
battalions from
crews of sunken
ships

Hundalen

Beisfjord

Narvik

April 10 & 13 German
destroyers sunk in naval battles.

April 29 -
Allies land.

OFOT FJORD

Skaanland

Rønnes

Hovnes

British destroyers

April 10 & 13

Br.

Harstad

British 24 6 Norwegian
Guards

April 15 - British brigade lands

10 miles

KAUFMANN

storms in the North Sea and snow over Norway. Only the French Alpins were equipped to brave it. The snow hindered the Norwegians, the Allies and the Germans alike, making the use of some airfields hazardous, while ice-covered lakes became potential airfields.

Early in the campaign, the Germans came out on the losing side of two important naval actions in the fjord leading to Narvik. First, on 10 April Captain Warburton-Lee, after being informed that 10 German destroyers were in the fjord, proceeded up it early in the morning with his five destroyers of the 2nd Destroyer Flotilla and sank two German destroyers and six merchant ships, then damaged two other destroyers at Narvik. Five German destroyers appeared from another fjord as Warburton-Lee's force withdrew, sinking two more ships. The Germans had not been able to close off the entrance to the fjord because, after they captured the Norwegian coastal forts, which they had intended to use for this purpose, they found they had not been completed or fully armed. The German divisional commander lost valuable supplies, including his ammunition, on the merchant ships. The Germans attempted, unsuccessfully, to fly in supplies by landing on a frozen lake where the aircraft sank through the ice. Their units at Narvik were in danger of being trapped.

On 13 April the British turned the Germans' worst fears into a reality. This time nine destroyers accompanied by the battleship *Warspite* entered the fjord. Despite the battleship's limited ability to maneuver in the narrow waterway, its big guns wrecked the remaining German destroyers and left the German ground commander in what appeared to be a hopeless position. At that point the British decided to withdraw leaving the Germans isolated, but still in possession of Narvik. On their way out of the fjord, the British escorts destroyed a U-boat lying in ambush.

On 15 April the 24th British Guards Brigade landed at Harstad and prepared to retake Narvik, under the command of General Pierse.J. Mackesy. The general waited for the French demi-brigade to arrive before proceeding, but he soon discovered it was being detached for the operation against Trondheim. According to Churchill, the general had no intention of striking at Narvik, even with naval support, and Admiral Lord

Cork, in overall command of the Narvik operation, could not force him to do so. On 17 April Lord Cork reported that General Mackesy was planning to wait until the end of the month when the snow melted and the French demi-brigade arrived. By 20 April Lord Cork was put in complete command of the Narvik operation in an unsuccessful effort to get General Mackesy to concentrate on land operations.

The men responsible for planning and leading from London prepared plans for naval and air units to bombard German-held ports and airfields in Norway, including a naval frontal assault on Trondheim. Unfortunately the men in London were too far away to coordinate the operation effectively and created additional problems instead.

Both the forces deployed against Narvik and Trondheim found themselves inadequately equipped since the convoy that was split was not loaded to support two different operations and most of the important supplies and equipment went on to the operation at Narvik. One indication of how bad the situation was in Norway was the fact that the commander of operations against Trondheim, General Massy, was stationed at the War Office in London since no facilities existed for him in Norway.

Central and Southern Norway

The three battalions of the 146th British Brigade, preceded by a naval landing force (Operation Henry), came ashore at Namsos on 15-16 April and the French 5th Demi-Brigade on 19 April in a command known as Mauriceforce under the command of General Adrian Carton de Wiart VC.

The 148th Brigade's two battalions had been removed from their ships on 7 April. They embarked later in the month on two cruisers and a transport. Fearing German air attacks, the troops on the transport disembarked at sea on two other cruisers, and then proceeded to land further south at Andalsnes on 18 April. This group, known as Sickelforce, had the mission of creating a pincer movement around the German enclave at Trondheim. The 148th Brigade arrived without mortar ammunition as part of its equipment was misdirected, adding to the confusion. The whole group was poorly equipped and had only a few tourist maps to find its destination. General Bernard Paget took command of this operation on 20 April after the first commander, General F.E. Hotblack, had a stroke on 17 April and his replacement died in an air crash. Paget's men appeared doomed from the beginning. Instead of skis, they found that their transport carried reindeer saddles.

In the meantime, a much larger German force advanced from Oslo, pushing the Norwegians back. New orders diverted Sickelforce from the pincer movement against Trondheim, directing it deep into Norway to aid their new allies between Lillehammer and Dombaas. The capture of a company of German paratroopers at Dombaas was overshadowed by a massive German force with tanks approaching the Allies near Lillehammer in mid-April. On 23 April the 15th British Brigade landed at Andalsnes and moved to support the 148th Brigade in the Gudbrandsal valley. Armed with inadequate anti-tank weapons, the 148th Brigade, on 23 April was overwhelmed by the Germans at Tretten. As the first elements of the 15th Brigade reached the front, the remnants of the 148th Brigade retreated by railroad. Constant air attacks pinned the bulk of the brigade for a whole day in a railroad tunnel concealed from German aircraft. General Paget pleaded for air support since the *Luftwaffe* threatened his supply line back to Andalsnes and applied constant pressure on the small port. Fortunately, the railroad, which aided the British withdrawal, miraculously remained in operation. Of 18 Gladiator aircraft flown in from the aircraft carrier *Glorious* on 24 April, 13 were destroyed on the frozen lake they had used as an airfield. The British 15th Brigade attempted to stop the German advance at Kvam, but was driven back by 28 April, while much of the 2nd Norwegian Division was destroyed.

The British evacuated their troops from Andalsnes by 2 May, under constant pounding from the *Luftwaffe*. Small units from the German *2nd Mountain Division* had already flown into Trondheim as reinforcements and some German troops there had advanced southward toward the Gudbrandsal which helped force the evacuation of Andalsnes.

The *Luftwaffe* quickly took command of the skies over southern Norway. Not only did they constantly harass and attack

British and Norwegian troops, but when the British cruiser *Suffolk* bombarded the Sola airfield on 17 April, the ship was attacked from the air for seven hours and badly damaged. Meanwhile, the main group of British and French units, Mauriceforce, landed at Namsos on 14-19 April and advanced to Steinkjer. Unfortunately, they arrived without anti-aircraft weapons and Namsos became a target for the *Luftwaffe*. The elite French Alpins also found straps missing for their skis which effectively negated their ability to move quickly over snow covered areas.

On 21 April a German battalion was carried up the fjord to Kirknesvaag by destroyer while a torpedo boat landed a company at Verdolsora. German bombers also destroyed the facilities at Namsos. The Germans could not be stopped and by 24 April the Allies had pulled back. By 3 May, the Allies had evacuated their troops from Namsos, and a few days later the Norwegian 5th Division (brigade) surrendered. The *Luftwaffe* discovered the evacuation fleet and placed it under attack for several hours scoring no hits on the transports, even though no Allied air units were available to deter them. German bombs hit and sank the British destroyer *Afridi* and the French destroyer *Bison* which carried the rear guard.

In the south the Norwegian 3rd Division (brigade strength) surrendered on 1 May. Other Norwegian units began to surrender in the south, some as early as 15 April, allowing German units to advance from Oslo along the south coast as well as westward from Oslo to Bergen.

Narvik

Meanwhile in the north, the German *3rd Mountain Division* at Narvik, one regiment strong with a naval regiment formed from about 2,600 sailors of sunken destroyers, continued to hold on through the month with little outside help. On 24 April the *Warspite* with three cruisers returned up the fjord to Narvik to bombard the town. The British warned the civilian population to evacuate, which they did together with the Germans. The bombardment achieved very little. The Norwegian 6th Division launched a four-battalion attack from the north only

ADVANCE OF THE
GERMAN 2nd MOUNTAIN
DIVISION–May-June 1940

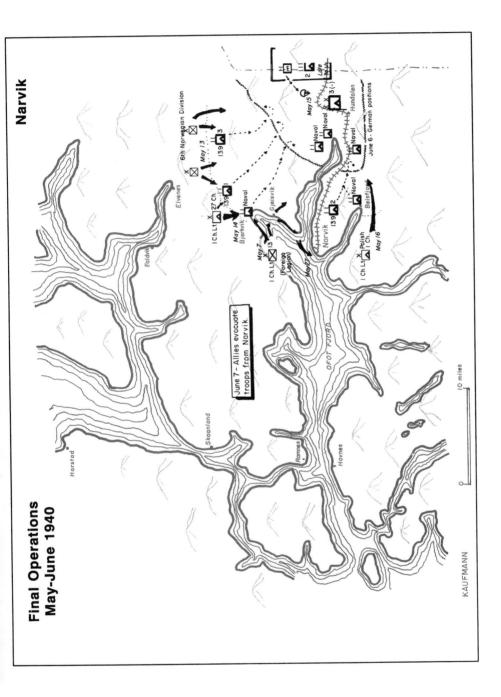

Narvik

Final Operations
May-June 1940

June 7 - Allies evacuate
troops from Narvik.

KAUFMANN

to be repulsed with the loss of most of a battalion after receiving no support from General Mackesy's troops. The German division at Narvik, isolated since 13 April, fought back but was desperate for supplies. Some were dispatched through Sweden via railroad, and the *Luftwaffe* made airdrops.

The Norwegian forces increased in size as the French and British landed additional units about 10 miles north of Narvik. The Germans checked initial attempts to advance southward, but in mid-May the Allies brought several battalions up the fjord towards Narvik and made successful landings. The German front began to fall back in the north and west, and by the end of the month Narvik was in the hands of the Allies. French troops, with the aid of the Polish brigade and the Foreign Legion, contributed to the Allied success. The German commander, General Edouard Dietl, contemplated retreating into Sweden.

The Allied operations against Narvik in May were a short-lived victory, for on 10 May the long awaited German offensive in the West began. As the situation on the Western Front grew critical, central Norway was abandoned and the Allies could offer only token resistance. British and French units attempted to fight a delaying action north of Namsos, as the Germans moved north, using amphibious operations to speed up their drive to relieve the troops at Narvik. By 7 June the Allies completed the evacuation of Narvik with a force of 3 cruisers and 16 destroyers for protection while the aircraft carriers *Ark Royal* and *Glorious* gave air cover. Shortly afterwards the Norwegian forces surrendered. King Haakon departed aboard the cruiser *Devonshire* with his government officials and gold reserves, permitting his Commander in Chief General Otto Ruge to surrender Norway to the invaders.

The *Scharnhorst*, *Gneisenau* and *Hipper* had been sent north before the Allies had departed, although they were unaware of the evacuation. This force sank the few ships it encountered while allowing a hospital ship to pass. On 8 June, after the evacuation of Narvik, they ran into a group including the British aircraft carrier *Glorious*. Two escorting destroyers and the aircraft carrier were sunk. In the course of the engagement a torpedo from the destroyer H.M.S. *Acasta* caused heavy damage to the engines and aft turret of the *Scharnhorst* before the German ship blew her out of the water. The German battle group was then forced to return to Trondheim where it was unsuccessfully attacked by Blackburn Skua dive bombers from the *Ark Royal*. A few days later, on 20 June, a British submarine torpedoed the *Gneisenau* causing significant damage. With the naval phase of the campaign concluded, the Norwegian campaign was finished.

The Results

German propagandists reveled in their success in the northern campaign, even before it was finished. In their propaganda magazine *Signal*, they boasted that in the first full month of operations they had sunk numerous Allied destroyers, submarines and a cruiser and had damaged a battleship. No doubt they had maintained air superiority, but their failure to destroy the railroads allowed Sickelforce to escape. Allied anti-aircraft weapons had been mostly absent in central Norway, and the guns of the warships had not been able to get sufficient elevation to offer protection inside the ports. The *Luftwaffe* certainly severely curtailed the effectiveness of the surface units of the British fleet. This was a portent of events on the Western Front. The Allies lost one aircraft carrier, two cruisers, a sloop, nine

The Norwegian Campaign Casualties				
Note: The following statistics are used in most accounts for total casualties, although no accurate figures can be given for the defeated:				
Army	KIA	WIA	MIA	Total
German	1,317	1,604	2,375	5,296
ALLIED				
British	--------1,896--------		2,500 lost at sea	4,396+
French-Poles	--------530--------		?	530
Norwegian	--------1,335--------		?	1,335
(Source: The German Northern Theater of Operations 1940-1945 by Earl F. Ziemke.)				

destroyers (including one French and one Polish) and six submarines (including one French and one Polish) with another five cruisers (including one French) damaged as well as two sloops and eight destroyers. This was actually insignificant compared to the German losses.

Germany had only one heavy cruiser (*Hipper*), two light cruisers and four destroyers in operation at the end of the campaign. The U-boats had little success during the campaign since the firing mechanisms on their torpedoes proved faulty, allowing several Allied ships to escape unharmed. Three cruisers, ten destroyers and eight U-boats were sunk and two battle cruisers, a pocket battleship and two cruisers were damaged. The victory cost the Germans much of their surface fleet with most of their ships either sunk or put out of action for months.

The Allies and Norwegians lost over 3,600 men while German casualties approached 6,000. Other than mountain divisions, the Germans had committed no elite units. For the Germans, loss of life was a small price to pay for the victory they achieved, but their naval losses crippled their small surface fleet, and may well have significantly contributed to preventing the launching of an invasion (Operation Sea Lion) against Great Britain.

Prime Minister Neville Chamberlain suffered a fate similar to Daladier of France who lost control of the French government for his earlier indecision concerning Finland. The events in Scandinavia brought down two rather weak leaders, unfortunately not soon enough to save the day for the Allies.

CHAPTER V

Hitler's Invasion Begins

As the first week of May 1940 drew to a close the fighting continued in Norway. The German commanders prepared to receive the code word for launching the long awaited offensive. For the first time, they were facing a battle in which they did not have a clear superiority over their opponents in men and weapons.

The armed forces of Belgium and the Netherlands awaited the inevitable while the French Army and the BEF prepared to implement the Dyle Plan. Despite the Mechelen Incident, King Leopold continued to deny the Allies entry into Belgium, although he had reduced the strength of his military forces on the French border from 50 percent to 10 percent and committed most of his army to the German frontier months earlier. Dutch military intelligence during April counted over 125 German divisions on the Western Front with an estimate that 85 were on the borders of Luxembourg, Belgium and the Netherlands. Of those 85 divisions, the Dutch identified 55 near their border. The Dutch realized that, despite his claims of peaceful intentions towards them, Hitler would strike through the Low Countries, and that they were definitely one of his objectives. Colonel Sas of the Netherlands received another warning from his contact in the *Abwehr*, but, after all the previous false alerts, no one took it seriously. Finally, in the early hours of 10 May 1940, the Western Front erupted as aircraft took to the air, guns blazed, and troops in field gray went on the attack. On the same

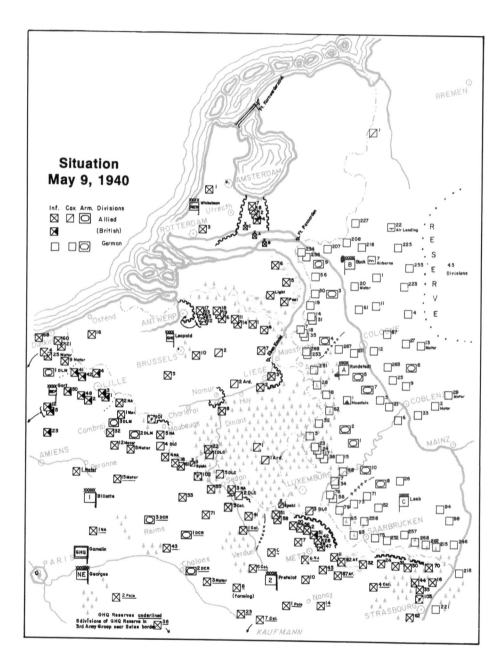

Situation May 9, 1940

Inf.	Cav.	Arm.	Divisions
⊠	⊠	◻	Allied
⊠			(British)
◻	◻	◻	German

GHQ Reserves underlined
8 divisions of GHQ Reserve in
3rd Army Group near Swiss border

day, Adolf Hitler proclaimed to the German people and the world that this was the beginning of a fight which would "...decide the fate of the German nation for the next 1,000 years."

Three German army groups deployed along the Western Front on 10 May. Leeb's *Army Group A* of 19 infantry divisions included *7th Army* along the Rhine and *1st Army* on the remainder of the Franco-German border. Bock's *Army Group B* with 29 divisions (3 panzer) had *18th Army* along most of the Dutch border (with one of the panzer divisions) and *6th Army* (with Hoepner's panzer corps) along the Maastricht Appendage of the Dutch border and the Belgian border in the vicinity of Aachen. Forty-five divisions (7 panzer) of Rundstedt's *Army Group A* occupied the smallest frontage, situated between the other two army groups and facing the Ardennes. The *12th Army* with Reinhardt's panzer corps (attached to *Panzer Group Kleist* was in the center of the *Army Group* with *16th Army* on the left flank which had *Panzer Group Kleist* (Guderian's panzer corps and *14th Motorized Corps*) under its administrative control and on the right flank *4th Army* with Hoth's panzer corps.

Reports on the early morning invasion of the Netherlands and Belgium indicated that the German operation was unfolding as General Gamelin had expected. The French general exclaimed, "The attack which we have been anticipating since October was launched this morning...[and] Germany has engaged us in a struggle to the death." When it received orders, the French 1st Army Group alerted its armies and they began to cross the Belgian border with mobile elements racing to the Dyle Line. The 12th Lancers at 1300 became the first unit of the BEF to cross the Belgian border. As the Lancers advanced, they met cheering civilians along their route. The Allies expected to engage the enemy in a decisive battle on the plains of northern Belgium but, unbeknownst to them, the main strength of the German Army was advancing into the Ardennes of southern Belgium and Luxembourg.

In accordance with the operational plan for the French 1st Army Group, its 2nd and 9th Armies facing southern Belgium moved a short distance into the Ardennes. The 2nd Army anchored the Army Group's flank from Sedan to the vicinity of the Maginot Line Proper and 2nd Army Group sent its two light cavalry divisions (DLC) forward into Belgium. The poorly equipped 9th Army, on the 2nd Army's left flank, with the mission to defend a stretch of the Meuse opposite a rugged region of the Ardennes, deployed a similar screen of mechanized and horse cavalry from its light cavalry divisions; the 1st and 4th DLCs. Neither army's units penetrated very far into the Ardennes. The mechanized cavalry of the 2nd Army, the 2nd and 5th DLC, was delayed by the flow of Belgian refugees. Soon, they began to encounter withdrawing elements of the Belgian Army. Units of the 2nd DLC reached Arlon only to be driven back by German armor. Enemy armor in the Ardennes! Something was terribly wrong.

On 3 March, 3rd DLC of 3rd Army, 2nd Army Group, had received the mission of occupying Luxembourg in the event of a German attack. When the first German troops entered the Low Countries on 10 May, the 3rd Army's headquarters was in a state of confusion. Several days earlier a French intelligence officer in Luxembourg, Captain Fernand Archen, had uncovered signs of a secret German operation. As the German special units went into action on 10 May, this agent repeatedly alerted his superiors at Longwy. Apparently, the messages were never forwarded to the 3rd Army Headquarters at Metz. That army's commander, General Charles Condé, and his staff received a flood of reports, but as late as 0530 he appeared to be uncertain of the situation and ordered an aerial reconnaissance. Finally, the 3rd DLC, with the attached 1st Spahi Brigade, received word to prepare and the division's commander reported that his men would be ready to move out by 0800 (two hours after being contacted). Almost four hours elapsed between the first time German units moved into Luxembourg and the time the first French units reached the border of the Grand Duchy.

Nasty Surprises

The events in southern Belgium and Luxembourg on the first day of the attack virtually guaranteed the success of the first phase of the German offensive. The Germans planned special operations to cover their advance through the Ardennes. German military intelligence, the *Abwehr*, had agents in Luxem-

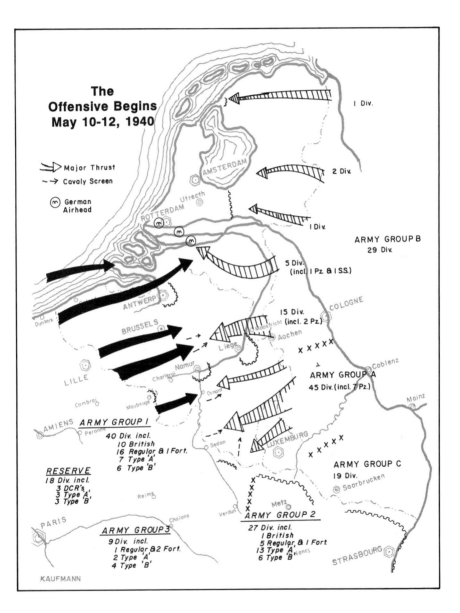

The
Offensive Begins
May 10-12, 1940

Major Thrust
Cavaly Screen
German Airhead

1 Div.

2 Div.

1 Div.

ARMY GROUP B
29 Div.

5 Div.
(incl. 1 Pz. & 1 S.S.)

15 Div.
(incl. 2 Pz.)

ARMY GROUP A
45 Div. (incl. 7 Pz.)

ARMY GROUP 1
40 Div. incl.
10 British
16 Regular & 1 Fort.
7 Type 'A'
6 Type 'B'

RESERVE
18 Div. incl.
3 DCR's
3 Type 'A'
3 Type 'B'

ARMY GROUP C
19 Div.

ARMY GROUP 2
27 Div. incl.
1 British
5 Regular, & 1 Fort
13 Type 'A'
6 Type 'B'

ARMY GROUP 3
9 Div. incl.
1 Regular & 2 Fort.
2 Type 'A'
4 Type 'B'

KAUFMANN

bourg, Belgium and the Netherlands with whom it organized special operations. Little information is available about these *Sonderkommandos* who formed an elite unit known as the *Brandenbergers* (named for the unit that captured Fort Douaumont at Verdun in 1916). As in Poland, these men were not in uniform and were assigned to secure vital objectives. In the Low Countries they prevented the demolition of bridges or sections of roads. One small group operating in Luxembourg included Germans who lived in the country and some Luxembourger sympathizers. It was rumored that they wore mechanics' coveralls over their uniforms so they could remove them in combat in accordance with the rules of land warfare, but some German sources claim that they never donned their uniforms. The second *Abwehr* group operating in Luxembourg crossed the border and had some success in rounding up gendarmes and seizing bridges. As early as 0410 the *Abwehr* units began their operations more than an hour before the first elements of German combat divisions had begun river crossing operations. One can assume that operations in Belgium had similar success although these missions were not well documented.

Some of the German commanders of *Army Group A* wanted paratrooper units to secure their front or aid their advance. However, the *Luftwaffe* which had assigned all its available airborne troops to operations against the Netherlands and the Fort Eben Emael in Belgium had none left for securing the routes through the Ardennes. Someone finally came up with the idea of using small observation aircraft to transport troops. Since the troops needed no special skills, the officers assigned the mission to selected volunteers from the *Grossdeutschland Infantry Regiment* and the *34th Infantry Division*. Late in the evening two groups prepared to land well ahead of the advancing armies. The special units boarded *Fieseler Storch* light aircraft which carried two passengers apiece. The smallest detachment of 125 men, divided into five 25 man groups, was assigned to Operation Hedderich. The planes flew low over the border and, at about 0455 landed in fields in close proximity to five key points near the border with Luxembourg and France. (Note: Some confusion exists concerning whether it was British or German time.)

The aircraft from the *Hedderich* groups returned to pick up

Fire! This German 150mm K 39 artillery piece discharges a destructive load on an enemy position.

additional troops. Most of the men landed by 0630 and began setting up road blocks and defensive positions. Their heaviest weapons were machine guns and mines. This daring operation was a success because the French 3rd DLC did not begin to move until after 0800. By that time the German special fast moving advanced parties, armed with heavier weapons, crossed the border; racing to reinforce four of these air landed units which had erected barricades near Esch. The second German group was closer to the German border and elements of the *76th Division* had only a short distance to move to reach them. The German *34th Division* moved on to Luxembourg City and then headed towards the German units at the border, the *17th Division* moving on its right flank secured the Luxembourg border of the German *16th Army*'s flank. The Germans repelled the 3rd DLC's advance elements all along the border preventing it from securing Esch, even with the use of H-35 tanks. The horse mounted Spahis advanced the furthest, although that was only a few miles, and encountered a larger German force advancing on all sides, forcing them to retreat grudgingly with almost 100 German prisoners. A French corps reconnaissance group, moving from Longwy to the border, withdrew later in the morning claiming that it had engaged German armor, when there had actually been none in the vicinity of southern Luxembourg.

The *Abwehr* and the *Hedderich Group* received little credit for their actions from the German commanders. Their intervention, however, prevented the French 3rd DLC from setting up blocking positions against the *16th Army*'s advancing infantry divisions, and possibly striking north and hindering the advance of Guderian's panzer corps. Although this theory appears far-fetched, it is not unreasonable since Guderian's tanks were already choking the few roads leading through the Ardennes and had to share at least one route with Reinhardt's panzer corps. As it turned out, the bold German move and the slow French reaction secured the southern flank of *Army Group A*.

Another 400 volunteers from the infantry regiment *Grossdeutschland* arrived in Belgium in the 98 light aircraft which made two trips. Operation Niwi had the objective of securing the villages of Martelange and Witry in Belgium and opening the route to Neufchâteau for Guderian's panzers. According to some reports, German agents of the *Abwehr* prevented prearranged demolition of some vital roads in southern Belgium, facilitating the advance of several of the panzer corps. In response to the German actions, the two Belgian divisions of Chasseurs Ardennais hurriedly prepared demolitions, successfully destroyed many key transportation points such as bridges, and withdrew from the easily defensible region as previously ordered. Early in the afternoon the *Niwi Group*, after having engaged Belgian chasseurs, finally opened the route to Neufchâteau, in spite of the cavalry screen of the French 2nd and 5th DLCs. Guderian's troops arrived later in the day.

Seven panzer divisions, divided into three corps, crossed the border running into the first obstacles in their path. General Erwin Rommel with the *7th Panzer Division*, his first major command, was part of General Hermann Hoth's *XV Panzer Corps*. He recorded that permanent barricades and deep craters obstructed all the main roads and forest tracks. Since few Belgian chasseurs remained behind, his division encountered few serious delays, simply moving around the obstacles by going cross country through the "impassable" Ardennes. By the second day, his advancing columns pushed back the French 9th Army's 4th DLC which made little attempt to hold its blocking positions. Rommel found that if his tanks fired indiscriminately with cannon and machine guns at suspected enemy positions, the Allied troops usually pulled out quickly. This procedure speeded up his advance.

General Heinz Guderian's *XIX Panzer Corps* of three divisions made good time through Luxembourg, and by the end of the first day it could not be stopped by Belgian demolitions. When General Ewald von Kleist, commander of *Panzer Group Kleist* which included *XIX Panzer* and *XIV Motorized Corps*, wanted to divert one of Guderian's panzer divisions to the south to meet the French 3rd DLC's counterattack, Guderian refused to comply, and, as it turned out, the French cavalry unit was already withdrawing towards Longwy after having run afoul of the air landed troops. The *XIX Panzer Corps* linked up with the *Niwi Group* on the afternoon of 10 May, but there were too many obstructions on its path. That night Guderian's men cleared the paths and roads, and the next day his tanks moved forward to meet the 2nd French Army's 2nd and 5th DLCs and the remaining Belgian Chasseurs at Neufchâteau. The Germans easily pushed back this Allied force, and went on to the Meuse at the end of 11 May.

General Georg-Hans Reinhardt's *XLI Panzer Corps* of two panzer divisions got entangled with the *XIX Panzer Corps* while operating on its right flank. This corps had entered the Ardennes on the heels of Guderian's and was to advance on his right flank. By 11 May all three panzer corps moved steadily towards the Meuse with few problems. The battle in the skies went the German's way as well. The Armée de l'Air took virtually no action, while the RAF sent in its light bombers, the Fairey Battles, with disastrous results. With the support of German anti-aircraft units, the *Luftwaffe* began dominating the air.

The paucity of roads in southern Belgium created bottlenecks with long columns of German vehicles strung out through the Ardennes, but the lack of resistance allowed the

German Tank Strength, 10 May 1940			
Tank Divisions	Pz I, II & command Vehicles	Pz 35t & 38t	Pz III & IV
ARMY GROUP A			
XIX Panzer Corps			
1st Panzer Division	130-180 (130)	---	96-146 (146)
2nd Panzer Division	130-182 (130)	---	90-146 (146)
10th Panzer Division	130-194 (130)	---	84-146 (146)
XLI Panzer Corps			
6th Panzer Division	50-60 (50)	106-132 (132)	26-36 (36)
8th Panzer Division	25-58 (50)	132-180 (132)	30-36 (36)
XV Panzer Corps			
5th Panzer Division	192-250 (250)	---	65-84 (74)
7th Panzer Division	50-109 (50)	48-132 (132)	23-36 (36)
ARMY GROUP B			
XVI Panzer Corps			
3rd Panzer Division	231-273 (250)	---	49-74 (74)
4th Panzer Division	250-290 (250)	---	64-76 (74)
XXVI Panzer Corps			
9th Panzer Division	175-185 (175)	---	38-90 (54)

Note: There is a considerable discrepancy between figures given by various sources, and these numbers represent some of the highs and lows given. Numbers in parentheses are from Bryan Perrett, Knights of the Black Cross, St. Martin's Press, NY 1986. These appear to be the most reasonable numbers which might have been set as a new table of organization for the spring of 1940, even if not actually achieved.

forward progress to continue and the German penetration of southern Belgium and the Ardennes progressed quickly. The Allies were unaware of the size of the force moving along the narrow roads of the hilly forested region. The special operations groups which had engaged the French cavalry units earlier were simply mistaken for a fifth column. In the Allied camp rumors were flying that disguised German agents were lurking everywhere, giving the impression that the fifth columnists instead of a major force were causing most of the problems in the Ardennes. Thus the Germans won the most critical part of the battle, obtaining a relatively unobstructed path to the Meuse, without having to fight.

All Eyes North

In the West, all eyes turned north of the Ardennes, towards the fields of Flanders where the French had anticipated the main German thrust. Here the Germans launched a dramatic assault on the main Belgian defensive line in front of Liege as well as against the Netherlands. Generals Gamelin and Georges were intent on reaching the Dyle Line in time to stop the Germans. Gamelin still hoped that the 7th Army would arrive at Breda in time to create a united front with the Dutch. The Allies anxiously watched the Belgian situation on the Albert Canal Line and in the Liege area, hoping they would have enough time to prepare defensive positions, but failing to recognize the role of the "secondary" German force advancing through the Ardennes.

Meanwhile, the Germans inaugurated new tactics against the Dutch defenses and the Belgian fort of Eben Emael. General Albert Kesselring took over the *2nd Luftflotte* in January 1940, after Hitler sacked General Helmut Felmy because of the Mechelen Incident. Kesselring was responsible for covering all the air landings and air operations in Northern Belgium and the Netherlands as well as over the North Sea. The Mechelen Incident also caused a change in German plans as Hitler and his generals believed their secret plans had been compromised when the Belgians seized the airborne operational plans from the downed aircraft. Fortunately for the Führer, he had kept the Eben Emael operation so secret that it had not been included in the captured plans. The air landings marked on the captured documents showed plans for an air assault on the Belgian National Redoubt formed by the Ghent Bridgehead and the Antwerp defenses, as well as a drop in the vicinity of Namur. Basically, the German airborne units were to breach every

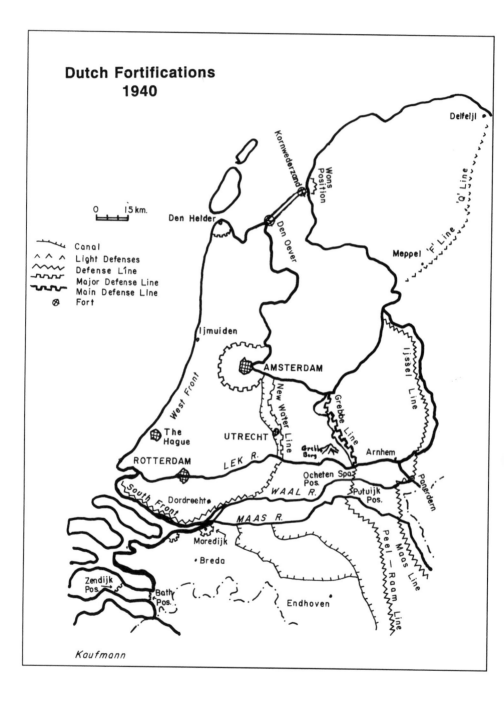

Dutch Fortifications
1940

Delfejl

Kornwederzand

Wons Position

'Q' Line

0   15 km.

Den Helder

Den Oever

Meppel   'F' Line

Canal
Light Defenses
Defense Line
Major Defense Line
Main Defense Line
Fort

Ijmuiden

AMSTERDAM

Ijssel Line

West Front

New Water Line

Grebbe Line

The Hague

UTRECHT

Grebb Berg

Arnhem

ROTTERDAM

LEK R.

Ocheten Spos. Pos.

Panerdern

South Front

Dordrecht

WAAL R.

Putuijk Pos.

MAAS R.

Moredijk

Peel — Raam Line

Maas Line

Breda

Zendijk Pos.

Bath Pos.

Endhoven

Kaufmann

184

German transport planes fly over Holland during the opening of the campaign in the West. German paratroopers took key objectives in the Netherlands and held them until relieved by advancing ground forces.

German Aircraft Available on 10 May 1940		
Note: Numbers approximated		
Plane	Model	Quantity
Fighters	ME-109	860
	ME-110	350
	Total	1,210
Bombers & Recon	HS-123, JU-87	380
	DO-17, JU-88, HE-111	1,300
	Recon Aircraft	640
	Total	2,320

major Belgian defensive line to aid the advance on the northern plains. Since Hitler adopted Manstein's plan after the incident, the northern operations were turned into decoys for diverting the Allies. Assuming that the Allies must already know the original objectives, the Germans scrapped all the air landing operations in Belgium with the exception of the top secret mission against the Eben Emael, in favor of a massive effort to breach Fortress Holland. The Germans hoped that this action would guarantee the quick defeat of the Netherlands, eliminate it as a potential staging area for the Allies, as well as draw Allied forces northward.

The German onslaught against the Netherlands began at dawn on 10 May with the air assault of several battalions of General Kurt Student's *7th Air Division* and *22nd Air Landing Division*. The parachutists were *Luftwaffe* troops under General Kesselring's air fleet, and, after having set idly in reserve waiting for action during the Polish campaign, they looked forward to their first real operation as a division. In Poland they had been meant to support operations underway, but the advance had gone so fast that they were never called up. This time they were to lead the way in the Netherlands and Belgium. Kesselring complained that not all the men of the *7th Air Division* had completed their parachute training and that all

German paratroopers dive from Ju-52 transport planes during attack on the Low Countries.

4,500 trained parachutists were going into action leaving no reserve for any additional missions. Other members of the division would land by different methods: in seaplanes or JU-52s. Many of the aircraft took off sometime after 0400, although there seems to be some question as to exact times and most of the airborne operations took place between 0430 and 0530 local time.

At dawn on 10 May, the *2nd Luftflotte* sent its fighters and bombers over the Netherlands in advance of the transports carrying the troops. Twenty-three Dutch aircraft stood ready at one airfield, but the Dutch airmen did not realize that the invasion was underway and the Germans wiped them out on the ground. Other Dutch fighters rose to intercept the superior

187

German fighter aircraft, but before the end of the day most of the Royal Dutch Air Force was a wrecked smoldering mass. Other fighters of the *Luftwaffe* escorted the JU-52s and gave them support on landing. The parachutists descended upon key crossings of the Maas (Meuse), Waal and Lek (Lower Rhine) Rivers, whose bridges offered a quick entry into the back door of Fortress Holland. Civilians living in the western end of the fortress zone awoke to the sound of gunfire, zooming aircraft, exploding bombs and a blue sky blossoming with the white mushroom shapes of parachutes.

The Germans attempted landings at the airfields around The Hague in order to capture the Dutch government in one of the boldest airborne operations of the campaign. The *22nd Air Landing Division* of General Graf von Sponeck, with a regiment of the *7th Air Division*, was ordered to land at points around the capital. But the operation ended in failure when many German aircraft attempted to land on airfields already obstructed by the Dutch, bringing about their own destruction, and some were forced to land on beaches and roads. Worst still, a number of men of the *22nd Division* were not able to land when their aircraft had to abort the mission. The Dutch fiercely contested the landings leaving the German parachutists and air landed troops isolated, suffering heavy casualties.

The *7th Air Division's 1st Parachute Regiment* and the *16th Air Landing Regiment* of the *22nd Air Landing Division* had the mission of securing a route to Rotterdam by capturing the bridges at Moerdijk over the Holland Deep, at Dordrecht across the Oude Maas, and in the center of Rotterdam on the Nieuwe Maas. Two companies from the *1st Parachute Regiment* landed on either end of the Moerdijk bridge, and successfully stormed it, securing the *2nd Battalion's* objective. A company from the regiment's *1st Battalion* seized part of the Dordrecht bridge, but the Dutch drove them back. Fortunately for the Germans, the Dutch, believing they needed the bridge for their own military movements, didn't destroy it and gave the Germans additional time to recapture it. At Rotterdam over a hundred men of a company from the *16th Infantry Regiment* landed on the river in a dozen Heinkel-59 seaplanes at either end of the two bridges. A small group of paratroopers dropped south of the bridges and moved up to join them. Meanwhile, the *3rd Battal-*

A Panzer I overlooks a Dutch bridge blown up to halt the German advance. Most Dutch bridges were captured by the Germans before they could be destroyed.

ion of the *1st Parachute Regiment* dropped near the Waalhaven airfield south of the city, and stormed it as the *3rd Battalion* of the *16th Infantry Regiment* was landing in JU-52s. The double assault overwhelmed the Dutch defenders of Waalhaven. Soon the German troops on the Nieuwe Maas bridges at Rotterdam received reinforcements from these units while some companies rushed south to recapture the Dordrecht bridge from the Dutch. Despite losses, the German paratroopers captured the vital bridges into Fortress Holland over the main Dutch river barriers. The air transports suffered heavily during these operations, especially near The Hague. All Dutch counterattacks in the next few days proved unsuccessful. Their reserve had to contain the bridgeheads, and they failed to seal the breach allowing the German sky troopers to stubbornly hold out until relief arrived.

At the end of the first day Radio Berlin announced that German parachutists had landed in Holland and Belgium "...in order to ward off the impending attack...[and] to safeguard the neutrality of these two countries." The Dutch claimed that they destroyed 70 German aircraft, then raised this number to 100

Allied Aircraft Available on 10 May 1940

Note: Numbers approximated

Country and Plane	Model	Quantity
French Fighters	MS-406	280
	Curtiss-75	100
	Block 151/2	130
	Dewoitine-520	20
	Potez 631	70
	Total	600
French Bombers & Recon	Potez 63.11	260
	Bloch 174	35
	Leo-451	55
	Breguet 691-2	45
	Other Types	1,000+
	Total	1,500+
British Fighters (in France)	Hurricane	60
	Gladiator	30
	Total	90
British Bombers (in France)	Battle	125
	Blenheim	60
	Whitley	30
	Lysander	120
	Total	335
Belgian Fighters	Hurricane	11
	Fiat CR.42	20
	Gladiator	15
	Fairey Fox (Biplane)	60
	Total Bombers and Rec.	106
Dutch Fighters	Fokker D. XXI	30
	Fokker GIA	23
	Total Incl. bmrs & Recon	53

and also announced that they recaptured airfields with 14 more German aircraft on them. During the operation the Germans lost, in fact, 170 aircraft and about the same number of their planes were damaged. In the following days the Dutch claimed that they were eliminating the parachutists which was largely true in regard to the *22nd Division*'s men whom the Dutch had trapped in pockets. But that was not the case for the *7th Air Division* which continued to hold the back door into Fortress Holland.

Also, early on 10 May special troops of the elite *Brandenburg* unit, dressed in Dutch uniforms, unsuccessfully attempted to capture key border crossings. The Dutch hailed their victories of destroying four German armored trains in these operations and blowing up most of the bridges on the Maas and Issel rivers. The Dutch reaction also prevented two trains from depositing a couple of battalions of infantry behind the Grebbe Line. Unfortunately it was too soon to claim a lasting success. At Gennep *Brandenbergers* in Dutch military garb escorted a party of "German prisoners" with concealed weapons and took the guards holding the bridge there by surprise while a German armored train approached. The *9th Panzer Division* followed and began its trek across North Brabant to relieve the paratroopers who were holding open the door into Fortress Holland.

As a result of these special operations, as in Luxembourg, rumors spread like wild fire about German "fifth columnists" who were active behind the front wearing a variety of disguises, from Allied uniforms to nun's habits. In a communique, the government of the Netherlands claimed that many German parachutists had descended upon their homeland wearing Dutch uniforms. As a result of these operations, the Belgians as well as the French turned their attention towards the sky with increased anxiety and deployed units to prepare against further airborne landings. Fearing German parachutists, the British took measures against them and alerted the civilian population not only in England, but also as far south as British Somaliland. Even the Swiss, noticing a German buildup on their northern border in the first days of the campaign, urged Boy and Girl Scouts and elderly women to watch the skies.

Everywhere belligerents and neutrals maintained a vigil against saboteurs.

The Dutch quickly withdrew their three infantry divisions of the III Corps and their only mobile division from the Peel-Raam Line, even before the Germans arrived. They had no hope of establishing a defensive link with the Belgians since earlier discussions with their neighbor had accomplished nothing. Also, Commander in Chief General Winkelman chose not to attempt to hold the whole frontier in force with his country's limited resources. Even in a more favorable situation, the Dutch would not have had enough troops to hold such an extended front on their own. Faced with the German airhead and the advance of the *9th Panzer Division*, the Dutch forces attempted to clear and hold Fortress Holland with everything they had. The French 7th Army rushed through Belgium and into the Netherlands to find Brabant abandoned and only a Dutch holding force in Zeeland since General Winkelman ordered the main elements of the Dutch Army back to Fortress Holland.

The Germans pushed back the Dutch on all fronts, and forced them to take up positions on their main defensive line in front of Fortress Holland; on 10 May the German *1st Cavalry Division* had quickly cut through the few outpost lines of Friesland to reach the Wons Position which covered the Great Dike and Fort Kornwerderzand on 11 May; it penetrated the Wons Position the next day.

On 12 May the *9th Panzer Division* drove into the heart of Fortress Holland with its armor. The same day signalled the collapse of the main Dutch fortifications of the Grebbe Line which had been under attack since the previous day by German infantry divisions and an SS regiment that penetrated the line and could not be driven back.

Even though the German infantry divisions deployed against the Dutch were not of the best quality, they were still better equipped and trained than their opponents and were able to overrun the Dutch positions with ease. The Dutch had hoped to employ traditional defenses of water obstacles and flooding to defend themselves, only to have the rapidly advancing Germans prevent them from putting this plan into action. Dutch mistakes compounded their desperate situation.

In the case of the Grebbe Line, the commander of the Dutch II Corps simply failed to prepare his troops for fighting in woodlands during the months before the invasion. J.S. van Wieringen, in his research on the Grebbe Line, recently discovered that a Dutch commander, General Harberts, failed to clear orchards to prepare fields of fire because both the military and civilians just did not believe the Germans would attack. Only when the invasion came did the Dutch begin to clear trees for fields of fire. These measures were both too late and too slow, giving the Germans use of the wooded terrain to shield their assault troops. In addition, the Dutch could not reinforce the Grebbe Line since their badly needed reserves were already engaged in containing the German airheads.

On 13 May the German X *Corps* with the *207th* and *227th Divisions*, reinforced by the *SS Der Führer Regiment*, breached a position on the Grebbe Line after three days of fighting, forcing the Dutch retreat to the weaker position of the New Water Line. The Germans enjoyed a rest from the intense fighting and did not even notice the withdrawal of the Dutch Army.

With the Germans' in position to seize total control of the Netherlands, the Dutch government leaders fled to England. A small force of British troops landed near The Hague to help evacuate the royal family and assist the Dutch in the demolition of vital port facilities. The day after the German invasion began, Queen Wilhelmina announced that, "I and my country will do our duty." On the fifth day General Winkelman announced that "our resistance has been broken by overwhelming power," and told his countrymen, "Hollanders, keep your faith in the traditions of our country," as he ordered an end to hostilities.

As the Netherlands collapsed one of the most unfortunate incidents of the war occurred. Before General Student was wounded at his command post at the Rotterdam airport, he had called for air strikes against strongpoints in Rotterdam while negotiations for the surrender of the Netherlands were going on. German bombers prepared for their mission and departed in the afternoon of 14 May when an agreement had already been completed. The resulting tragedy is the source of some debate. Hitler may have wanted the bombing mission to take place anyway in order to demonstrate to his enemies the kind

Though making a valiant defensive effort, the Dutch were forced to surrender after a week of fighting.

of devastation he could wreak upon those who resisted him. Or perhaps many of the aircraft never got the signals to abort. Whatever the reason, Rotterdam suffered massive devastation from bombing with destructive fires breaking out and spreading throughout the city. First reports indicated 100,000 casualties, though actually only about 1,000 people died.

As General Winkelman surrendered the army in Fortress Holland, the Dutch forces in Zeeland continued to resist with the support of elements of an infantry division of the 7th French Army which had arrived by sea a few days earlier. On

18 May the French divisions of the 7th Army fell back on Antwerp and soon the Germans penetrated the last defensive positions of Zeeland.

There was only one bright light in the fading hours of Dutch resistance. As the *German 1st Cavalry Division* swept through the few small weak lines of resistance in Friesland and moved on through the Wons Position, it came across Fort Kornwerder-zand which defended the northeastern end of the Great Dike. One assault after another ended in failure. Stukas and shock troops attacked the fort with no success, and the Germans were not able to occupy the fort until General Winkelman ordered it to surrender. Because of this fierce battle, the men of the German cavalrymen named the fort the Dam of Death.

The Big Push?: Penetration into Northern Belgium

While most of the battalions of the German *7th Air Division*'s two parachute regiments descended upon the Netherlands, several smaller detachments launched daring assaults on a series of objectives which led to a breach in the main line of Belgian defenses and the capture of Fort Eben Emael. These units were part of *Assault Group Koch.*

Although Hitler liked Manstein's Ardennes operational plan, he chose to include these special air assault landings. The operation against the key Belgian fort, probably more than any other, caught Hitler's fancy. What a propaganda coup if a handful of men could take one of the strongest forts in the world with daring new tactics. The plan required a spearhead of the *4th Panzer Division* to break through to relieve the attacking airborne troops. This operation, as hoped, deceived the Allies into believing that it was the main thrust of the invasion and that the Schlieffen Plan was back in operation causing eyes to remain turned away from the Ardennes on the first critical days.

Assault Group Koch departed just before dawn from its air base with JU-52s hauling the assault teams in DFS 230A gliders which carried up to 10 men and their equipment. The gliders were cut loose before reaching the border and began soaring

A Belgian ACG-1 tank knocked out after engaging invading German forces.

A large non-eclipsing turret of Eben Emael with two 120mm guns. The Belgian fort was thought to be invincible, but was easily taken by German glider-borne troops.

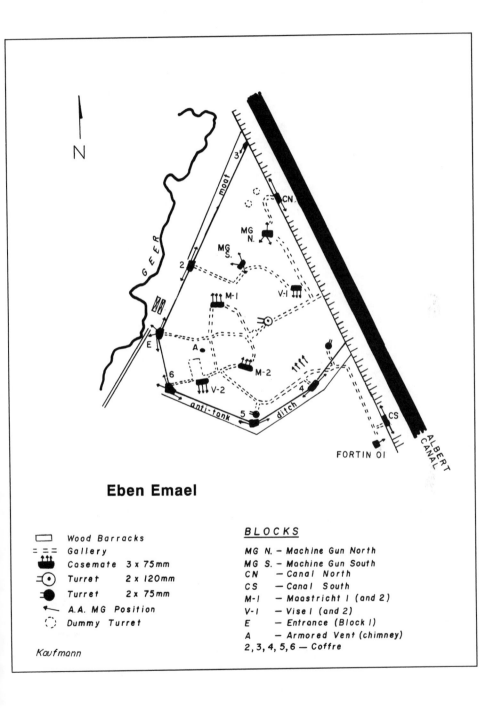

Eben Emael

◻ Wood Barracks
≡≡≡ Gallery
⛫ Casemate 3 x 75mm
⊕ Turret 2 x 120mm
● Turret 2 x 75mm
← A.A. MG Position
⊙ Dummy Turret

Kaufmann

BLOCKS

MG N. – Machine Gun North
MG S. – Machine Gun South
CN – Canal North
CS – Canal South
M-I – Maastricht I (and 2)
V-I – Vise I (and 2)
E – Entrance (Block I)
A – Armored Vent (chimney)
2, 3, 4, 5, 6 – Coffre

Aerial photo of Eben Emael. 1. Area armed outside the fort. 2. Block Canal North on Albert Canal. 3. Block with 75mm gun turret and weapons covering anti-tank ditch. 3a. Fortin. 4. Water filled anti-tank ditch. 5. Temporary surface barracks.

over the Maastricht Appendage towards the Albert Canal, although Dutch anti-aircraft guns opened fire on them before they reached their objectives. The group was divided into 4 small detachments of glider troops of which 3, in 10 gliders each, attempted to capture 3 of the key bridges over the Albert Canal under the guns of Fort Eben Emael. They succeeded in taking 2 bridges, but the garrison had time to blow up the third as the remaining detachment of 12 gliders, carrying the combat engineers, landed right on top of the fort. The assault troops carried special hollow-charge explosives in addition to their assault weapons.

Most of the 11 gliders carrying troops sailed past the Dutch defenses of the Maastricht Appendage and skidded across the top of the Belgian fort while 4 did not reach the target including the one with the commanding officer, Lieutenant Rudolf Witzig. However, this was airborne again later in the day and arrived during the heat of the action. Even though the fort's garrison was alerted more than an hour before the landing, the silent descent of the Germans took it by surprise. The great fort had open anti-aircraft machine gun positions on its surface, but the gliders approached too quickly for the gunners to fire upon them. The German troopers had already scrambled out of their gliders and were moving toward their objectives across the fort's surface before the garrison reacted. One by one, the assault engineers knocked out each of the fort's combat blocks and the 75mm gun turrets by using the new and still secret hollow charges. Amazingly, the 120mm gun turret withstood the new type of demolitions, and it was later rumored that sabotage had taken it out of action before the arrival of the German assault troops. The Belgian artillerymen occupying the fort had no infantry training and ended up abandoning their casemates as the Germans breached them, and sealing internal galleries to prevent penetration from above. Thus they locked themselves in an underground prison with all their guns out of action. A nearby Belgian infantry division failed to launch a successful counterattack to relieve the fort. Although the Eben Emael still had not surrendered, on 10 May Berlin announced the awarding of the Iron Cross to Captain Koch and Lieutenant Witzig with no explanations given.

The next day the spearhead of the *4th Panzer Division* finally reached the Albert Canal after bridging the Maas in the town of Maastricht where the Dutch had blown up the bridges. The link-up with the small party of paratroopers on the Eben Emael gave the commander of the garrison no choice but to surrender the largest and best known of the Belgian fortifications on the afternoon of 11 May.

The fall of Fort Eben Emael broke the main line of Belgian defenses. Soon the Germans invested the other three forts of the main line and the second line of old forts around Liege. The last of these forts fell to the Germans several days later, but the

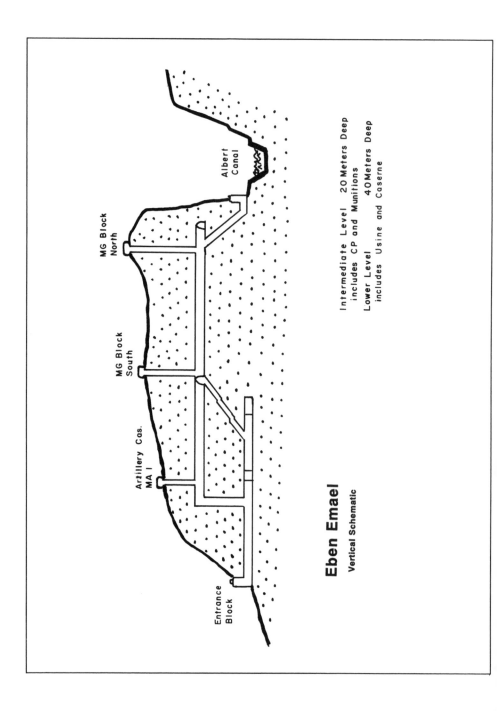

Eben Emael
Vertical Schematic

Entrance Block

Artillery Cas. MA I

MG Block South

MG Block North

Albert Canal

Intermediate Level 20 Meters Deep includes CP and Munitions
Lower Level 40 Meters Deep includes Usine and Caserne

Hitler visits a Belgian bunker as his forces sweep across the Low Countries and northern France.

true success of the operation was in convincing the Allies that the main German thrust was coming through the Belgian Plain.

Meanwhile, the Germans continued to roll through the Low Countries. They began to move toward the partially defended Gembloux Gap located between the Meuse and the end of the Dyle Line. The French 7th Army, as previously mentioned, had already reached Antwerp with its mobile units, where its armored elements detrained and began moving towards Breda hoping to link up with the Dutch. As the French 1st and 7th Armies and the BEF advanced, General René Prioux's Cavalry Corps of light mechanized divisions (2nd and 3rd DLMs) dashed to cover the Dyle position and Gembloux Gap. The Allies soon discovered that the Belgian defenses were largely incomplete and the Germans were close by. The bridges destroyed by the Dutch at Maastricht had held up Hoepner's panzer divisions on 10 May, but on 11 May, the *3rd* and *4th*

A jubilant Fuhrer poses with some of the troops who took Eben Emael. They wear Iron Crosses awarded for their spectacular feat.

Panzer Divisions resumed their advance, crossing the Albert Canal and engaging advancing armored elements of the French Cavalry Corps well behind the canal line. The move to the Dyle Line went on unhindered. The *Luftwaffe*, engaged in attacking Dutch, Belgian and French air bases, did not interfere with troop movements and allowed the Allied armies to settle down in their new positions. In the meanwhile, the bulk of the panzer force was rapidly moving through the Ardennes.

The first major engagement of German and French armor had mixed results, proving that the French armor was a force to be reckoned with. General Prioux's Cavalry Corps withdrew, having successfully completed its covering mission, but the Belgian withdrawal from the Albert Canal and the Liege area left the French force exposed. The Germans occupied the battlefield and proceeded to recover and repair damaged vehicles. Gamelin directed the French heavy armored divisions (DCRs) from his reserve toward the 1st Army which was

A Belgian railroad destroyed by air attack.

French motorcycle troops race across the Belgian border to meet invading Germans. Little did they know that they were playing into their enemy's hands.

already effectively checking the German drive across northern Belgium. The DCRs were unable to reach the 1st Army, finding themselves strung out behind the 2nd and 9th Armies when the events in the Ardennes caught up with them.

The Dutch had incorrectly estimated that there were as many as 55 German divisions on their border, while the news media correctly alleged that there were, in fact, 29 divisions advancing against the Netherlands and northern Belgium. These were all units of General Fedor von Bock's *Army Group B*. However, as noted, this was not the main thrust. In reality it was what B.H. Liddell Hart called the "Matador's Cloak," and it successfully fooled the Allies. The French and the British continued to rush into the trap, while their leaders seemed to have no idea about the whereabouts of *Army Group A's* 45 divisions.

Courage, Energy, Confidence

On the day the Germans struck at his country, King Leopold informed the world that, "The Belgian cause is pure and with the help of God will triumph." Unfortunately his public speeches were more effective than his military directives. When he saw that his main line was threatened in front of Liege, he recalled most of his troops in the Ardennes, leaving the heavily wooded and hilly region with its tortuous roads virtually undefended. As noted, this was the situation the French cavalry found when it arrived on the first day.

The seven panzer divisions of *Panzer Group Kleist* spearheaded the drive of the three armies of General Rundstedt's *Army Group A* through the Ardennes, pushing aside all opposition. The Belgian 1st Chasseurs Ardennais Division withdrew to defend the main line in the north, while the 2nd Chasseurs Ardennais Division retreated without coordinating with the French, leaving the Ardennes virtually undefended. The Allied air forces joined the action, seeking targets, but the *Luftwaffe* was able to mask the approaching German forces. Belgian obstacles and demolitions succeeded in hindering not only the progress of the Germans, but also the advance of the French cavalry divisions. The French 2nd Army's cavalry, driven back by the advancing Germans, soon joined the flood of refugees

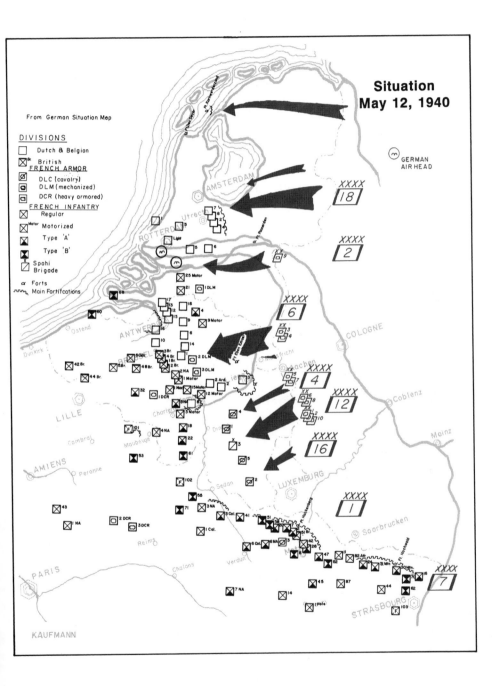

Situation
May 12, 1940

From German Situation Map

DIVISIONS

☐ Dutch & Belgian
☒ British
FRENCH ARMOR
◪ DLC (cavalry)
◉ DLM (mechanized)
▣ DCR (heavy armored)
FRENCH INFANTRY
☒ Regular
☒ Motorized
☒ Type 'A'
☒ Type 'B'
▨ Spahi Brigade
α Forts
⌇ Main Fortifications

GERMAN AIR HEAD

KAUFMANN

from the vicinity of Arlon which had slowed its progress in the opposite direction.

The German deception worked perfectly. Air reconnaissance reports from 10 May and initial contact by scouting elements still failed to convince the French High Command that a major threat was materializing in the Ardennes. *Luftwaffe* fighters and flak units helped deter prying eyes as well as air attacks on German ground forces. While the headlines and radio reports buzzed with news of small actions in front of the Maginot Line, the campaign against the paratroopers in the Netherlands and the fall of the Eben Emael, other coverage was sketchy. Bombs falling on Switzerland as a result of an aerial engagement between French fighters and German bombers, violent fighting in northern Belgium and claims of the fall of Liege also received the lion's share of news media attention. The only news from the front between the border of Luxembourg and the Liege defenses was a German report of heavy fighting around Malmedy, near the border with Germany, and the occupation of Luxembourg, interpreted as a possible move to reach or outflank the Maginot Line.

On the night of 11/12 May General Corap committed a serious error by withdrawing his 9th Army's cavalry divisions to the Meuse. Some of Corap's infantry formations had not yet arrived at their new positions on the Belgian section of the Meuse River while others still needed time to prepare to allow the remainder of the army several days to set up the new defensive line. Corap ordered all the bridges from Dinant to the vicinity of Sedan blown up.

The decisive day in the campaign came on 12 May as the whole of the Allied effort was diverted to the Netherlands and the major armored battle occurred between the 3rd DLM and the *4th Panzer Division* in Belgium. The superiority of the French artillery decided the tank battle, even though the *Luftwaffe* dominated the air. In spite of this victory, the French suffered heavy losses because of the inadequacy of their small unit tactics and inefficient one-man tank turrets. The next morning, the French withdrew in anticipation of a more decisive tank battle.

The 1st DCR, with its formidable Char B tanks headed toward the battle, but was soon diverted by developments in

German troops inspect a British Battle, brought down during failed Allied attempts to destroy German crossings in the Ardennes.

the Ardennes. The Belgian Army began its complete withdrawal from the Albert Canal on 12 May and took up positions with the Allies on the Dyle Line. Meanwhile the previously mentioned clash of armor began leaving the French Cavalry Corps exposed. Elements of the three panzer corps in the Ardennes closed on the Meuse, as the Allies remained thoroughly entangled in northern Belgium.

Guderian's panzer corps bounced the cavalry units of the French 2nd Army from the Ardennes by 12 May. Before the day was done Guderian set up his headquarters near the winding Semois River in the ancient town of Bouillon, overlooked by the castle of the first great leader of the Crusades, Geoffrey of Bouillon. A few remaining Belgian aircraft made an unsuccessful raid on this picturesque town and a tank park situated there. Guderian's tanks found all the bridges over the Semois demolished, but located many other fordable points as the divisional engineers began to erect bridges. By evening his troops had reached the banks of the Meuse, the last major barrier before the open terrain of northern France. The Germans also quickly stormed Sedan, the site of Prussia's first great victory over the French in 1870.

General Charles Huntziger, the French commander of the 2nd Army, realized the gravity of the situation since in earlier war games he had used a plan similar to that being employed by the Germans in the Ardennes. Believing that the Germans intended to outflank the Maginot Line, General Huntziger posted his best units on the flank of the fortifications since that was his main mission, and the inferior Category B divisions of his 2nd Army he moved to the extreme left, near Sedan, to protect what was to become the critical sector of the Meuse front.

Rommel's *7th Panzer Division* followed the retreating French cavalry right up to the Meuse, only to find the bridges at Houx and Dinant blown up. Still the French forces on the other side of the river, Corap's 9th Army, were weak and over extended. Despite good defensible terrain, it was manned with too few Regular units and saddled with too many Category B divisions, many of which had performed only labor functions during the winter, lacked equipment and weapons, and were in desperate need of additional training. Some, such as the 61st Division, didn't even have the anti-tank guns they had requested months earlier and been promised in March by General Georges. To aggravate the situation, Corap had been forced to send his divisions up to defensive positions on the Meuse on 10 May where they found themselves in unfamiliar Belgian territory, rough terrain and, on the 12th, confronting panzer units. When Corap advanced into Belgium he left his Category B divisions holding the line of the Meuse on the positions prepared in French territory during the winter. These unprepared units were given large frontages they couldn't possibly defend. And one of the Regular units, the 102nd Fortress Division, received more than twice the frontage of the already overextended B Divisions. The widely dispersed 9th Army also found its flank linked to the similarly weakened front of the 2nd Army near Sedan as it attempted to defend the Meuse. This overextended, ill-equipped army most certainly could hardly be expected to achieve the success of Marshal Foch's famed 9th Army of 1914.

During the month of November, General Alan Brooke, ob-

A Panzer III crosses a pontoon bridge during the offensive through the Low Countries.

serving General Corap's troops at a commemoration of the 1918 Armistice, noted, "Seldom have I seen anything more slovenly and badly turned out..." and that the men had a "...complete lack of pride in themselves or their units." Assuming that the whole French army was in equal state of disrepair, he expressed doubts as to their ability to withstand the test of war. For the army he observed that was, unfortunately, the truth. Gamelin's directive on 10 May was, "The orders are, for France and her Allies: Courage, energy, confidence." No one

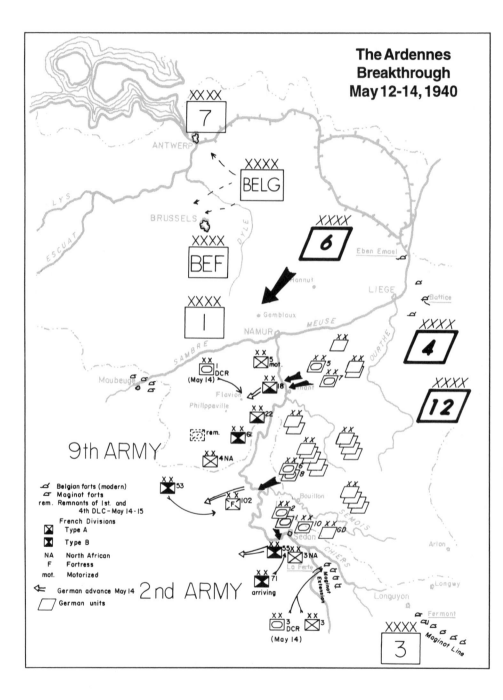

The Ardennes
Breakthrough
May 12-14, 1940

XXX
7

ANTWERP

XXXX
BELG

BRUSSELS

XXXX
BEF

XXXX
6

Eben Emael

Hannut

LIEGE

Battice

XXXX
I

Gembloux

MEUSE

NAMUR

SAMBRE

XXXX
4

OURTHE

XXXX
12

X X
DCR
(May 14)

X X
5 mot.

X X
5

X X
7

X X
18

Dinant

Moubeuge

Flavion

Philippaville

X X
22

X X
61

rem.

X X
4 NA

9th ARMY

Belgian forts (modern)
Maginot forts
rem. Remnants of 1st. and
4th DLC-May 14-15

French Divisions
Type A
Type B

NA   North African
F   Fortress
mot. Motorized

German advance May 14
German units

X X
53

X
F 102

Bouillon

X X
2

1 X X
10 X X
GD

Sedan

Arlon

X X
55 X X
A   3 NA

La Ferte

X X
71

2nd ARMY arriving

Maginot
Extension

Longwy

Longuyon

Fermont

X X
3 DCR
(May 14)

X X
3

XXXX
3

Maginot Line

expected the 9th Army to carry it out, but many men did their best to follow it and became the forgotten heroes of France!

On 12 May, the Allied air forces made a serious effort to stop the advancing columns in the Ardennes, but they had just as little success as in their attempts to knock out key bridges along the Albert Canal. This was also the date on which the *Luftwaffe* demonstrated air superiority. During the days that followed British and French air units suffered severe losses attempting to stem the German tide.

General Georges, on 12 May, dispatched the 1st North African Division with the 43rd Division to reinforce the 101st Fortress Division in the Maubeuge sector, neglecting to place additional first-rate units between Dinant and Sedan. The town of Sedan, on the wrong side of the river, quickly fell to the Germans that day. That evening Huntziger's 71st Division (Category B) took over part of the front from the 55th Division (Category B). The poorly equipped divisions changed fronts, and the disruption caused by this movement left the sector disorganized and vulnerable. The French hoped that the Germans would delay their river crossing operations for a few days until their artillery could catch up with their rapidly advancing units. They would have been dismayed to know that the advance through the Ardennes had progressed with such speed that Guderian, deciding not to wait for the arrival of the guns, had hurriedly relabeled some old orders from a training exercise, issuing them for his planned attack. Panzer cannons and aircraft like the Stuka dive bomber acting as flying artillery would give the necessary supporting fire. That evening German columns were streaming through the Ardennes with lights blazing. The panzer units of all three corps prepared to make the decisive breakthrough as soon as bridgeheads could be established.

On 13 May, the Germans denied the French the one element they needed the most: time. While the French slowly began to take action to support the front on the Meuse, the aggressive black beret tank commanders of the panzer divisions anxiously waited for their infantry to cross the Meuse so they could press on before the French got an opportunity to react.

To the north, the French 7th Army had withdrawn from the Netherlands, and at Antwerp its mechanized units and some B

Category troops drove the Germans back. The Belgian Army took up positions between the BEF and the French 1st Army, and all three threw back German infantry assaults the next day. Further south, the Cavalry Corps savagely reengaged the *3rd* and *4th Panzer Divisions*. French artillery once again punished the enemy and both sides took losses of upwards of 100 tanks. Both the French and Germans claimed victory, but the latter held the battlefield and again recouped some of their losses. All these French successes, however, lost their significance when the three panzer corps on the western edge of the Ardennes began their assault across the Meuse that day.

CHAPTER VI

Critical Days

The main assault crossings of the Meuse began on the morning of 13 May, preceded and accompanied by several hours of bombardment by the *Luftwaffe*. The French units resisted fiercely in some sectors and fell apart in others. By evening each panzer corps had established a bridgehead. Hoth's *XV Panzer Corps* crossed near Dinant at Houx, Reinhardt's *XLI Panzer Corps* at Monthermé, and Guderian's *XIX Panzer Corps* at Sedan. The French 22nd Division (Category A) of XI Corps occupying defensive positions in the rugged terrain on the Meuse above Givet showed signs of collapsing before a single German infantry division and was pushed back on 14 May.

According to some accounts of the battle, the Germans routed the inferior French reservists and advanced unchecked. In reality the Germans had to fight hard to gain most of their bridgeheads on 13 May, and in some instances almost failed. Many French troops refused to withdraw after the Germans made their crossings, and had they been better equipped, they might have repelled them. In one case French troops of X Corps near Sedan panicked when they heard a rumor that there were tanks in the area. Ironically, the tanks turned out to be French. Some French artillery units which had devastated the Germans earlier, exhausted their ammunition before they gave up and in many instances were overwhelmed by attacks from Stukas. General Georges ordered his three DCRs with additional divisions to prepare a counterattack. Not only did these reinforcements fail to arrive in time, but no one arranged to coordinate their attacks. Gamelin's strategic reserve, the 1st DCR under General Bruneau, moved into a position behind the northern flank of the 9th Army, after receiving orders canceling its original mission to Gembloux by General Georges; the 2nd DCR began to assemble behind the 9th Army; and the 3rd DCR arrived on the left flank of 2nd Army near Sedan. These three heavy armored divisions took up positions on three sides of what some news reports called the "Battle of the Bulge," as the Germans broke out of their bridgeheads on 15 May. Meanwhile, General Billotte, apparently blind to the situation, remained reluctant to send the reserves of his other two armies to help the 9th Army until the situation became hopeless.

First Bridgehead on the Meuse

On 14 May the Allies witnessed not only the surrender of the Dutch and the terror bombing of Rotterdam, but also the breakout from the German bridgeheads over the Meuse. Rommel's *7th Panzer Division*, held up by the French 18th Division near Dinant, finally crossed the Meuse with its tanks and penetrated the French line. The day before, Rommel had watched French gunners shooting up his infantry's rubber assault boats that were attempting to cross the Meuse. Despite French harassment, his motorcycle battalion finally got a foothold on the west bank while Rommel brought up his medium tanks to give fire support so his troops could enlarge the bridgehead. The general personally crossed the Meuse to take charge of the operation and his forces successfully repelled tanks of the 1st DLC which restored confidence to his troops shaken on 13 May. The French 18th Division (Category A) and, further north, the 5th Motorized Division seriously hampered the advance of Rommel and the remainder of Hoth's panzer corps.

As Rommel's position improved during 13 May, the French counterattacked on the next morning with the 5th Motorized Division and 4th DLC, but they failed to restore the situation for the French 9th Army. Even though Rommel managed to bring a number of tanks across the river by 14 May, he still

Dinant today. The future "Desert Fox," Erwin Rommel, pushed his **7th Panzer** *Division across the Meuse River here while under fire from French forces on the opposite bank.*

found his men hemmed in by the French. Early on 14 May Rommel received a report that one of his units was surrounded at Onhaye, about 3 miles (5 kilometers) west of Dinant. Rommel personally led the relief force of tanks only to find that the report had been incorrect, and that his troops, far from being surrounded, had taken the town instead. Many French soldiers had surrendered as his troops pushed forward, but the resis-

German troops make a river crossing while under shell fire.

tance of most can only be described as tenacious. The French continued to resist Rommel's advance and kept the troops of the *7th Panzer Division* bottled up for the remainder of the day. As a result, even Rommel became a casualty when he was slightly wounded. Nevertheless, the German general had succeeded in cracking the French river line. General Julien Martin, the commander of the XI Corps, with General Corap's permission, ordered his tired troops back from the Meuse before the line disintegrated. The French resolved to set up a "Stop Line" at Philippeville, a final position from which they wanted to contain the breakthrough.

Finally, the 9th Army's 4th North African Division, and the 1st DCR came to reinforce the 9th Army by moving towards Corap's stop line on 15 May, but it was already too late. Rommel's panzers pressed forward, breaking through the position, and caused thousands of French soldiers to retreat pell-

Tanks of the formidable Panzer arm of the German Army. A Panzer II and Czech made Panzer 38 advance side by side.

mell from the front. Corap ordered his units to fall back to the French border. Displeased with Corap's decisions, commander of the 1st Army Group, General Billotte, called in General Giraud, commander of the 7th Army, to replace him. However, the existing situation was mainly due to the fact that the higher echelons had failed to send reinforcements in a timely fashion; Corap just happened to be a convenient scapegoat.

If many of the withdrawing units were on the verge of disintegration, it was due to the fact that they were battle weary, and not because of lack of nerve. Other commands attempted to attack. The 1st DCRs tank units struggled forward, past columns of refugees, leaving their supporting elements and artillery behind. The division attempted to proceed

A trio of knocked out Renault FT tanks. The one on the right has been literally blown to pieces.

toward Philippeville and launch a counterattack against the advancing Germans on 15 May. But also left behind in the rear echelons during this poorly organized assault were fuel trucks. Predictably, the 1st DCR's armor were helplessly stranded when they ran out of gas and came under air attack while waiting for their fuel trucks. Finally, the French tanks were refueled, and the armored units proceeded to join the battle, although they went into action piecemeal. The 1st DCR's attack against Rommel's *7th Panzer Division* from the north near Flavion demonstrated the superiority of the French heavy tanks against German light tanks, Czech tanks and Panzer IIIs. Although Rommel called it a brief encounter, it might have developed into a more serious battle if the 1st DCR had been better prepared for the operation. General Bruneau's armored division actually succeeded in threatening the flank and rear echelon of Rommel's division only to have the assault fail. This was partly the result of the poor design of French DCRs which made them unsuitable for offensive action without sufficient infantry and service support, and partly because these heavy formations were only a few months old and their commanders still had many problems to work out. A key problem for most of the French armored units was lack of radio communications between units and individual tanks, making coordination extremely difficult.

The French claimed that the 1st DCR knocked out as many as 100 German tanks. Even if the French exaggerated, the Germans had a rough time dealing with the Char B tanks whose armor was impenetrable to most German weapons. Finally the French division withdrew with less than two dozen tanks, having left behind many disabled vehicles with shot out tracks or lacking fuel, and virtually ceased to exist as a fighting unit. General Bruneau reformed the remnants of the division the next day, and prepared to reenter the battle.

Meanwhile, the 4th North African Division arrived only to run into the chaos of withdrawing French units and advancing panzers, making it unable to set itself up properly before being shattered by the Germans. Rommel's victorious division continued plowing forward, its tanks firing on the move and overtaking remnants of several of the French units which had fought so well. The remainder of Hoth's panzer corps helped continue the breakout. The German *32nd Division* expanded the breakthrough, driving back the remnants of the French 22nd Division. Severely battered, the French forces opted to retreat behind their old frontier defenses.

While Rommel forged the first bridgehead on the Meuse on 13 May, troops of Reinhardt's panzer corps strove to establish their own crossing at Monthermé in the face of tenacious resistance, causing them a long delay to throw up a bridge and break out. For a while troops from the corps were literally trapped on a peninsula formed by a bend of the Meuse and dominated by French troops of the 102nd Fortress Division on higher ground. Rommel's advance and the growing threat to Sedan diverted the attention of the French from the crossing at Monthermé especially since the situation in that quadrant appeared well contained. The French felt that Reinhardt simply could not break through the well defended positions which kept them pinned down. On the morning of 15 May, Rein-

A key to German success in France was the ability to quickly cross and bridge rivers, often under enemy fire. Here German infantry pass over a pontoon bridge.

hardt's panzer corps, taking advantage of the diversions created by Rommel's successes in the vicinity of Dinant and Guderian's near Sedan, finally made its breakout at Monthermé. The determined troops of the 102nd Fortress Division had received virtually no reinforcements since 13 May. Despite the fierce resistance of the command, it was over-extended, out-manned, out-gunned, and soon overwhelmed by Reinhardt's men who made an additional crossing further down river. The German attack caused other commands to fall apart as well. The untested and ill prepared 61st (Category B) simply collapsed and reeled back. The 9th Army's XLI Corps

The Sedan citadel today. Sedan was the site of France's defeat to Prussia in 1870. Seventy years later, the Germans crossed the Meuse near the town to continue their invasion of France.

disintegrated, leaving a gaping hole on the front through which Reinhardt's panzers rushed unimpeded.

Sedan and Disaster

Reinhardt's *XLI Panzer Corps* succeeded mainly thanks to the larger breakthrough at Sedan by Guderian's *XIX Panzer Corps*. On the western side of the river there was General Huntziger's left flank held by weaker units since the French commander thought Guderian was moving against the flank of the Maginot Line. After the *1st* and *10th Panzer Divisions* reached the north bank of the Meuse on the night of 12 May, Guderian prepared them for the river crossing on the next morning.

The assault began late in the afternoon of 13 May with heavy

German troops occupy Sedan. The citadel can be seen in the rear.

air support. Although the *Luftwaffe* did not go totally unchallenged, it successfully brushed aside all opposition. Initially the crossing of the Meuse was somewhat of a challenge. From the heights of Marfee, French observers had a commanding view of the enemy and could identify tank concentrations. This allowed their artillery to again demonstrate its deadly effectiveness and forced enemy vehicles and troops to seek cover everywhere. Although the Germans found the fire devastating, it was actually a limited effort according to General C. Grandsard of X Corps who claimed the gunners were assigned a limited quota of shells for each mission because the higher command did not expect the big attack to take place on that day. Guderian asked German pilots to specifically deal with the French artillery so his troops could make the river crossing. Wave upon wave of DO-17 bombers, and then JU-87 Stuka dive bombers, and even fighter aircraft, concentrated on the French guns with an almost continuous air assault. Many of the French pieces were blown from their rather newly-established and not well-prepared positions, but most of the damage appeared to be on the morale of the gunners. After four hours of intense bombardment, the guns were subdued and the river crossing proceeded with little interference from French artillery.

All available German artillery and flak concentrated on helping the *1st Panzer Division* cross the Meuse, in the sector defended by the French 55th (Category B) Division. The German gunners, with the aid of the *Luftwaffe*, blasted most of the French blockhouses. Without assistance from the air there was little the 2nd Army could do to withstand the mighty assault. General Billotte directed the French air commander to give the 2nd Army assistance, but due to some confusion most of the French aircraft flew to other sectors including that of 9th Army to the north. With help not forthcoming from their own airforce, Huntziger's troops could also expect no assistance from the RAF since it had sustained heavy losses in previous attacks. Thus, the *1st Panzer Division*'s infantry regiment, reinforced by *Infantry Regiment Grossdeutschland*, successfully crossed north of Sedan encountering little resistance. Even Guderian took a trip across the Meuse to witness the buildup. The French troops were in disarray, although some desperately held out. Although some French artillery pieces continued to fire, panic spread when the corps artillery commander ordered a withdrawal. Without effective resistance, the Germans consolidated their positions, and a motorcycle battalion cleared the Ignes Peninsula allowing an expansion of the bridgehead.

Meanwhile, the *10th Panzer Division*, with less support, had some difficulty making its crossing at Wadelincourt, south of Sedan. Many of its problems were caused by French 75mm cannoniers of the 71st Division covering the 55th Division's front. Still, the 55th's front collapsed before the advance of the *1st Panzer Division*'s infantry. The French division's flanks continued to hold despite the setback though German infantry

A small victory for the Allies, a downed German Dornier 17 bomber. The **Luftwaffe** *suffered heavy aircraft losses in France.*

resumed its advance toward the Marfee Heights, relieving pressure on the *10th Panzer Division*'s infantry. By evening both Panzer divisions had firmly established bridgeheads across the Meuse while reconnaissance elements of the late arriving *2nd Panzer Division* had forced a crossing earlier at Doncherry.

General Grandsard of X Corps attempted to rush forward his two reserve infantry regiments with two battalions of FCM infantry support tanks to hold back the Germans, but they were caught in the debris of the retreating 55th Division. Even reinforcements caused difficulties for the French when friendly tanks arriving in Bulson caused a general alarm among the rear echelons who thought they were being attacked by panzers from behind. The 55th Division's commander, General Lafontaine, with some other officers, did all he could to keep the broken elements of his division in place, but the panic spread even to the neighboring 71st Division. Despite the stampede, enough French soldiers stayed in the line to contain the Ger-

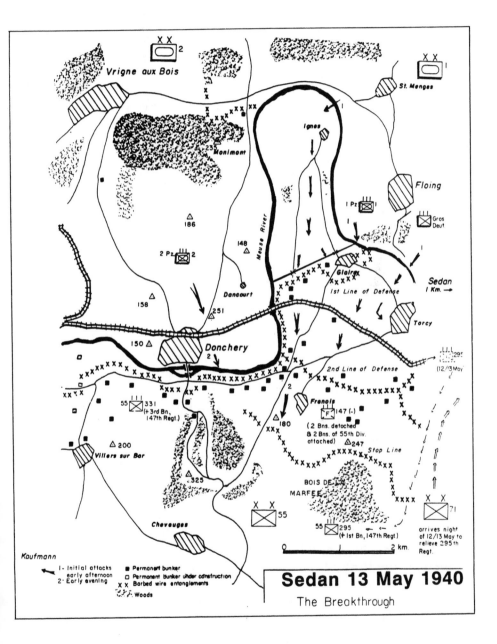

Sedan 13 May 1940

The Breakthrough

mans a little longer. On 13 May the results at Sedan were not yet decisive, but Guderian's panzer corps would hold the upper hand if it managed to get its tanks across the river to support the infantry.

The French 2nd Army tried to carry out to the letter the orders of General Gamelin of 13 May: "Fight to the finish, no retreat, if the enemy makes a breach, counterattack." When Grandsard's reserves finally approached the front during the early hours of 14 May, General Lafontaine ordered them to attack at dawn, but their commanders claimed they were not ready. After several hours, at about 0700, some of the units went forward. The French troops had nothing to fear from the *Luftwaffe* because Guderian had been informed on the previous day that he would have no air support. Unless he could get some tanks and guns across the river, his men would be unsupported. The delay in the French assault gave him the opportunity to have his panzers cross the river on bridges his engineers had laid the night before. One of the French infantry regiments and a tank battalion attacked, but after some initial success it was repelled by the German armor. As the *1st, 2nd* and *3rd Panzer Divisions* began their breakout, the 55th and 71st Divisions disintegrated and the battle of Sedan came to an end.

For the French, only one hope remained. In the early hours of 14 May General Doumenc came to report to General Georges at the La Ferté headquarters only to find the commander of the Northeast Front a broken man. When Georges informed Doumenc that the Germans had pushed in the front at Sedan, Doumenc consoled him and suggested that he send in the three heavy tank divisions to break the German bulge in its front. Georges accepted the plan and sent the appropriate orders, but there was too much confusion. As mentioned, the 1st DCR's attack from the north on 15 May against Hoth's panzer corps only ended in disaster. Meanwhile, the 2nd DCR moving up behind the front of the 9th Army attempted to assemble right in the path of the advancing panzers. The 3rd DCR was already near Sedan and had not launched the counterattack as instructed by Georges on 13 May. If the 3rd DCR had been able to attack immediately with the 3rd Motorized Division (they both formed the XXI Corps), it might have had enough time to throw back the Germans before they became stronger. The unit

French infantry on the advance. Their helmets distinguish them as motorcycle troops.

had only been created in March so that, despite the high quality of its troops, it lacked training.

Because Grandsard's reserves failed in their counterattack at Sedan, his X Corps collapsed. General Huntziger allowed the commander of XXI Corps with the 3rd DCR to cancel his own attack and set up instead a defensive line to contain the breakout. In the meantime the *XIX Panzer Corps* pushed 6 miles (10

French Armored Divisions and Smaller Armored Units in May 1940									
Note: Numbers approximated									
Armored Units	#	R-35/40	H35/39	FCM	D2	B1	S35	2C	FT
Total AFV		945	690	90	85	337	280	6	534
Tank Battalions	31	810	90	90				6	504
Independent Companies	12		30		40	57			30
Divisions:									
DCR (Heavy)	4	135	270		45	280	40+		
DLM (Light)	3		240				240		
DLC (Calvary)	5		60						

kilometers) forward from its bridgehead to cross the Bar River and Ardennes Canal to the west. The *1st* and *2nd Panzer Divisions*, with the help of the *Infantry Regiment Grossdeutschland* and the *10th Panzer Division*, secured the heights at Stonne to the south where they engaged the French XXI Corps.

As 14 May came to an end, the situation appeared bleak. General Georges' Northeast Front was on the verge of breaking wide open. At Sedan, Guderian's panzer corps had firmly established itself across the Meuse, while near Dinant, Hoth's panzer corps, led by Rommel's division, finally secured a position on the Meuse and began to advance. For the French High Command, the situation was as critical as on the Marne in 1914, but this time the Germans made no major miscalculations, and the French had no massive reserves to plug the gap. Early in the evening, Prime Minister Reynaud sent a message to Winston Churchill, who had become the British prime minister on May 10, informing him that the front was broken and the situation serious. Churchill, in turn, contacted Generals Gamelin and Georges who assured him that the French forces would close the gaps and hold the line.

The next day, 15 May, a special detachment formed under General Robert Touchon to fill the gap that had been torn open between the 2nd and 9th Armies. This formation became 6th Army and took over the XXIII Corps which was part of the reserve. Touchon was also allotted 14th Division, the 2nd DCR and 9th Army's XLI Corps (53rd and 61st [Category B] Divisions, 102nd Fortress Division, and 3rd Spahi Brigade). He was also promised three additional divisions after 15 May. His forces attempted to close the gap around the crumbling 9th Army. General Georges began withdrawing divisions and tank battalions from the 2nd Army Group to meet the crisis. Colonel Charles de Gaulle also began assembling the new 4th DCR east of Laon, but it was not fully equipped at the time.

The day of 15 May heralded a complete disaster for the Allies on the Western Front as the French desperately attempted to seal the collapsing front. Instead of launching counterattacks, newly arriving units were dispersed by local commanders to plug the gaps while others failed to do much of anything. General Giraud, who replaced Corap, attempted to retreat the shattered elements of the 9th Army. The terrible situation he

Tank Strength of French Armored Divisions			
Note: Numbers Approximated			
Armored Units	1st Division	2nd Division	3rd Division
DCR	90 H-35/39 70 Char B	90 H-35/39 70 Char B	90 H-35/39 70 Char B
DLM	80 H-35/39 80 S-35 100 additional tracked & wheeled AFV	80 H-35/39 80 S-35 100 additional tracked & wheeled AFVs	140 H-35/39 80 S-35 40 Wheeled AFVs
DLC	12 H-35/39 32 tracked & wheeled AFVs	12 H-35/39 32 tracked & wheeled AFVs	12 H-35/39 32 tracked & wheeled AFVs
Armored Units	4th Division	5th Division	
DCR	135 R-35/40 45 D-2 Char B	945	
DLM		810	
DLC	12 H-35/39 32 tracked & wheeled AFVs	12 H-35/39 32 tracked & wheeled AFVs	

Note: The above is based on data from French Infantry Tanks: Part II By Major James Bingham. (Profile Publications Ltd., 1973) and Blitzkrieg by Steven Zaloga (Arms and Armor Press) faced was somewhat alleviated by reinforcements. The 2nd DCR, receiving conflicting orders from Giraud and Touchon, became paralyzed.

Most Allied attention focused on Guderian's huge expanding bridgehead, while the XXI Corps and the 3rd DCR merely held their positions near Stonne, without launching a major counterattack. As all efforts were directed toward stopping Guderian, Reinhardt's breakout at Monthermé swept forward, tearing open the French front and driving deep through the French lines towards Montcornet. The 2nd DCR which lay along the German axis of advance was split and scattered, leaving Touchon to reorganize its remnants in an effort to form a stop line.

By the end of the day, the Allies were facing a disaster because the divisions of *Panzer Group Kleist*, moving in a westerly direction, were threatening to cut off most of the 1st Army Group up to the north. The French perceived the German drive as a direct threat to Paris and by the next day that city's population was in a state of alarm.

Early on 15 May, Reynaud telephoned Churchill to declare that the Allies were beaten. Late that night, Churchill received another message from the French premier stating again: "Last evening we lost the battle." The British prime minister flew to France the next day. At Vincennes, Churchill asked Gamelin about his strategic reserve only to have the French general sadly inform him that there was none.

Despondent or not, the French commanders did what they could to halt the German drive. Official communiques from the French High Command became shorter, sometimes barely including a couple of brief paragraphs. On the morning of 16 May, Communique No. 511 indicated that something was very wrong:

> The battle from the Namur region to the Sedan region has assumed the character of a war of movement with both sides participating with motorized elements and aviation.
>
> In the superior interest of conducting operations we cannot furnish at the present time precise information concerning the action in course.

Debacle: Panzer Country

As 16 May dawned, the extent of the disaster which had befallen the French on the Meuse became apparent. The Germans had broken out into the open rolling farmlands of France. Amazingly, both Rommel and Guderian, influenced by French and German propaganda, expected the defenses of the Maginot Line to hinder their breakouts. Rommel, who mistakenly thought he had broken through the Maginot Line, expressed his disappointment in the famous French fortifications, declaring them insignificant. Guderian, on the other hand, having expected the guns of the Maginot forts to impede his progress, was relieved to find that their range was not nearly as great as the propaganda had claimed. As they emerged from the Ardennes, the Germans found themselves in the open where the Allies would no longer be able to channel and delay their columns, and, most importantly, no more French artillery blocked their path. The plains of northern France were perfect for tank maneuvers. It might have been the ideal place for Gamelin's original plan for cutting off and isolating an armored breakthrough. If only the French had not scattered and squandered the resources of their DCRs and DLMs early in the campaign. If only the shattered divisions of the 9th Army had held on to their positions. If only the strategic reserve, including armor, had not already moved up to the front.

What cohesive units were still available were thrown into battle while the French High Command ordered Paris to prepare for its own defense. Panic began to set in and the flow of refugees away from the invaders increased. Desperately the French attempted to counterattack. The French 9th Motorized Division of the 7th Army was the only intact formation moving into the breach to face a renewed German thrust. General Billotte, commanding the French 1st Army Group, rushed the 1st DLM (from 7th Army) and 1st North African Division (released earlier to the 1st Army from the strategic reserve) to assist the 9th Motorized Division on his right flank. In an attempt to secure the flank of the 1st Army on the Oise River, the 1st North African Division was ordered to occupy Anor (near Hirson) on the border in the vicinity of the St. Michel Forest. It failed to reach its goal in time. The remnants of the

A snag in the blitzkrieg. An armored column is held up at a bridge when a Panzer IV slips off the road. The lead tank in the picture is a Czech made Panzer 38.

1st and 2nd DCRs with the 1st DLM were ordered to attack the German flank.

Meanwhile, the *XVI Panzer Corps* pressed on through the Gembloux Gap with its two panzer divisions, striking at the 1st Army's III Corps (2nd North African and 1st Motorized Division) and IV Corps (1st Moroccan and 15th Motorized Divisions). Both corps contained good divisions which might have made a difference if they could have been disengaged and sent to seal the breach created by the breakthrough on the Meuse. As it was, the 1st Moroccan Division took over 50 percent casualties, while the 15th Motorized Division repelled the *4th Panzer Division*. While 1st Army held off the *XVI Panzer Corps*, the remainder of the Allied forces on the Dyle Line received orders to withdraw that night in a four day staged retreat.

To the south, Rommel's division hit the 101st Fortress Division and the remaining elements of the 1st DCR defending the

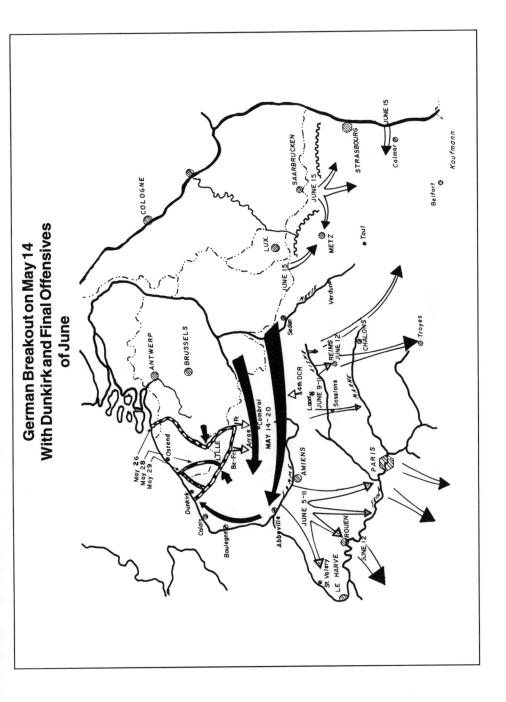

German Breakout on May 14
With Dunkirk and Final Offensives
of June

A German crew works an 80mm mortar.

Maubeuge area. The 1st DCR had little more than a dozen tanks left, but went into action about half way between Anor and Maubeuge, at a place called Solre-le-Cateau where it was hit by Rommel's panzer division on 16 May. Initially the two French divisions succeeded in checking the German advance but by evening their supporting artillery ran out of ammunition and the remnants of the 1st DCR moved back to Avesnes. On 17 May the panzers breached the front held by the fortress division and destroyed the last of 1st DCR's armor. What Rommel encountered was fairly typical. Some French troops caught up en route and confronted by the fast advancing German columns surrendered, while others fought on, even when the situation appeared hopeless. The tanks of the 1st DCR presented Rommel with a challenge, their armor being too thick to penetrate, but the troops, having suffered one defeat after another, had finally become demoralized. Rommel claimed that he captured over 10,000 troops and 100 tanks, but undoubtedly many of these men came from broken units already overwhelmed by a hopelessly confusing situation and many of the tanks were also without fuel. The French commanders frantically attempted to create some order out of the prevailing chaos, but were foiled by the Germans who did not allow them time to recoup.

Further down the front, on the afternoon of 16 May, the 2nd DCR advanced upon the headquarters of the *1st Panzer Division*, but when its tanks ran out of fuel, its unsupported attack petered out. Most of the 2nd DCR remained strung out over a large front, lying right in the path of the German advance.

Between May 13 and 16, the Germans began to clear their lines of communications and secure their left flank near Sedan. Several of the forts of Liege came under attack beginning on 13 May. On 16 May, as the first of the Liege forts fell, the Germans made their first real attempt to capture a fort of the Maginot Line. German air and ground units attacked the petit ouvrage of La Ferté on the Maginot Extension. The German *71st Infantry Division* bombarded La Ferté with supporting heavy artillery including 210mm cannons and Stukas. The French 6th Infantry Division received reinforcements in the form of heavy tanks.

On the night of 15 May General Kleist, commander of the panzer group, ordered the *XIX Panzer Corps* to halt its advance to allow the infantry to catch up. General Guderian convinced Kleist to allow him to continue his advance for another 24 hours only to receive another order to halt on the morning of 17 May. A fuming Guderian, sensing that a great victory was about to slip from his grasp because of Kleist's ignorance, met with his superior and requested to be relieved of his command.

A shattered Char B1.

While Kleist was quite willing to take one of Germany's ablest panzer leaders out of action, Von Rundstedt, commander of *Army Group A*, would not hear of it. Having been told that the order came from *OKH*, Guderian managed to wrangle from his superiors permission to continue a reconnaissance in force. This would allow no respite for the French, since Guderian's probing force was composed of nothing less than the combat elements of the *1st* and *2nd Panzer Divisions*.

The order to halt had come from Hitler, who like some of his generals in the field could not believe the incredible success of his forces. The Führer did not want to take any risks with his panzer units that might cause a reversal, so he directed them to stop their advances in order to consolidate the position. His decision would have allowed the French time to fill in the breach in their lines, but Guderian was determined to prevent this from happening.

On 17 May, the panzer advance continued almost unchecked until General de Gaulle's newly formed 4th DCR with about 150 tanks (two battalions of R-35 and one of Char B tanks) struck at the German spearhead, hit the rear echelons of the *1st Panzer Division* of Guderian's corps and penetrated over 20 miles (30 kilometers) to occupy Montcornet. The *10th Panzer Division* was brought in, and Stukas, unopposed by Allied air power, counterattacked, finally driving off the French tanks. Guderian considered this attack to be little more than a nuisance, even though it was one of the best efforts of the enemy's armored units.

In desperation, Gamelin ordered his soldiers to fight to the death, while Georges tried to plug the gaping breach in the front. The 3rd DCR, or what remained of it, continued its two-day-old struggle to secure the flank of the 2nd Army at Stonne, but it lacked the capability to breach the expanding German spearhead at its base. The 1st (twice destroyed) and 2nd DCRs, which had been severely mauled earlier, had no time to regroup as the *7th Panzer Division* rapidly advanced, until the nervous Führer called it off on 17 May. The French 25th Motorized Division, recently withdrawn from Antwerp, raced to head off the *7th Panzer Division*.

The Germans continued their westward advance towards the Channel. Guderian's *2nd Panzer Division* took St. Quentin in the morning and his *1st Panzer Division* crossed the Somme River early in the afternoon. Reinhardt's panzer corps brushed aside the remnants of the 2nd DCR while further north Rommel's *7th Panzer Division* took Cambrai. Meanwhile, the remainder of Hoth's panzer corps found itself engaging the 1st DLM which had recently returned from Belgium with its

German troops clearing a bridge over the Somme Canal.

SOMUA tanks on railroad flat cars. A sharp battle ensued on 17 May in the Mormal Forest. On 18 May there was a short respite after the German armor cleared the forest, but on 19 May, elements of the 1st DLM reengaged them. The encounter ended before the next morning.

Northern Belgium and the Retreat: Mid-May

The forces in Belgium remained blissfully unaware of the disaster that had taken place to the south. Since arriving on 10 May and taking up positions during the night of 10/11 May on the Dyle Line, the British troops felt confident. The BEF deployed in echelons, with the 1st and 2nd Divisions of I Corps in line, and the 48th Division behind in support, while the II Corps had 3rd Division on line and 4th Division behind it. The

4th and 48th Divisions arrived on 13 May. The 1st Army Tank Brigade took up position behind the 2nd Division of I Corps. The Belgian Army, much of it arriving on 13 May after disengaging from the Albert Canal Line, held the left flank of the BEF to the north of Louvain and the French 1st Army the southern flank, south of Wavre. The 5th and 50th Divisions were in reserve while the 42th and 44th Divisions remained in the rear on the Escaut Line. Even if British commanders did not find the Belgian divisions very effective in combat, they managed to work with them. The men of the Belgian Army and BEF saw the Germans reach the Dyle Line on 14 May. The next day they repulsed attacks by the German *IV* and *XI Corps*. Only at Wavre did the British pull back because the French had moved back on their left to the Lasne, a tributary of the Dyle.

The events of 15 May illustrate the desperate situation the Allied forces in Belgium were in. Rommel's panzer division had already broken out of the bridgehead and caught and destroyed most of the armor of the 1st DCR and the piecemeal attacks of French armored divisions and independent tank battalions were totally ineffectual. The 9th Army had been routed that morning and only shattered elements of the 9th Army remained while the 61st (Category B) and 102nd Fortress Divisions began to break up. If the Allied armies did not pull out of Belgium quickly, they would soon have to surrender.

On 16 May, the order for a withdrawal went out. Both British and Belgian troops found the order to retreat equally discouraging. For the Belgians and their king it meant abandoning their capital and most of their country at a time when the Allies appeared to be holding the Germans in check in northern Belgium. The soldiers had little news of the events of the disastrous campaign to the south except for bulletins and official communiques which reported little beyond the then supposed successes of the Allies. Even the men of the French 1st Army, who were successfully holding off the *XVI Panzer Corps*, could not understand why they must withdraw. Those in the higher echelons were also ill informed. They could hardly comprehend the serious situation that had developed in the Ardennes and that a dangerous gap had been opened in the Allied lines and was widening.

On the same day the withdrawal order went out, the Germans began an assault on General Montgomery's 3rd Division front at Louvain. Again, the British held on. That evening they began an orderly withdrawal, for which they had been prepared by Montgomery during the Phony War. General Bock, commander of *Army Group A,* planned a major assault on the Allied front on the Dyle between Wavre and Louvain for 17 May, but the night of 16/17 May the British and Belgian troops had already withdrawn to the Senne Line running from Charleroi to Brussels and on to the Willebroeck Canal.

On 17 May the British prepared a mixed force called Macforce, after its leader General MacFarlane, consisting of infantry from the 42nd Division and support elements as well as the 1st Army Tank Brigade which would arrive later to protect the right flank of the BEF in the event the 1st French Army caved-in. In addition, the British set up a garrison consisting of the 1st Welsh Guards and assorted units, including some light armor, to defend their General Headquarters at Arras. General Gort relieved the 12th, 23rd and 46th Territorial Divisions from their work duties on the lines of communications and sent them to occupy defensive positions. The 12th and 23rd Divisions took up positions on the Canal du Nord between the Scarpe River and Peronne, occupying positions behind the 9th Army and between the 1st and 7th Armies. On the night of 17/18 May the British withdrew to the Dendre Line (Maubeuge to Mons to Ath and the Dendre River to Termonde), but a gap formed between them and the Belgian army through which the Germans had penetrated. During the withdrawal, the 4th Division found itself involved in heavy fighting. The roads, crowded with Belgian refugees fleeing after the Germans had reached the Dyle Line, did not make the retrograde movements any easier. On the night of 18/19 May the British and Belgians fell back on the Escaut Line.

Desperation

During the three critical days of May and on 16 May the French had hoped their British ally would send more troops, and especially aircraft. Even though the British 1st Armored Division was already en route, and some RAF squadrons were

French formations of tanks such as this Char B1 were no match for the German Panzer divisions.

released, only a coordinated effort on the part of the French could save the day. The French had to find a way to stop the armored thrust towards the Channel and reestablish the front before the BEF and the 1st Army Group became hopelessly trapped. General Gamelin began the preparations, but was faced with a dearth of resources since he was unable to organize an effective striking force within a short time. The Germans, on the other hand, pressed on their advantage denying the French an opportunity to work out their problems. They continued widening their breach and securing their rear areas in order to open additional supply lines.

The Germans, in an attempt to widen their left flank, continued their attack on the Maginot fort of La Ferté, subjecting it to heavy bombardment. The small fort received support from three nearby infantry divisions and a neighboring gros ouvrage of the Maginot Extension. The fort's garrison, having no weapons larger than 25mm guns, 47mm AT guns and 81mm mortars, attempted to ward off a major assault. Soon the fort's only retractable turret, equipped with 25mm guns, was disabled and the defense fell to fixed positions of cloches and casemates. On 18 May German combat engineers assaulted each of the two blocks and soon found that all resistance had ended. Later the garrison was discovered in the gallery below, asphyxiated from the diesel fumes of its own usine (power station).

On the main front, there was a glimmer of hope. Georges, despite his pessimism, tried to organize a counterattack and positive results came from the advance of the 1st DLM and 1st North African Division in the Mormal Forest where the *5th Panzer Division* was engaged. The DLM's SOMUAs discovered a number of abandoned Char B tanks, but were unable to establish contact with headquarters to recover these valuable vehicles. Throughout the rest of the campaign, the Germans continued to find a good number of abandoned French tanks which were unserviceable or simply had run out of fuel.

Prime Minister Paul Reynaud was meanwhile forced to make changes in his command. He finally decided to replace Gamelin with General Maxime Weygand who returned from Syria on 18 May, as Gamelin was trying to seal the German penetration. Meanwhile the Prime Minister was also faced with reorganization of his cabinet. He called on the old war hero Marshal Philippe Pétain to serve in his government and hopefully restore confidence. Nothing, however, could avert disaster. The Belgian king, ready to give up, withdrew his army to the last corner of his kingdom. British concern regarding the fate of the BEF and its survival intensified. By 19 May, the Germans were already establishing bridgeheads over the Somme River which was rapidly becoming untenable as a defense line for the French. The problem facing the French High Command was how to defend the ever-expanding front when already up to one third of its forces, including allies, were destroyed or trapped in the North.

Gamelin hoped to take advantage of the vulnerability of the

French Air Groups		
May 1940		
Air Divisions	**Quantity**	**Breakdown**
Fighter Groups	28	15 of MS 406 8 of Bloch 151/2 4 of Curtiss 75 1 of Dewoitine 520
Bomber Squadrons	33	7 (Leo 45, Breguet 693, and Martin 167) and 20 converting including Amiot 354
Recon Groups	15	Potez 63.11
Observation Groups	48	Potez 63.11

German spearhead and send his troops against its shoulders which would disrupt the lines of communication behind the panzer units. He ordered the 2nd Army to launch an offensive action in the vicinity of Sedan, and commanded the units of the main body of the 1st Army Group to attack further southwards towards Cambrai. Before the preparations for these actions could be effected, Gamelin was replaced by Weygand on 20 May who decided to make his own evaluation of the fluid situation before going on the offensive. The French, now as ready as they could be, lost more time awaiting the decision of the new commander.

The day of 19 May only brought a few encouraging moments for the Allies as the overall situation of the 1st Army Group deteriorated. De Gaulle's 4th DCR, now comprising about 150 tanks, struck again at the Germans, and this time hit Guderian's left rear in the vicinity of Laon. Mines, anti-tank guns and Panzer IVs finally brought de Gaulle's armor to a halt at Crécy (not the town where the French were defeated during the Hundred Years War). As on 17 May, the French division was hard hit again by the *Luftwaffe*. In a tragic error, the Armée de l'Air assigned to protect them didn't show up until after the

Stukas had turned back the French tanks because of a change in the scheduling. Though Guderian later claimed the action had given him some uncomfortable hours, the beaten attack was not hardly enough to stem the almost irresistible tide. The whole incident did demonstrate though just how effective French armored units might have been if only they had had a more adequate divisional organization and better coordination between units. Afterwards, the French Cavalry Corps attempted to reorganize its DLMs.

Despite the Allies' best efforts, the Germans breached the line of the Escaut River adding to the difficulties of the encircled 1st Army Group. To make matters worse, the French abandoned the remaining three ouvrages of the Maginot Extension, fearing that these forts might suffer the same fate as La Ferté since they had not been designed to be defended in the same way as the Maginot Line Proper. As a result, the Germans firmly secured their flank at Sedan. To add to the woes of the French, both General Giraud, commanding the 9th Army, and General Bruneau, who had fought with his 1st DCR to the end, fell into German hands.

In a renewed offensive on 20 May, Guderian's corps, in conjunction with Reinhardt's and Hoth's, overran the British 12th and 23rd Territorial Divisions holding the line of the Canal du Nord. General Gort had requested and received these two poorly trained divisions late in April to use mainly as a labor force. General Ironside had directed him to make sure they received additional training, but he failed to do so. The German breakthrough forced Gort to move them into the line in order to block the German drive to the sea, a hapless move since neither unit was assigned the three artillery regiments or the anti-tank regiment that were the normal components of a British infantry division. Their infantry battalions were also poorly armed. Each had three rather ineffective Boys anti-tank rifles, with five rounds of ammunition each and even then few of the men were experienced to operate them. For the moment, these divisions represented the only forces available to bar the German thrust. The *2nd Panzer Division* quickly cut through the British line and soon reached the coast at Abbeville, sealing the trap for the 1st Army Group and the BEF. Meanwhile, the French command ordered the British 5th and 50th Divisions

French General Henri Giraud in the hands of the Germans. Giraud, commander of the 7th Army, was captured as he rushed to take command of the crumbling 9th Army. After his country surrendered he escaped to join the Free French.

with the 1st Army Tank Brigade to prepare for Gamelin's earlier planned attack together with the remaining armor of the French Cavalry Corps. Since the British were not able to load their tanks onto trains, they had to drive them most of the way out of Belgium, which gave rise to numerous maintenance problems.

On 21 May Weygand finally decided to launch assaults from both sides of the German spearhead in hopes of cutting it off and relieving the encircled units of the 1st Army Group. In other words, he simply followed Gamelin's strategy, after having delayed its implementation. At a conference held at Ypres, Weygand ordered Billotte to launch an attack towards the south, in the vicinity of Bapaume, with the forces he had available. A similar operation would be initiated with units on the Somme. Billotte's limited resources included the remnant of his DLMs. His last remaining DCR had been eliminated as a fighting unit. General Besson, commanding the French 3rd Army Group on the Somme, was still building up his new front with the 6th and 7th Armies. He had the 3rd DCR, which had been rebuilt from training units and depots, and the 2nd DCR with less than half of its original equipment, but neither of these units was ready for an offensive move. Weygand's new orders to attack pushed the date back to 26 May, causing a delay which could have been avoided by going ahead with Gamelin's original plans. No attacks took place in the end, partly because French morale had been shattered by 25 May.

During the day of 21 May, as Guderian's *XIX Panzer Corps*, after securing a bridgehead on the Somme, advanced on Boulogne and Calais, the British attempted to reinforce the motley French garrisons of those ports. The 20th Guards Brigade, consisting only of the 2nd Battalion Irish Guards, the 2nd Battalion Welsh Guards and an anti-tank battery arrived at Boulogne. It soon faced the *2nd Panzer Division*. Another two battalions from the 30th Infantry Brigade, with the 3rd Battalion of the Royal Tank Regiment from the 1st Armored Division, a former motorcycle battalion and an anti-tank battery, completed the British force defending Calais. According to General Ironside, these were the last Regular Army troops left in England. Initially, Guderian sent the *1st Panzer Division* against this force.

As Guderian's panzers began to advance on the left wing of the German spearhead, the British began an offensive against Hoth's panzer corps on the spearhead's right flank. The weak British 1st Army Tank Brigade, with its 58 Mark I tanks armed only with machine-guns, and 16 of the slow but more formidable Mark II Matilda infantry tanks armed with 40mm guns, launched the only Allied attack of 21 May. The 3rd DLM, with its 60 SOMUA tanks, joined the British raid, advancing on their right flank as they moved south of Arras. Of the two British divisions assigned to this offensive, only two infantry battalions arrived. The Allied attack spread panic among the still green troops of the *SS Totenkopf Division*, convincing Rommel that his *7th Panzer Division* was under attack by upwards of five divisions. The shaken general took personal control of the situation, throwing back the Allies at the battle of Arras. Rommel recounted that when his *6th Rifle Regiment* failed to stop

Even more menacing when wearing gas masks, these German motorcycle troops speed down a dusty road in France.

the British tanks with its anti-tank guns and began to take heavy losses, his divisional artillery intervened, bringing the attack to a stop and destroying 28 tanks. His 88mm anti-aircraft guns eliminated another seven light tanks and one heavy tank. Finally Rommel's *25th Panzer Regiment* joined in taking the British in the flank and rear. Seven more Matildas were knocked out for a corresponding loss of three Panzer IVs, six Panzer IIIs and a number of light tanks in the resulting tank battle. This action caused the Germans much greater concern than the 19 May attack of de Gaulle's armored division, even though the latter could have inflicted more serious damage if it had succeeded in cutting off German supply lines.

On the evening of 21 May, after completing his conference at Ypres, Weygand found it impossible to return to his headquarters by air and had to take his leave from the isolated army group on a destroyer. Meanwhile, an automobile accident took Billotte's life. This created further problems because his replacement, General Georges Blanchard, the commander of the 1st Army, lacked the authority and personality to direct the British and Belgian forces. Blanchard was unable to marshal the units needed for the planned offensive and his army group no longer had the needed mechanized units to stage an offensive, as many units had wasted away in piecemeal actions. The best the French could hope to achieve at this point was to maintain a defensive position. Since this would only be a temporary solution, the remnants of 1st Army Group were doomed.

Each day the situation grew worse. On 22 May, the French 1st Army's V Corps began its own offensive. Instead of the required divisions, the V Corps mustered a single regiment with some armor support for the assault. The offensive thus degenerated into a raid in the direction of Cambrai. It achieved some success, reaching the outskirts of Cambrai only to be driven back by a superior German force. While it was again too little too late, the effort demonstrated that the French had the men and equipment for mechanized warfare, but lacked the proper leadership in the higher echelons.

The French 1st Army struggled to maintain contact with the BEF and the remnants of 1st Army Group. In the vicinity of Maubeuge, several old forts, which had been converted into Maginot-type ouvrages of the smaller type, resisted German assaults, but they all fell. Meanwhile in Belgium, the fall of forts Battice and Neufchâteau, and the old forts around Liege, opened the major access routes in the German rear area. At the same time the defenses of Namur were breached, and its forts began surrendering, removing the last major obstacles behind the lines. German armor had shown its ability to penetrate enemy lines while bypassing strong points and holding the enemy at bay until their own line of communications could be cleared. As a result, the German spearhead received more reinforcements and became less vulnerable on 23 May. Such expedients as flying small aircraft to the front with fuel for the

After making a run across France, a soldier in a Sd. Kfx armored car pauses near Abbeville to look across the English Channel. The German drive through northern France left thousands of French and British troops cut off at Dunkirk.

tanks were no longer necessary since the logistical elements were able to catch up with the panzer divisions.

With 23 May came the loss of Boulogne after the Germans broke through the old town wall with an 88mm anti-aircraft

A modern monstrosity: a British Cruiser Mark 1a CS (A-9) with a thrown track.

gun, even though the fighting continued until 25 May. After the position of Boulogne could no longer be held, Churchill ordered an evacuation of both British and French troops from the town. Eight destroyers began the rescue during the night of 23 May, successfully evacuating 5,000 men from Boulogne by the afternoon of the next day. By the evening of 23/24 May the BEF's position at Arras became tenuous, and it pulled out the 5th and 50th Divisions, against the wishes of the French. The French even offered to put a British officer in command of the 1st Army Group in place of Blanchard, but the British believed it was a ploy to throw the blame for the defeat upon them. On 24 May Besson immediately used the British withdrawal as an excuse to cancel the 3rd Army Group's offensive north of the Somme, while the situation in the pocket became critical. On 24 May the *10th Panzer Division* cut off Calais, and the *1st Panzer Division* reached the Aa Canal establishing a bridgehead, thus threatening the right flank of the Allied pocket.

Winston Churchill sent a letter to General H.L. Ismay, his representative to the Chiefs of Staff Committee, asking why a regiment with 21 light and 27 cruiser tanks, was "boxed up" in Calais by the nearby German field guns. He expressed concern as to why General Gort could not spare at least a brigade to help clear the rear and relieve Calais. He noted that British tanks pulled back in the face of German field guns, whereas the crews of British field guns were loath to take on German tanks. He believed that Calais must be held till the end.

The Germans succeeded in isolating and attacking the port of Calais. Only the small port of Dunkirk remained open to the Allies, and the German advance on it ceased. On 24 May, the Führer ordered the panzer assault to a halt, supposedly at the urging of Göring, who wanted the honor of destroying the pocket with his *Luftwaffe*, and Rundstedt and others who believed that the marshy terrain in the area would hinder a renewed tank thrust. Although Guderian wanted to continue with the final drive against the town, he again had to comply with orders he disagreed with. As the panzer divisions used this time to reorganize, the Allies took advantage of the respite to consolidate their crumbling perimeter and secure their last port at Dunkirk.

On the other side of the pocket, German infantry divisions put the Belgian Army under heavy assault on 25 May. Leopold III desired to hold on to the Ghent Bridgehead, since to abandon it would leave him occupying only a tiny corner of his kingdom. The effort proved too much for his overmatched army. Defeat appeared inevitable as the Belgian line gave way with their forces facing a collapse in strength and morale.

The next day, Hitler canceled the order to halt, and General Gort felt obliged to withdraw part of the BEF which left the French 1st Army in a precarious position around Lille. This led Weygand to try to vindicate his own failure to attack by claiming that the British ruined his plans. At this time, the Germans demanded that Brigadier General C.N. Nicholson, the British commander in Calais, surrender, to which he replied: "The answer is no, as it is the British Army's duty to fight as well as it is the German's." On the night of 26 May, Nicholson received instructions from his superiors to hold Calais as long as possible, a decision Churchill wrote made him feel ill.

Every hour you continue to exist is of the greatest help to the B.E.F. Government has therefore decided you must continue to fight.

Have greatest possible admiration for your splendid stand. Evacuation will not (repeat *not*) take place....

The brigadier carried out his orders to the letter, so that the Germans had to fight their way into the city against stiff resistance. Guderian claimed to have taken 20,000 prisoners of which over 3,000 were British. The surrender came on 27 May, although according to Guderian it was 26 May which was before Churchill's message even arrived. General Ironside believed that the evacuation from Durkirk succeeded only because of the heroism of the men at Calais, and he stated that the "historic name of Calais should be written once more on British hearts."

As the fighting raged north of the Somme, the British and the French did not stand idle south of the river. General A.B. Beauman, commander of the British troops in the rear, mostly the Line of Communications troops, organized various rear echelon elements into a defense force. The survivors of the 12th Division's 35th Brigade, which attempted to stop the German advance to the coast, made it back to Rouen where they reorganized. They represented slightly less than half of the brigade's 2,400 men. Various other units formed a defensive force. These troops also included elements from numerous garrison units which had protected supply dumps and bases in the rear for months, and, by and large, had little training.

More substantial support came from Great Britain when the first elements of the British 1st Armored Division arrived in mid-May. The division's Support Group, consisting of artillery and infantry, came first, followed by the 3rd Armored Brigade, which arrived at Cherbourg on 23 May, and moved forward to join its other formations. By that time, the Germans had established a major bridgehead on the Somme at Abbeville and captured bridges near Amiens. General Roger Evans, commander of the 1st Armored Division, launched an attack with his 2nd Armored Brigade against German bridgeheads on the Somme, west of Amiens on the morning of 24 May (the 3rd Armored Brigade was en route). Even though the Germans heavily defended the bridges in the area, the Support Group's infantry managed to capture one and advanced to St. Sauveur. Unfortunately, the armored brigade could not get any tanks across the damaged bridge, and eventually the unsupported

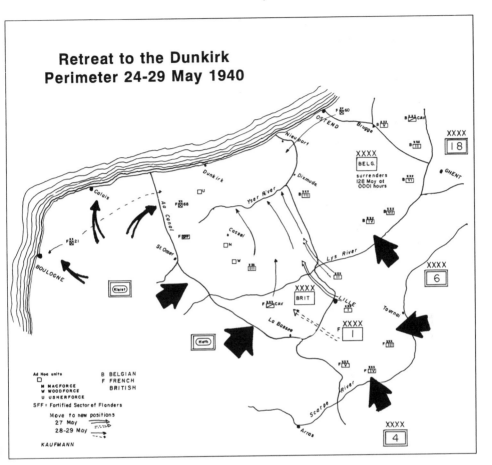

**Retreat to the Dunkirk
Perimeter 24-29 May 1940**

infantry had to retreat back across the river. The Germans had firmly established themselves in the area and the Allies just did not have the ability to dislodge them.

As the situation seriously deteriorated, the French tried to fill in the Somme Line. The British organized a divisional size force called the Beauman Division under General Henry Karlslake after 25 May. The general scrapped together all available resources in the rear echelon from garrison battalions to new Matilda II tanks sent as replacements for the 1st Army Tank Brigade which was already trapped in the pocket. He even found guns sent back for reconditioning as well as others abandoned on airfields for his artillery. The Beauman Division was to guard the valuable stores south of the Somme, while the

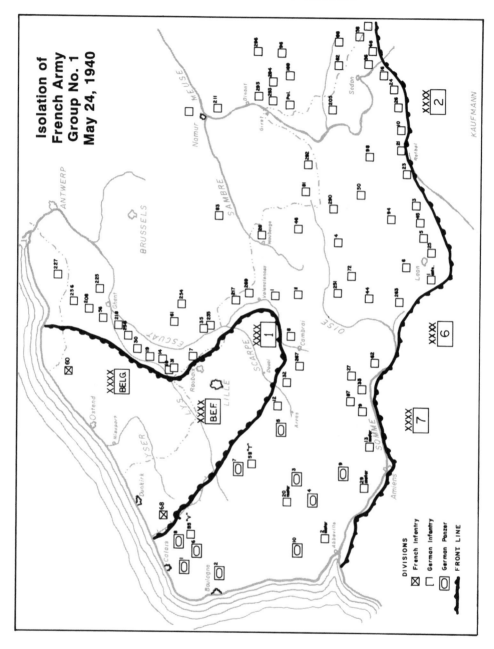

Isolation of
French Army
Group No. 1
May 24, 1940

British Spitfires helped ward off the **Luftwaffe** *in the skies over Dunkirk to successfully cover the evacuation there.*

51st Highland Division withdrew from the Maginot Line to take up positions on the new front.

On 26-27 May Guderian's panzers pushed forward towards Dunkirk, making some progress, while Rommel's *7th Panzer Division* of Hoth's corps pushed north from Arras to cross the La Bassée Canal. Although the British did not heavily defend the canal, their troops stationed there put up a stubborn defense causing Rommel some problems. In addition, the numerous sunken barges in the river seriously hindered the laying of

British Tommies withdraw from Dunkirk in one of the most dramatic moments of World War II.

a bridge across the canal. Despite their spirited resistance, the British had also lost many of their heavy weapons and could not hold out much longer, but the panzers were slowed on all fronts. By 29 May both Hoth's and Guderian's panzer corps received instructions to pull back in preparation for the final campaign on the Somme-Aisne Line.

The Belgian Army, on the verge of collapse, warned the Allies on 27 May that it would surrender the next day. The king dispatched a French division to the Allied lines and withdrew his own troops before he surrendered on 28 May. General Montgomery, moving his 3rd Division quickly to fill in the gap left by the surrender of the Belgian Army, was instrumental in securing the Allied left wing of the Dunkirk perimeter.

The capitulation also left the French 1st Army in an untenable situation because Gort had to pull back the 5th and 50th Divisions to help fill the new gap in the lines. In the desperate situation, another important French general, René Prioux of the Cavalry Corps, was captured by the Germans. Despite bad luck and hardship, the surrounded units of the 1st Army fought

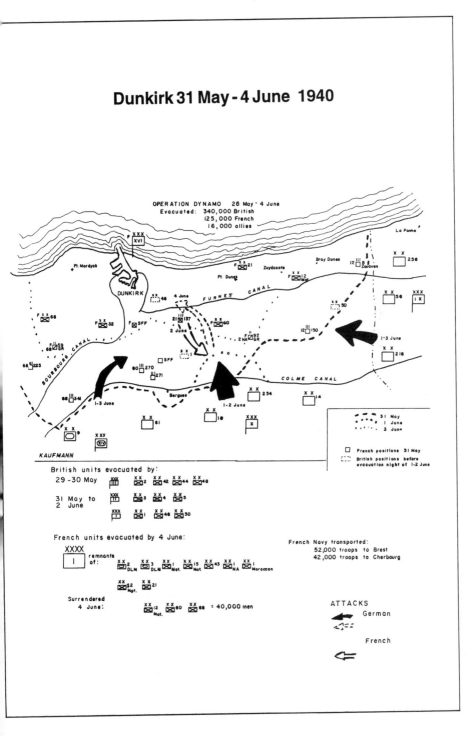

Dunkirk 31 May - 4 June 1940

OPERATION DYNAMO   26 May - 4 June
Evacuated: 340,000 British
125,000 French
16,000 allies

hard until the very end under the leadership of General Molinié. Its resistance took some pressure off the troops at Dunkirk. On 1 June, with no other alternative, they surrendered at Lille, although in the tradition of another age, the Germans gave them the honors of war. The 1st Army's III Corps, instead of remaining in the trap, chose to break out of the pocket and cut its way through to the Dunkirk perimeter. After the Belgian surrender the Allied enclave was shrunk to half its size.

On 26 May, the British put into effect Operation Dynamo, which involved the evacuation of the BEF using the British Royal Navy and many small privately owned vessels. Since Calais had fallen, only the small port of Dunkirk remained available for the operation. Forty British destroyers, later augmented by fifteen French warships and hundreds of smaller vessels (a total of about eight hundred and sixty vessels), evacuated over sixty thousand men in three days. Because of bad weather the *Luftwaffe* was unable to launch an aerial assault until the end of May and on 1 June devoted its full attention to the rescue ships and forced the Allies to limit the evacuation to the hours of darkness. But now German air supremacy was effectively challenged over the battlefield by the RAF with the new British Spitfires proving decisive in the defense of Dunkirk.

The evacuation continued until 4 June. Although thousands of troops streamed to the beaches, the retreat was basically conducted in an orderly manner. The British ships managed to pluck troops not only from the port of Dunkirk, which was under heavy air assault, but also right from the beaches. Between 27-29 May about 72,000 men withdrew by sea. During the next 3 days the little fleet transported huge numbers of troops ranging from 53,000 to 68,000 daily and then about 26,000 a day for the last three days. The British III Corps with four divisions (three Territorial) went out on 29-30 May. The British II Corps (three Regular divisions) departed on 31 May and 1 June. Most of the three divisions (two Territorial) of the I Corps were taken off by 3 June. The organizers had not dared hope to save so many men, but before the operation ended on 4 June, over 330,000 men, one third of them French (mostly rear echelon personnel), were rescued. Losses in ships was heavy, over 240 in all although most of these were small craft. Finally,

Dunkirk Statistics

Ships employed by the Allies during the evacuation:

Ship Type	Sunk*	Damaged	Total Employed
A.A. Cruiser	-	1	1
Destroyers	9	19	56
Sloops	-	1	6
Corvettes	-	-	11
Minesweepers	5	7	38
Torpedo Boats	-	-	15
Naval Transports	-	-	3
Armed Merchant Ships	1	2	3
Hospital Ships	1	5	8
Cargo Ships	3	-	13
Ferry Boats	9	8	45
Tug Boats	6	-	40
Trawlers	23	2	230
Dutch Skoots	1	-	40
Yachts	1	-	27
Barges	4	-	48

Note: Several hundred smaller craft were also used.
* Sunk or Damaged by S boats, aircraft or artillery. Destroyers, ferries, mine sweepers, trawlers, and sloops took 75% of the men off the beach.

on 4 June the Germans took Dunkirk and captured 40,000 troops who remained behind, most of them French. The Allies had saved the majority of their men, but lost most of their equipment. The beach area and environs of Dunkirk were cluttered with abandoned vehicles and weapons. The so called "Miracle of Dunkirk" mainly came about thanks to Hitler's whim which prevented his armies from destroying the pocket while they had the chance. (This was the same man who had berated his generals for their lack of aggressiveness.) While the operation was the greatest Allied success in the fight in France and gave the British some measure of cheer, as Churchill somberly noted in a speech to the House of Commons on 4 June, "Wars are not won by evacuations."

While the fighting raged around Dunkirk, the French attempted to break the German hold on the Somme crossings. The British 1st Armored Division came under the command of General Robert Altmayer's French 10th Army as the 2nd and 5th DLCs arrived on 26 May to strengthen the front. The French, after ordering the British 1st Armored Division to lead an attack against the German bridgehead at Abbeville (which extended to St. Valéry-sur-Somme at the mouth of the river), sent their own two armored formations in behind them. The attack began on 27 May and ran into heavy opposition. In a disaster for the Allies, the British lost 110 tanks out of 257 (over half of these were knocked out by the enemy, but the rest simply broke down) and the armored element of the division's 2nd Armored Brigade was largely eliminated in this action. The French continued their own attacks against the bridgehead on 28 May, but, even with the help of 4th DCR, were unable to break the German's hold. On 29 May the French requested the British 51st Division join in the operation, but received only a few of its battalions. More forces were committed when the 31st Alpine Division and the 2nd DCR joined the fray. The battle raged on from 31 May to 4 June, but in the end, the Germans managed to break out. The French 40th Division arrived as the French 10th Army found itself with no choice but to pull back on 5 June as the new German offensive in the West began. As the French vainly tried to break the German hold on the Lower Somme and the battle at Dunkirk drew to a close, the German panzer divisions moved back from the coast to prepare a new offensive across the Somme and Aisne Rivers. With Case Yellow completed, the Germans launched the final phase, Case Red, which became the battle for France.

CHAPTER VII

Battle for France

The destruction of the French 1st Army Group left the Germans in complete control of the Low Countries and a small part of northern France north of the Somme and Aisne Rivers. The *Wehrmacht* had successfully completed Case Yellow which had only called for a limited victory securing the position of the German forces occupying northern France. Next came Case Red, which called for the destruction of the remaining Allied forces in France and the occupation of the whole country. The final operational plan was drawn up during the last 10 days of May, and soon put into action. In preparing the plan the Führer apparently believed that even after the loss of northern France, the French would resist to the bitter end. He therefore aimed to isolate the French behind the Maginot Line so that his forces could cripple their industrial production. His idea did not cause the *OKH* any major problem since General von Brauchitsch and Chief of Staff Halder concluded the French would hold on to the Maginot Line, since it gave them a sense of security and its loss would bring about a collapse in morale. So the plan was to concentrate the panzer forces on the Aisne River, with the aim of driving towards Reims and Verdun, cutting off the French Army from the Maginot Line and build up along the Somme to drive a wedge between the French and the coast. After *Army Group A* and *Army Group B* developed the invasion of France's interior as called for in Plan Red, *Army Group C* would attack the Maginot Line and the Rhine Defenses

A Sd. Kfz 232 heavy armored car followed by a Sd. Kfz light armored car and motorcycle pass through a French village.

in operations named Tiger and Bear. Tiger mainly involved an attack by the German *1st Army* on the Maginot Line from Alsace and Lorraine. Bear was the plan for the German *7th Army*'s crossing of the Upper Rhine. *OKH* conceived a scheme to bring an Italian army into Operation Bear, but political considerations forced it to abandon that option. At the end of May, Hitler informed *OKH* that Italy planned to enter the war, but he did not want the Italians to become involved until after Case Red began.

Before beginning their offensive, the Germans had to give their panzer divisions a few days to receive reinforcements, rest and refit. The campaign in the West was only three weeks old and the Germans had to depend on battlefield repairs of damaged tanks to replace their substantial losses. Many of the surviving tanks had travelled distances of up to 300 miles (480 kilometers) on their tracks during the campaign and it was beginning to show. Moreover, Case Red required some units to

German Air Strength and Losses, May-June 1940

Note: the Luftwaffe had over 4,500 aircraft available on 10 May 1940, with over 3,500 on the Western Front.

Types of Planes	Available	Lost	Damaged	Total
Bombers	1,300	521	203	524
Dive Bombers	380	122	28	150
Fighters	1,210	367	179	546
Recon	640	166	39	205
Total	3,530	1,176	449	1,625
Transports	450	213	27	240

Note: Over 30 percent of the Luftwaffe's engaged aircraft were damaged or destroyed

move 150 miles (190 kilometers) or more to their assembly points and would travel many more miles than in Case Yellow before the end of the campaign. Since the Germans deployed virtually all of their armor on the Western Front when the campaign began, there was a small pool of replacements: 500 rather ineffective Panzer Is, about 150 other better models of light tanks and Czech tanks (Panzer IIs and 38ts). New ones would not be forthcoming. According to General Heinz Guderian, the German war industry produced only 125 tanks of all types in the month of May. Fortunately for the Germans, their field maintenance service was highly efficient, getting tanks suffering from light damage or mechanical breakdowns quickly back into action. On 31 May, General Halder noted in his diary that 50 percent of the army's tanks were ready for immediate operations, but by 5 June that figure rose to 70 percent after the service units completed minor repairs. He also concluded that a large number of their tanks, because of their limited useful life, would be out of action after about 190 miles (300 kilometers). This, he believed, would be sufficient to complete the final campaign, and if necessary a large number of captured French tanks might be pressed into service.

The *Luftwaffe* also sustained substantial losses in the first few weeks, but the Allied air forces suffered more serious losses. The superior German planes continued to maintain an advantage over most types of Allied aircraft. In addition the Allies handicapped their effective air strength by holding back fighter units to protect their capitals and rear areas during the first phase of the campaign. But now in the second phase of the German campaign the front lines would be closer to Paris.

In the French capital, the Reynaud government struggled desperately to find some way to save their country overrun by a seemingly unbeatable enemy. At the end of May, Prime Minister Reynaud had considered creating a "Breton Redoubt," but no divisions could be spared to prepare the position. Churchill hoped that the French, instead of surrendering, would still fall back on Brittany. Reynaud, for his part, tried to convince Churchill to commit more aircraft to the Continent at the beginning of June, claiming these would be crucial to the fight. The British prime minister refused by insisting these aircraft would be decisive for the impending battle of Britain. Reynaud also sought more aid from President Roosevelt and received promises of equipment, although the United States categorically refused to enter the war.

The military situation for the Allies was bad not only because they had lost the northern corner of France, but also because the Germans had destroyed so many of their divisions and inflicted heavy casualties on those that had survived. The hopes for the survival of France and the Allies now hinged on the ability of Weygand to defeat or at least hold back the Germans in the north of France. With his battered forces, the general would make his stand on the Somme and Aisne Rivers.

Reinforcements were drawn in from other fronts. Troops were called in from the German frontier and the Southeastern Front to shore up their defensive positions along the Somme and Aisne Rivers. The Alpine Front with Italy was also stripped, after all, it was considered the last "impassable" barrier, and at this point the French could afford the risk. More reinforcements came when French soldiers evacuated from Dunkirk returned from England, and the British prepared to dispatch more divisions to reinforce the two still in France.

The new defensive position, which anchored itself with the Maginot Line, was called the Weygand Line after their new commander. The French troops deployed in strong points along the line with the intention of defending wooded areas

Armed with an FM 24/29 machine gun, a pair of French troops take cover in a barn.

and towns behind the front. The strong points were called hedgehogs: a small defendable area armed with weapons for an all-around defense including at least one 75mm gun to be used as an anti-tank weapon. The forces that could be scraped together were assigned the task of maintaining the gaps between strong points and throwing back any German penetrations and the defenders had orders not to retreat under any circumstances. Many of the French units manning the Weygand Line were reservists, since the best elements of the French Army had been lost with the 1st Army Group. However, a fair number of combat veterans still remained.

On the new defensive position stretching along the Aisne and Somme, the French had about 40 infantry divisions plus an assortment of mostly reconstituted armored divisions of all types. From the northern end of the Maginot Line to the Swiss border the French deployed 17 divisions, only one of which was a Regular unit. The French Army now totaled over 60 divisions in France from the English Channel to the Mediterranean, but most were seriously weakened. Against this force Weygand estimated that his army faced between 130 to 150 enemy divisions, not taking into account the possibility that Italy's more than 70 divisions, mostly concentrated in Europe and Libya, might enter the war at any time.

Along the Somme from the Channel to the Oise River, the French deployed the 10th and 7th Armies, the former with the second BEF. The sectors along the Aisne River to its bend east of Rethel were defended by the 6th Army. These forces served as the 3rd Army Group under Besson. General Huntzinger commanded the new 4th Army Group of the 2nd Army, holding the gap between the Aisne River and the Maginot line, and a reserve force from the Maginot line, the 4th Army, in position at Troyes. Prételat's 2nd Army Group held the frontier regions with the added responsibility of the upper Rhine.

Each of the 3rd Army Group's divisions defended fronts of up to 10 miles (15 kilometers) which was about twice the normal divisional frontage and the situation for the divisions of Huntziger's newly created 4th Army Group was not much better. De Gaulle tried to convince Weygand to form more armored divisions with his remaining tanks, or at least rebuild those that remained, but Weygand refused. While De Gaulle claimed France still had 1,200 tanks left, the 2nd, 3rd and 4th DCRs had less than 150 tanks among them, the newly created 7th DLM another 174 tanks. These were scattered about the Weygand Line. All in all it was a paltry force to send up against the destructive panzers of the Germans.

The defense would be a desperate gamble. The Weygand Line was no Maginot Line and did not have the ability to resist for more than a few days simply because the fortified positions had limited supplies and not enough mobile units or reserves to maintain all the gaps through which the Germans might penetrate. The very set-up of the line itself had problems. The Germans had already established major bridgeheads over the Somme and could not be driven north of the river while the French held positions in advance of the Aisne Line. Still, Weygand and his superiors agreed that this would be the last stand of the French Army. They could do little else since they did not have enough troops to effect a withdrawal and take up successive positions in the rear.

An effective air force would be instrumental in supporting their line. General Vuillemin had reorganized a French Air Force about 2,350 aircraft strong on 5 June, or almost 175 more aircraft than on 10 May, with 1,000 aircraft being delivered to units after the campaign began. Unfortunately, only about 600 of these were operational. The French air chief also withdrew French air units from the army commanders' control for ground support operations and centralized his command against General Georges' wishes. The British had already withdrawn most of their surviving air units to England, although they maintained a significant air element in France. Unlike the situation at Dunkirk where their forces were within range of fighter units operating from England, British forces south of the Somme were much further distances away and would be unable to receive air support from bases across the Channel. The Armée de l'Air managed to muster almost 1,000 aircraft for the next series of battles, while the RAF committed an additional 100 of its remaining planes in France.

As Weygand prepared to make his stand, his position began to suffer from a disturbing development: the relations between the two Allies were becoming strained. The French leadership never seemed to fully recover from the German breakthrough in the Ardennes sector and pleaded for additional British support, especially in the air, believing that only more British fighter squadrons could save the situation. The British had already suffered severely in the air providing tactical bombers, mostly the inadequate Battles, in the early phase of the campaign. Like the French, such planes made almost suicidal attacks against a vastly superior enemy, suffering high losses, but the Allies were simply incapable of gaining control of the air. The British did what they could, also attempting to carry on a strategic bombing campaign against Germany which might have helped morale. Such efforts proved hardly enough to stem the victorious Nazi tide. At Dunkirk the RAF fighter squadrons successfully held back the *Luftwaffe* even though the German aircraft managed to penetrate as far as the beaches and port area, creating havoc, and making the British troops feel abandoned by their own air force. While the French criticized their allies for holding back needed squadrons, the British, for their part, did not feel that the French had contributed enough with their Armée de l'Air and were equally displeased with its reluctance to engage in activity. The French continued to request more RAF fighter squadrons, but the British refused to supply them, explaining that they could not strip their home defenses.

Weygand was not optimistic about his chances. After all, his 60 odd divisions had to defend a long line stretching from the English Channel to the Swiss border against the demonstrated skill and might of Germany's panzer and infantry forces. Although Weygand did not believe he could win, he took positive action ignoring past doctrine, determined to make a last stand to safeguard the honor of France.

Case Red

Case Red had *Army Group A* and *Army Group B* penetrate the Weygand line while *Army Group C* kept French units on the Maginot line pinned down. Bock's *Army Group B* faced the Somme front and his primary responsibility was to crack the defenses along the river. To the left was Rundstedt's *Army Group A*, concentrated between the Aisne and Meuse Rivers. It would smash into the Weygand Line along the Aisne after Bock opened his offensive.

Army Group B began Case Red on 5 June. It was assigned six panzer divisions, including four from *Panzergruppe Kleist*, to penetrate the Somme sector of the Weygand Line. Although some of the German units were driven off by Weygand's hedgehogs, Rommel's *7th Panzer Division*, leading *Hoth's Panzer corps*, forced a passage. Rommel's troops encountered French colonial and African troops which put up a determined fight and delayed his advance. The French artillery attempting to interdict caused some problems. This scene was repeated at many points along the front. The French finally put up a determined fight all along their line, but now they lacked the numbers and resources to make a stand for more than a few days at the most. As he advanced with his division, Rommel discovered that the French had barricaded almost every village

Rommel's command vehicle for the 7th Panzer Division, a Sd. Kfz 251/6, moves forward through France followed by an armored radio vehicle.

and key crossing behind the front, and the French appeared determined to hold these positions. Rommel opted for a rather novel and daring solution to penetrate the French line by having his vehicles, tracked or not, leave the roads and move cross country. He simply bypassed the French strong points until he encountered rear echelon units which showed less determination to fight. The advance of the *7th Panzer Division* began to drive a deep wedge which split the French 10th Army. Slowly Allied troops began to fall back from their line. Rommel's troops encountered a few retreating units of the British 1st Armored Division escaping across the Seine River and the French IX Corps with the British 51st Division fell back along the coast. On 8 June Rommel raced his lead elements towards

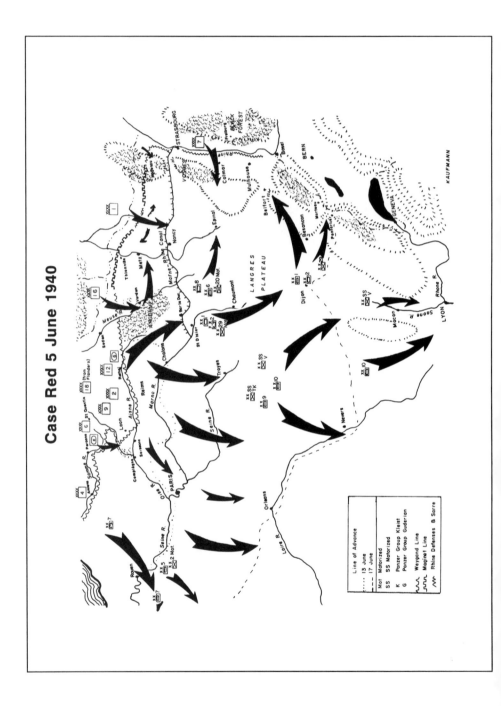

Case Red 5 June 1940

Rouen. He hoped to capture by surprise the bridges at Elbeuf, southwest of Rouen in a loop of the Seine, but arrived in the early hours of 9 June only to find that he was too late. However, the bridges were still standing so he ordered his troops to storm them, but before they could make a move the French blew all the bridges on the Seine. Despite this, the Germans succeeded in making a few crossings of the Seine south of Rouen that day. The French had a brief reprieve on the Seine while Hoth's *XV Panzer Corps* took up new positions and the infantry caught up. The *7th Panzer Division*, followed by other corps units, then moved towards the coast to destroy the French IX Corps before it could be evacuated.

Advancing behind and to the left of Hoth's corps was General Manstein's *XXXVIII Corps* consisting of three infantry divisions and the *1st Cavalry Division*. Manstein's divisions crossed the Somme in pneumatic boats on 5 June and established bridgeheads in the face of determined resistance from French troops and some of their colonial units. As Manstein's corps advanced towards the Seine its reconnaissance located a concentration of about 100 French tanks. The *Luftwaffe* swooped in to break it up and no ground contact with the force took place. After Manstein's divisions reached the Seine, the French armor reappeared and attacked their flank, hitting the *1st Cavalry Division*. The *XIV Panzer Corps* on his left could offer little help since it had been held up in Amiens by French resistance. On 9 June Manstein sent his *6th Division* to force a crossing at Les Andelys, and the *46th Division* to do the same at Vernon. In both cases a river crossing operation was necessary because the French blew the bridges and by the next day both divisions had established solid bridgeheads over the Seine. On 11 June Manstein ordered his three infantry divisions to cross the Seine (the *1st Cavalry* was reassigned to *I Corps*). The *46th Division* received serious attacks from French armor units, sustaining significant casualties. The RAF placed "the two weak pontoon bridges" at Les Andelys and Vernon under attack several times according to Manstein, temporarily putting the one at Vernon out of action. The next day, Manstein received reports that the French had massed 110 tanks for another counterattack. He received permission to attack first and, as he went into action, the *46th Division* was struck by

In what became a familiar scene in Europe for the next five years, a Panzer I travels through a village destroyed in the crossfire between Allied and Axis forces.

about 50 to 60 French tanks which it again beat off one more time.

Meanwhile, the four panzer division *Panzergruppe Kleist*, the main spearhead of Bock's *Army Group B*, assaulted the French 7th Army on the Somme, between Amiens and Péronne. The French 16th Division kept Kleist's *XIV Panzer Corps* from penetrating more than 6 miles (9 1/2 kilometers) at the German bridgehead at Amiens on 5 June. His *XVI Panzer Corps* had no more success trying to break out of the Péronne bridgehead. The French 7th Army held back the main panzer thrusts aimed at Paris, but Rommel's drive against 10th Army exposed its flank. Matters for the 7th became worse when the 6th Army on its right flank was pushed back across the Aisne, exposing that flank. The French 7th Army then began to fall back and had to move across the Oise River as the French 10th Army attempted to defend the Seine. The 7th's move was made all the more difficult when most of the Oise bridges were destroyed by comrades before the force could cross. By 9 June the 7th Army managed to reach a new line, but the Germans had already gained a bridgehead at Soissons on the Aisne against the French 6th Army. Contrary to Weygand's initial plan to make the last stand on the Somme and Aisne before giving up, his armies continued to fight and pulled back when necessary to continue resisting.

On 6 June, with slow progress being made against the front of the French 7th Army, Bock decided to send the *XIV Panzer Corps* to join the more successful *XVI Panzer Corps*. The same day *OKH* considered pulling the *XIV* and *XVI Panzer Corps* of Kleist's group out of the front line, but *Army Group B* reported making progress. On 7 June Brauchitsch informed Halder that these two panzer corps were only slowly advancing and that the *XVI Panzer Corps* already had lost 30 percent of its tanks and both needed personnel replacements because of combat losses due to heavy French resistance. On 8 June Hitler issued his Directive Number 14, where he stated that "The enemy is offering stiff resistance on our right flank and the center of [the German] 6th Army." He directed the *XIV Panzer Corps* to withdraw from the Amiens bridgehead and take up a position on the left flank of the German *4th Army*. Finally, *Panzergruppe Kleist* shifted its two corps to the left flank of *Army Group B* and the right flank of *Panzergruppe Guderian*.

During those first days of the June German offensive the French Armée de l'Air was thrown into the battle, striking at advancing German columns and attempting to destroy the bridges over the Somme, but it had no success and furthermore, many of the planes were hit with ground fire. As the Germans opened the offensive of *Army Group A* on 9 June, the French air arm had been already greatly depleted, and a few days later the high command had transferred many of its units into southern France. As the situation rapidly deteriorated, the

The German 88mm anti-aircraft gun was probably the greatest anti-tank gun of the war. It proved its destructiveness on many of the great battlefields of World War II.

RAF returned most of its squadrons to England in the middle of the month, beginning with the bomber units.

Rundstedt's *Army Group A*, with only four panzer divisions under the new panzergruppe commanded by Guderian, opened the assault on the Aisne River defenses on 9 June with spearheads that found it difficult to break through the French line. On the first day Guderian's troops secured only two small bridgeheads on the Aisne, west of Rethel. On 10 June his troops bypassed the French hedgehogs and met little resistance, leaving the infantry that followed to deal with the French resistance centers. Guderian ran into General Jean de Lattre de Tassigny's 14th Division which fought fiercely for the better part of two days. The 3rd DCR launched a fanatical counterattack with 86 Char B's, H-35 and H-39 tanks at Juniville, and managed to destroy about 100 German armored vehicles of the *1st Panzer Division* before the Germans drove it back following a two hour battle. Guderian himself recorded how his own efforts to de-

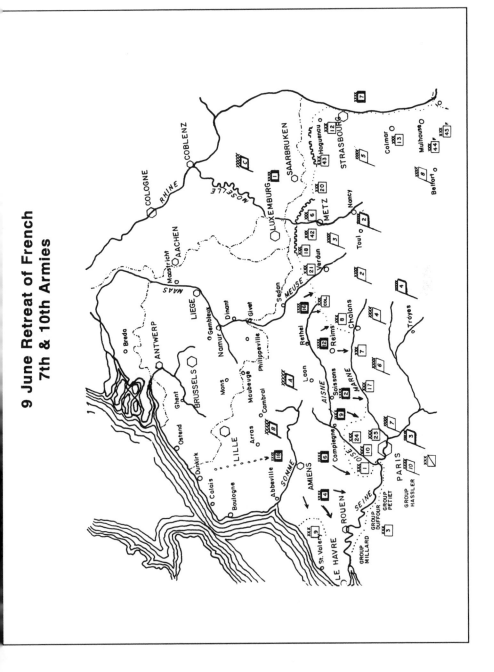

9 June Retreat of French
7th & 10th Armies

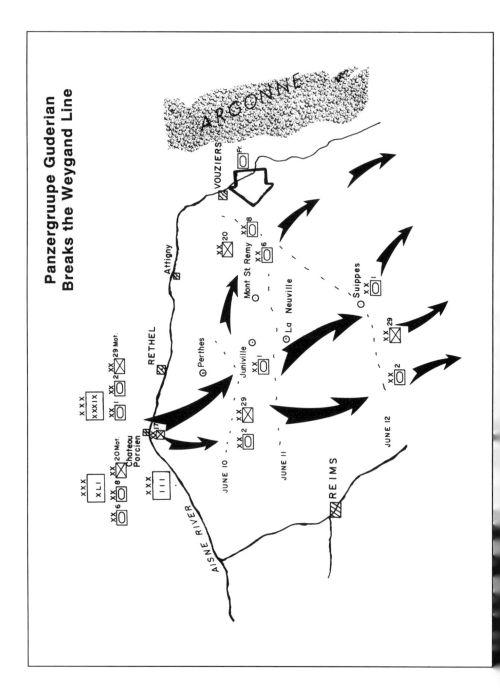

Panzergruupe Guderian
Breaks the Weygand Line

ARGONNE

VOUZIERS

Attigny

RETHEL

Chateau Porcien

Perthes

Mont St Remy

La Neuville

Suippes

Juniville

REIMS

AISNE RIVER

JUNE 10

JUNE 11

JUNE 12

Wreckage of war. Abandoned Allied vehicles, like these French H-39 tanks were restored or modified for German service. Others too badly damaged were sent to the scrap heap.

stroy a French Char B with a captured 47mm anti-tank gun had proved fruitless. Fortunately for the Germans, the French had few reserves left to throw into the battle. Guderian's advance continued towards La Neuville, a few miles south of Juniville, where the 3rd DCR had retreated. Meanwhile the *2nd Panzer Division* took Reims on the Aisne.

On 11 June the *1st Panzer Division* moved south from La

Neuville to Suippes where the new French 7th DLM counterattacked with 50 tanks. General Buisson's armored group, 3rd DCR and 3rd DLC continued to counterattack *Panzergruppe Guderian's* flank from the Argonne Forest and hit Reinhardt's *XLI Panzer Corps*. The Germans again repulsed all the French attacks and continued their advance.

Panzergruppe Kleist reached the Aisne on Guderian's right a couple of days after his crossing and also threw its two corps across the river. Two panzergruppes with eight panzer divisions began the breakout west of Rethel and, by 11 June, the Weygand Line began to crumble. The French 3rd Army Group, once on the Somme, was already pushed back to the Seine by the advance of Hoth's *XV Panzer Corps*, and the French 4th Army Group on the Aisne were breaking up. The Allies' situation was rapidly becoming hopeless as the Germans raced forward to exploit their penetrations. By 12 June, *Panzergruppe Guderian* established a bridgehead over the Marne at Châlons. As his first troops began to cross the bridge, it blew up, yet his panzers relentlessly continued their advance, arriving at Besançon on 16 June effectively cutting off General Prételat's 2nd Army Group defending the Maginot fortifications.

Last Stand

The French government evacuated Paris on 10 June as the Germans pushed the French 10th, 7th and 6th Armies back and Reynaud had to face the prospect of surrender. Churchill flew to France to meet with the French prime minister and his cabinet at Tours on 11 June. The alliance was on the verge of collapse. The French were just about ready to submit: Reynaud was despondent, Weygand wanted to surrender, and although de Gaulle wanted to continue the fight, Pétain, recently appointed to the cabinet, advocated capitulation.

Adding to the mounting problems, Italy declared war on France on 10 June. In response, the RAF sent Wellington bombers to southern France to attack Northern Italy. However, the French government denied permission for the assault, going so far as to block the airfields when the attempt was made. Meanwhile, the two prime ministers continued to confer. Chur-

A German officer inspects a battered French Char B1 tank.

chill still hoped for a union of the two nations, but the French leaders were not interested. After the meeting, the government moved to Bordeaux, and Allied cooperation came to an end.

As Churchill returned home on 12 June, Rommel's clean-up operations north of the Seine wound down. While the *5th Panzer Division* took Rouen, his *7th Panzer Division* rolled on to the coast, driving right down to the sea between St. Valéry and Fécamp on 10 June. Having heard from a prisoner that the 51st Division was to be evacuated from Fécamp by sea that very afternoon, he moved against that port. The next day he moved back towards St. Valéry to engage the remnants of the French IX Corps with its British division. His troops drove into the town and forced the Allied troops to surrender including Gen-

French civilians pass by a reminder of their armed forces' defeat, a knocked out Char B1 tank.

eral Ihler, the commander of IX Corps, and soon after General Fortune, the commander of the British division. Among the approximate 40,000 prisoners, there were remnants of two DLCs and 8,000 men of the Highland 51st Division (only about 2,000 had been successfully evacuated). Rommel's tanks even engaged British destroyers during these operations. Rommel recorded that the French population of the region was glad to be done with the war while French civilians from the Somme to the sea happily greeted his soldiers often believing they were British. His formations moved back to prepare for the next offensive.

More bad news followed for the Allies each day. On 13 June the government declared Paris an 'Open City' as thousands of refugees fled. The Germans occupied the city on the next day. On 14 June Churchill ordered the withdrawal of the remnants of the BEF still in France: the 1st Armored Division, weakened by heavy losses during operations between the Somme and the Seine, the recently landed 52nd Lowland Division and the 1st Canadian Division. These units pulled back with all their support troops to ports in Brittany and Cherbourg on 15 June. The British also had time to evacuate some valuable stores, including some ammunition, chemical weapons and even well over a hundred guns, all items badly needed for the defense of Britain. One brigade of the 52nd Division, forming part of *Normanforce* with elements of the 1st Armored Division's 3rd Armored Brigade and units of the Beauman Division, took part in the final operations in Normandy with the French III Corps. On 17 June they disengaged and fell back on Cherbourg for evacuation. When General Weygand became aware that the second BEF, no longer taking orders from his 10th Army, was preparing for evacuation from the Continent, he decided the British decision released him from any obligation to protect their soldiers. The new French government felt the same way and accused the British of abandoning them. Despite Weygand and his superiors, the British escape from France was made possible by the cooperation of French units and their commanders.

The British carried on more Dunkirk-like operations at Brittany while the Germans advanced and the French began to capitulate. On 18 June 136,000 British support troops and elements of three divisions with various formations of the Beauman Division reached England with about 50,000 Czechs, Poles and French after being evacuated from Cherbourg and ports in Brittany. The British embarked almost 31,000 men at Cherbourg, over 21,000 men at St. Malo and over 32,000 at Brest. The only incident to mar this successful evacuation was the sinking of the *Lancastria* by German bombers, resulting in the loss of about 3,000 men. Interestingly, many of the French troops in Brittany and Normandy had recently returned from Dunkirk and found themselves covering again the escape of their ally. Several destroyers, six liners plus other ships assembled off southern Brittany, near the mouth of the Loire, waiting to rescue more troops, including Allies from St. Nazaire and Nantes. On 16 June 12,000 men came out, another 23,000 men followed on 18 June. A convoy made mostly of ships found in

Rommel poses with General Fortune who surrendered the British 52nd Division at St. Valery.

the harbor, departed La Pallice with 10,000 troops on 18 June. Another 2,000 men, mostly Polish troops, were lifted from the Loire area on the same day and on 19 June another 4,000 more Poles embarked. The evacuation of civilians and Allied troops (mostly French, Polish and about 5,000 Czechs) continued from ports in Southwest France like Bayonne, Le Verdon and Saint Jean de Luz until the armistice. As the British evacuated the Continent, Hoth's *XV Panzer Corps* began a new offensive on 17 June with Rommel's "Ghost Division" in the lead. The French had ceased to resist vigorously by now and Rommel soon discovered from his prisoners that the new prime minister, Pétain, had requested an armistice. The *7th Panzer Division* simply raced past the French troops and turned into the Cotentin Peninsula, driving towards Cherbourg. In a single day his division advanced from the Seine to La Haye-du-Puits, west of Carentan. Though on 18 June he found that the French troops to the north had not heard of the proposed armistice and

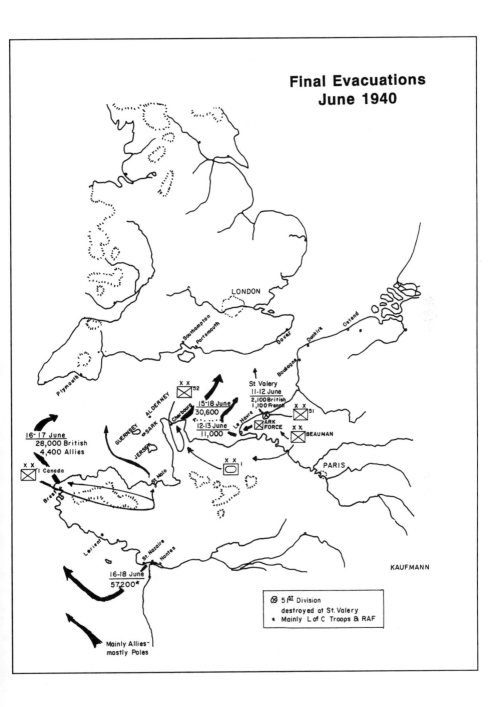

**Final Evacuations
June 1940**

French refugees fleeing the fighting during the campaign in the West.

were preparing to resist him. He began his attack against the forts of Cherbourg the next day. Finally, a French delegation of officers, without the approval of Admiral Abrial, surrendered the city and its forts informing Rommel that they had only given up because of a lack of ammunition. Fortunately, the British troops had already been evacuated before the German attack, but left behind many new vehicles in the port area.

Meanwhile, the remainder of Hoth's *XV Panzer Corps* drove on to take Rennes on 18 June, capturing General Altmayer, the commander of the 10th Army. That same day Hoth's troops from the *5th Panzer Division* reached Brest. The previous day the last French naval units had departed followed by a British demolition team which attempted to destroy the port facilities. Behind the fleeing allies was the wreckage of a dozen warships under repair at Brest, including nine submarines.

Army Group B began to move its divisions south to cross the Loire. On June 16 Manstein's *XXXVIII Corps* headed for Le

Mans only to run into the remnants of the French DLMs, which had been evacuated from Dunkirk halfway between its objective and the Seine. The ensuing clash lasted until evening. Having disposed of this last serious attempt at resistance, Manstein's troop moved through Le Mans and reached Angers by 19 June. On 22 June they crossed the Loire.

Meanwhile, *German Army Group C*, with 17 divisions, prepared for its long awaited offensive against the Maginot Line and the Rhine Defenses. The 17 German divisions no longer faced 50 French divisions, but only 17, of which 10 were Category B. Until then, the Germans had put little pressure on the Maginot Line, only increasing patrols and bombardments when the panzer force reached the Meuse. This activity fooled Gamelin in May into believing that the Maginot Line was the real target of the German offensive, causing him to keep forces of the 2nd Army Group there instead of having them move north to meet the real threat. While panzers rolled across the Low Countries and France, the Germans limited their actions on this front until 14 June, when the *Army Group C* commander, General Leeb, gave the orders for the attack. Leeb thus advanced the assault date after discovering that Weygand had ordered the withdrawal of the 2nd Army Group on 12 June as Guderian's panzers drove south. The move was a desperate ploy by Weygand to prevent the Germans from occupying more territory before an armistice.

The main attack against the Maginot Line was delivered by the German *1st Army* against the lightly defended Sarre Gap between the two RFs of the Maginot Line on 14 June. The German *7th Army* launched an amphibious assault across the Rhine the next morning. French divisions occupying the intervals had already begun their withdrawal, slowed for want of transport, as *Army Group A*, with *Panzergruppe Guderian*, approached to trap them from the rear. *Army Group C's 1st Army* was initially checked in the Sarre region by the remaining divisions, but as the French began their retreat, the German divisions quickly passed through the area, spreading out to encircle each of the RFs.

A single German division, the *215th Infantry Division*, attacked the line of casemates in the Vosges in the RF of the Lauter. The gros ouvrages of Grand Hohékirkel, Four à Chaux

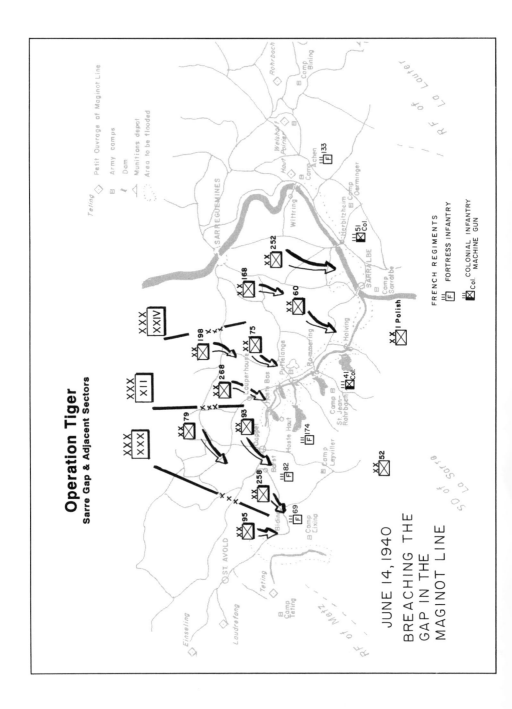

Operation Tiger
Sarre Gap & Adjacent Sectors

JUNE 14, 1940
BREACHING THE
GAP IN THE
MAGINOT LINE

German troops cross the Rhine to assault the Maginot Line. Surprisingly, the bank of the river lacked obstacles to stop such an attack.

and Hochwald, flanking the region, put down heavy supporting fires, but they were unable to hold the position without the presence of interval troops. The *215th Division* penetrated the weakly held line on 15 June, moving to encircle the large ouvrages of Four à Chaux, Hochwald and Schoenenbourg, and was reinforced with an assortment of heavy artillery, including a Czech 355mm gun and the last 420mm Big Bertha from World War I. Though the Germans subjected these ouvrages to an intense bombardment with artillery and aircraft, in the closing days of the campaign, the big guns and Stukas did little damage to the forts, even though a few heavy rounds scored hits. The French continued to resist, ignoring the hopelessness of the situation as well as initial orders from the government to surrender after the armistice.

As the fighting heightened in the Vosges, the 11 German divisions, breaking through the Sarre Gap, began to reduce the

German troops attack one of the Rhine casemates with a flamethrower.

petits ouvrages which protected the flanks of this sector and were located well out of range of the artillery ouvrages. The small forts fought back as best they could while the Germans positioned artillery weapons, including 88mm guns, behind

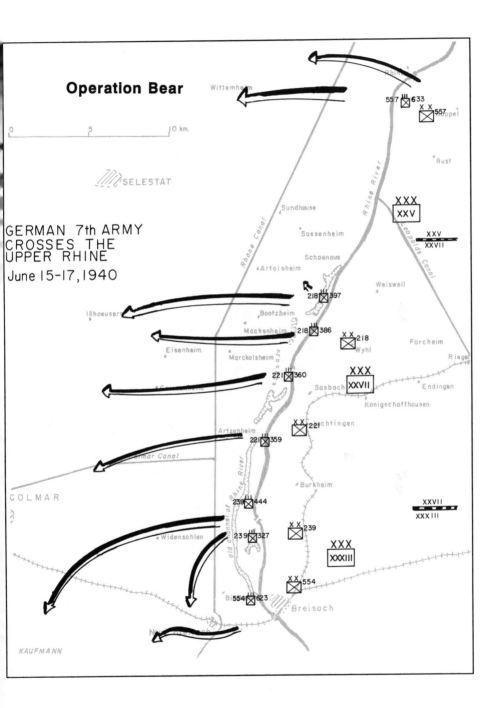

Operation Bear

GERMAN 7th ARMY
CROSSES THE
UPPER RHINE
June 15-17, 1940

A German 280mm Bruno K heavy railway gun goes into action against French fortifications.

them in order to hit their weak rear-facing walls and force their surrender.

The French XX Corps having failed to stop the German breakthrough in the Sarre Gap, continued to resist until it was hopelessly trapped. Its 1st Polish Division was eliminated after a battle lasting from 17 to 18 June at Lagrande.

Meanwhile, German units led by the *169th* and *183rd Infantry Divisions*, swept around the end of the Maginot Line at Lon-

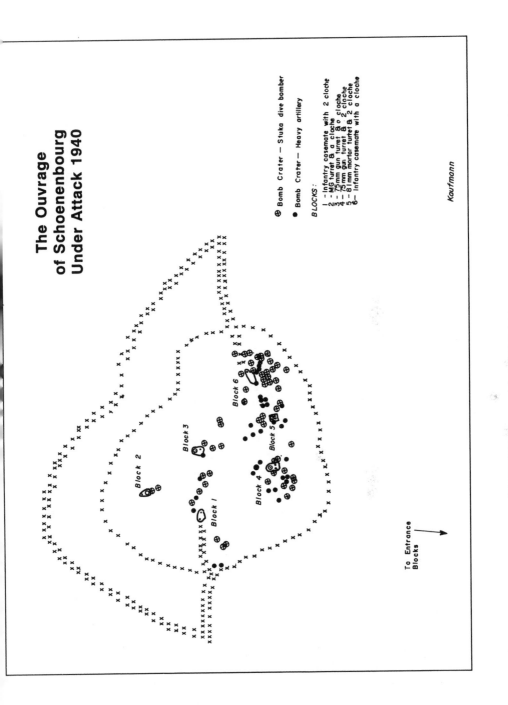

The Ouvrage
of Schoenenbourg
Under Attack 1940

⊕ Bomb Crater — Stuka dive bomber

● Bomb Crater — Heavy artillery

BLOCKS:

1 — Infantry casemate with 2 cloche
2 — MG turret & a cloche
3 — 75mm gun turret & o cloche
4 — 75 mm gun turret & 2 cloche
5 — 81 mm mortar turret & 2 cloche
6 — Infantry casemate with a cloche

Block 6

Block 3

Block 2

Block 5

Block I

Block 4

To Entrance
Blocks

Kaufmann

guyon, moving towards the Sarre region to encircle the RF of Metz. An unsuspecting supply column of the *183rd Division* following the advance was devastated by the 75mm gun turret of the Ouvrage of Fermont on 15 June. On 17 June a German detachment with an 88mm gun almost penetrated the fort's artillery casemate (Block 4) adjacent to the ready rounds for a 75mm gun. The Germans had been firing repeatedly at the same spot from a position behind the fort, but they finally gave up their effort, unaware that one further round would have broken through, allowing the French to seal up the damaged wall after the Germans withdrew.

On 18 June Guderian's men occupied Belfort, thus closing the trap, while his *29th Motorized Division* pushed on to the Swiss border leaving not even a torturous exit for the French through the Jura Alps. The French XV Corps, including the 2nd Polish Division managed to break out by moving into Switzerland where they were taken into internment. Many others however were now prisoners of the Reich. Guderian passed long columns of surrendered French vehicles and although there were thousands of prisoners in the area, the resistance continued at Belfort, since the town's old forts refused to surrender without a fight. The defense did not last long. Belfort's citadel and remaining forts finally surrendered to the *1st Panzer Division* late in the day after an afternoon assault was launched against them. German losses in the operation were light. Further north Épinal fell to the *6th Panzer Division*; each yielded about 40,000 prisoners according to Guderian (Belfort may actually have had only 10,000 men). On 19 June Guderian's units linked up with the German *7th Army* which had already crossed the Rhine.

From 18 June through 20 June German field artillery engaged with the Ouvrage of Fermont in a duel, and on June 21 the fort was bombarded by several huge 305mm guns and 210mm howitzers as well as other artillery for four hours. Just like the other gros ouvrages in the RF of Lauter, which underwent bombardment by even bigger guns, Fermont kept all its turrets eclipsed. When the firing stopped, the ouvrages' combat positions opened fire on the German infantry working its way through gaps blown in the anti-tank rails and barbed wire obstacles surrounding the fort. The 75mm guns of the ouvrage

The fosse wall of this infantry block at Schoenenbourg was breached by a Stuka divebomber while the fort was under bombardment by heavy artillery.

of Latiremont joined the action and the German assault was broken up. A 47mm German anti-tank gun pounded the Men's Entrance (EH), causing the death of a single French soldier, the only member of the garrison to die during the battle. The Germans, having learned that an assault on a *gros ouvrage*, even an isolated one, was a futile task, broke off the attack. It became evident that the large forts could not be taken as easily as the smaller ones.

As *Panzergruppe Guderian* began its advance behind the French 2nd Army Group, the German amphibious operation on the Upper Rhine appeared to be a major success. The German *7th Army*, having bombarded the French positions with over 600 guns, including 240mm and 280mm railway guns, crossed the river with elements of three infantry divisions on the morning of 15 June. In spite of all the years of preparation, there was still a dearth of obstacles in key spots along the Rhine Front. The French had tried to fill the gaps with barbed wire, unknowingly facilitating German landings by apparently giving them something rather solid on the river banks to establish

German officers and a Japanese observer ponder the amazing victory being won by the Axis forces in France.

a foothold on. The positions on the river line fell quickly, and soon the assaulting troops were at the main line of casemates.

Though vigorously defended, these positions were inadequately supported and soon began to fall, so that by 16 June the French had to withdraw to the Vosges to continue the battle. The Germans succeeded on the Upper Rhine because the French 104th Fortress Division was overextended, covering over 50 kilometers (30 Miles) with no transportation at their disposal. The French counterattacked vigorously, but soon ran out of troops. Throughout this operation, the Germans maintained complete control of the air since the defenders had neither aircraft nor AA guns. By 16 June the Germans completed the first pontoon bridge across the Rhine and sent their

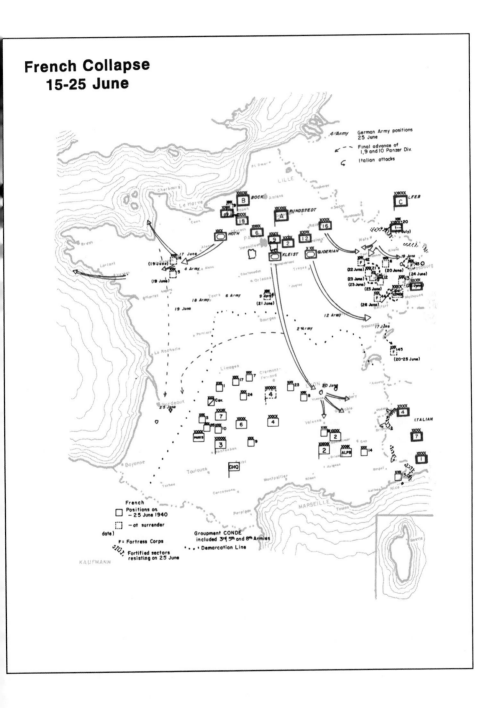

French Collapse
15-25 June

An abandoned SOMUA is a roadside monument to the French defeat.

heavy equipment over it. Only the French units in the Vosges checked their advance.

On the same day, Reynaud resigned from the French government at Bordeaux, and Pétain took charge, immediately seeking an armistice. German units continued to race across France even as the French government was surrendering, reaching as far south as Lyon and as far west as Saumur by 19 June while overtaking masses of refugees. At Saumur cadets from the cavalry school valiantly brought the German *1st Cavalry Divi-*

The old railroad car where defeated German officials had surren-dered during World War I was used for the armistice of June 1940. This time it was the French who gave up.

sion to a halt on 19 June, but they had to surrender the next day after expending their ammunition.

On the 20th, the Italians, 10 days after declaring war, had begun their offensive through the Alpine passes.

The next day, French officials under General Huntzinger arrived at Compiègne, the site of the armistice of 1918, to begin talks. There they found their German hosts had engaged in a bit of ironic staging: negotiations were to be conducted in the same railway car where German officials had surrendered in World War I! General Huntzinger was given terms that were not open to discussion: occupation of Northern France, payment of occupation costs, demilitarization and incarceration of troops captured during the 1940 campaign. Huntzinger reluctantly accepted.

On 22 June the French signed the armistice, but the cease-fire would only take effect on 25 June if Italy and France completed negotiations. Over 400,000 French troops in the Vosges Pocket

On 22 June, General Huntziger (left) and General Keitel (right) signed the armistice documents to take France out of the war. Free French forces under Charles de Gaulle continued to fight elsewhere.

were ordered to surrender to Guderian and *Army Group C*, but a number of the ouvrages of the Maginot Line refused to do so. In some cases it took until July for representatives of the French government to arrive and arrange for the surrender of the forts.

Battle for the Alps

Mussolini, having told his Chief of Staff Marshal Badoglio at the end of May that he needed several thousand dead Italian soldiers so he could sit at the peace table, jumped into the war on 10 June 1940. The next day his air force bombed French bases in Tunisia and Corsica. The RAF jumped into the fray on the night of 11/12 June, launching a long distance raid from England against factories at Turin. Of the 36 Whitley bombers assigned to the mission, 23 had to turn back due to bad weather over the Alps. Nine aircraft bombed Turin, but hit the rail yards instead of their targets, while two others hit Genoa. Their

298

mission was facilitated by the fact that the Italians had taken no measures to black out their cities. More British raids took place in the following days, but without much effect. Little else was done until 18 June when Mussolini met with Hitler at Munich, only to be disappointed when he found out that he was not going to get a share of France's colonial empire. Although the Duce was not ready to fight on any front, he found it necessary to launch an offensive soon if he was to get a share of the spoils from the Allied defeat. Still, the Alpine Front remained quiet.

In the final week of the war, the truculent General René Olry, commander of the French Army of the Alps, refused to give up without a fight, despite facing an impossible situation. The

Small Italian L-3 tanks during the invasion of southeastern France. Though badly defeated in the north, French forces on the Italian border easily stopped the poorly equipped attack.

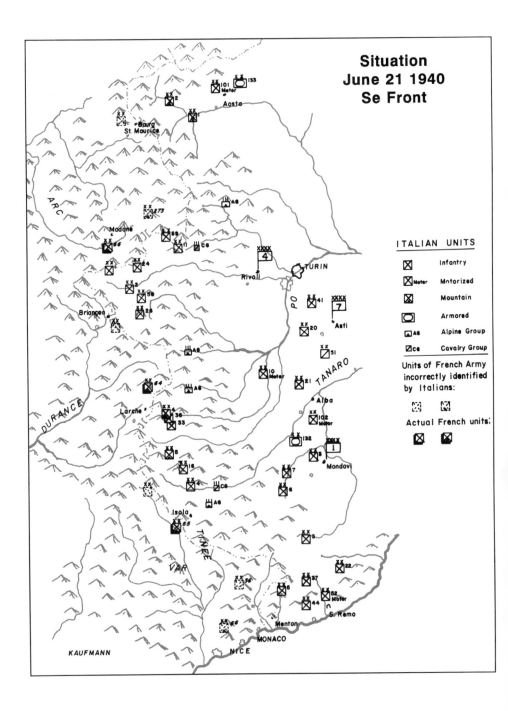

**Situation
June 21 1940
Se Front**

ITALIAN UNITS

⊠	Infantry
⊠ Motor	Motorized
⊠	Mountain
⬡	Armored
⊡ AG	Alpine Group
⊠ cs	Cavalry Group

Units of French Army
incorrectly identified
by Italians:

Actual French units:

KAUFMANN

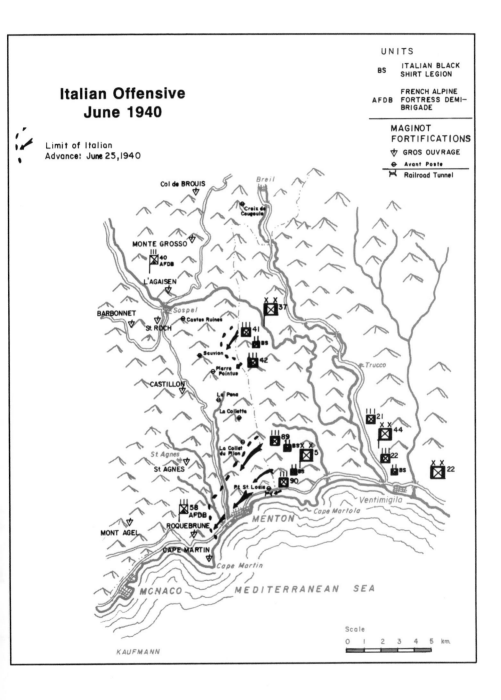

Italian Offensive
June 1940

UNITS

BS ITALIAN BLACK SHIRT LEGION

AFDB FRENCH ALPINE FORTRESS DEMI-BRIGADE

MAGINOT FORTIFICATIONS

⍌ GROS OUVRAGE
⊖ Avant Poste
🚊 Railroad Tunnel

Limit of Italian
Advance: June 25,1940

Col de BROUIS

Breil

Creix de Coupoule

MONTE GROSSO

III 40 AFDB

L'AGAISEN

Sospel

BARBONNET

Castes Ruines

St. ROCH

Scuvion

X X 37

41 BS

42

Pierre Pointue

Trucco

CASTILLON

La Pena

La Collette

III 21
X X 44

89
BS X X 5
22

La Collet du Pilon

BS

St Agnes

St AGNES

III 90
BS

22

BS

Pt. St. Louis

Ventimigila

58 AFDB

Cape Martola

MONT AGEL

ROQUEBRUNE

MENTON

CAPE MARTIN

Cape Martin

MONACO

MEDITERRANEAN SEA

Scale
0 1 2 3 4 5 km.

KAUFMANN

301

general not only had to contend with the Italians to the east, but also with German troops moving down the Rhone Valley. Lyon's mayor had already declared it an "Open City," and the Germans were allowed to use its bridges to cross the Rhone by 19 June, to the chagrin of Olry, who desperately scraped together troops and equipment from the rear echelons to stop the German advance.

On the next day, the Italians finally began their offensive. The seven French divisions along the Alpine Front managed to halt an Italian army group of more than 30 divisions, at the Little Maginot Line's line of avant-postes, or outposts. Along the Mediterranean coast, bypassing and never capturing the avant-poste of Pont St. Louis, the Italians reached the city of Menton on 20 June before they were stopped by the gros ouvrages on the other side of the city. The isolated avant-poste continued to interdict the coastal route until the armistice. A naval armored train mounting four turrets of 150mm guns being brought in to reduce the French forts was destroyed by the guns of the ouvrage of St. Agel as it emerged from the railway tunnel to bombard the ouvrage of Cap Martin on 22 June. Further north, in the vicinity of Briançon, a four-gun heavy battery of 280mm mortars, with the assistance of the observation posts of the ouvrage of Janus and other positions, engaged in a four-day artillery duel with the Italian fort of Chaberton, destroying its six 149mm gun turrets on 21 June. Fort Jafferau's mounted 149mm guns in open positions to the north was unable to offer any relief to Fort Chaberton's plight.

The Italians requested that the Germans advance down the Rhone and towards the Alpine positions to aid their attack against the Little St. Bernard Pass and the Italian General Staff urged Halder to begin pushing on to Grenoble and Chambéry to help them. But the German general expressed little confidence in the Italian operation. That night the OKH made the decision to begin the advance the next day. German units approaching from the Rhone Valley were temporarily checked as they entered the Alps and moved towards the rear of the French Alpine Army's positions. Fortunately for the French soldiers of the Alps, they did not have to face military defeat, as their government had finally succeeded in negotiating an armistice with Italy so that their peace with Germany could go

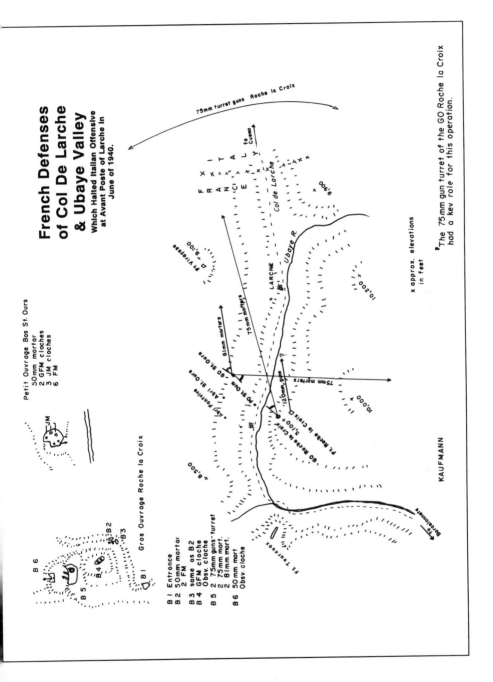

French Defenses
of Col De Larche
& Ubaye Valley

Which Halted Italian Offensive
at Avant Poste of Larche in
June of 1940.

75mm turret guns Roche la Croix

to Cuneo

F R A N C E
I T A L Y

Col de Larche

9,900

x approx. elevations
in feet

*The 75mm gun turret of the GO Roche la Croix
had a key role for this operation.

Pt Viraysse
+ 9,100

81mm mortars

75mm mortars

LARCHE

Ubaye R.

10,200
x

GO St. Ours

Abri Fontvive

120mm gun

GO St. Ours

75mm mortars

10,000
x

KAUFMANN

Pt Roche la Croix
5,100 +

GO Roche la Croix

Petit Ouvrage Bas St. Ours
50mm mortar
2 GFM cloches
3 JM cloches
6 FM

JM

Gros Ouvrage Roche la Croix

8,500
+

to Barcelonnette

Ft Tournoux

B 6

B 2
B 3

B 4

B 1

B 5

B 1 Entrance
B 2 50mm mortar
     2 FM
B 3 same as B2
B 4 GFM cloche
     Obsv. cloche
B 5 2 75mm guns-turret
     2 75mm mort.
     2 81mm mort.
B 6 50mm mort
     Obsv. cloche

303

into effect as scheduled. On 24 June Halder noted that the Italians wanted to send several battalions by air to the vicinity of Lyon so they could negotiate for rights to occupied French territory, a strategem he described as "...the cheapest kind of fraud." As the battle for the Alps developed, Allied units were in the process of leaving southern France by air and sea.

The fighting came to an end on 25 June 1940, and slowly the last French units surrendered. The battle for France was over. Now the war would shift to Great Britain.

CHAPTER VIII

The Alliance Breaks Up

The relationship between the Allies was already strained before the capitulation of the French. The French bitterly blamed the reluctance of their comrades from across the Channel to provide enough troops and airpower to stem the German tide. For their part the British claimed the French had given in too easily and expected their army and air force to bear the brunt of the fight on the Continent. The evacuation of the BEF and the French surrender led to an uneasy relationship between these powers that had once fought side by side, a relationship that now had sometimes violent consequences.

After the surrender terms were presented to the French, it was widely speculated that France would be forced to turn its colonies and formidable fleet over to the Axis. Although Admiral Darlan promised them that the French fleet would not fall into German hands, the British remained skeptical. The admiral, true to his word, ordered his captains to keep the Germans from taking over their ships. Before the armistice took effect, the Western media made it known that the British and Americans were concerned about the fate of the French fleet and colonies. In the meantime, General Nogués in French North Africa and General Mittelhauser in Syria indicated that they would not allow the Axis to occupy their territory and would continue to resist the Axis. The British continued to withhold their assent to a French surrender, setting up General de Gaulle at the head of his own French Legion in London to

A graveyard of wrecked British Fairey Battles. This so-called fast bomber proved to be a failure and many such planes were lost during the campaign in France.

Dejected French prisoners of several nationalities captured during the German advance. Many of these soldiers would wait out the war in Germany in prison camps.

A German trumpeter sounds the cease fire after the signing of the armistice at Compiegne.

continue the fight. From England, de Gaulle exhorted his countrymen to continue the struggle.

During the last week of June, after the French surrender, a verbal war began between the two former allies. As France now sought to rebuild its captive nation, a task for which it was hoped American aide would be forthcoming, Pétain attempted to justify his government's decision to surrender by heaping the blame on the British. Such sentiments are to be found in a 25 June speech by the old war hero along with the hope that the British would accept the new political situation, "We would like for our British friends to respect our sorrow and examine their own conscience." He also chided the British for failing to send the 26 divisions promised in the first months of the war, a commitment he felt contributed to the final defeat.

The best weapon the British had in this verbal battle was General Charles de Gaulle. De Gaulle's broadcasts to France fell largely upon deaf ears in the early days, but they made good propaganda. On 26 June de Gaulle addressed a message to Marshal Pétain on the BBC expressing his dissatisfaction with the Marshal's justifications, and spelling out his own theory on the French defeat:

> ...But what was the cause of (our) inferiority? It was brought about by a bad military system. France has been struck down, not by the number of German effectives, not by their superior courage, but solely by the enemy's mechanized force with all its offensive power and maneuverability.

Casualties: Campaign in the West			
Army	KIA	WIA	POW & MIA
French	90,000(+)	200,000(+)	1,900,000
British	6,475	20,000(?)	15,000(?)
Belgian	7,550	15,850	?
Dutch	2,890	6,889	?
German	27,074	111,034	18,384
Italian	631	6,029	

(Sources: To Lose a Battle by Alistair Horne, The Collapse of the Third Republic by William Shirer, France: Summer 1940 by John Williams and Nazi Europe by Marshall Cavendish Ltd.)

He accused Pétain of preventing the French army from creating a mechanized force and pointed out that the old marshal had been the dominant military figure in France until the mid-1930s and that he "...never supported, demanded, insisted on the indispensable reform of this rotten system." Then he accused Pétain of using his past status to help forge an armistice which:

> ...is dishonorable. Two-thirds of our territory handed over to the occupation of the enemy—and what an enemy!—our whole Army completely demobilized, our officers and soldiers, who are now prisoners, kept in captivity. Our Navy, our aircraft, our tanks, our armies are to be handed over intact, so that the enemy may use them against our own Allies. Our country, the Government, you yourself reduced to servitude. Ah! in order to obtain and to accept such an act of enslavement there was no need for you...anyone would have done.

The general went on to describe the losing game Pétain played with the enemy, bemoaning that France was now under the "German jackboot and the Italian dancing pumps." De Gaulle closed his scathing speech with the warning that France would rise again. Pétain's government retaliated against de Gaulle by demoting him and relieving him from active service, but these efforts had little effect on the battle of words over the radio air waves.

Meanwhile, news from the French colonies was positive later in the month. At first most French colonial officials indicated they would not turn their territories over to the Axis, and that the war was not over for them. However, one by one they yielded to the new government at Vichy. Soon some of the governors were replaced. Despite earlier efforts to resist, General Noguès felt compelled to remain loyal to the Vichy government, but continued to express his intention to prevent an Axis occupation. The governor of French Somaliland, backed by the local military commander, General Legentilhomme, continued to defy orders from Vichy allowing his 10,000-man force to become an important element in future British plans for action against Italian East Africa. Later an official of the Vichy government usurped his power and the colony was neutralized, but the general escaped to join the Free French.

On 28 June, the last major force, that of General Mittelhauser

German troops parade in review through Paris.

in Syria, announced its acceptance of the terms of the armistice. Although General Mittelhauser and his officers wanted to resist, their troops were reluctant. The *London Times* explained that the problem was that most of the officers had their families with them, but the enlisted men did not, and they feared for their loved ones still in occupied France. Mittelhauser thus gave in and, later in the next year, when the British invaded Syria and Lebanon, many of his troops chose repatriation to France rather than joining the Free French.

A major concern to the British Admiralty and Churchill was the fate of the French fleet. In accordance with the armistice, Darlan also began to demilitarize naval bases at Toulon (France), Bizerte (Tunisia), Oran (Algeria) and Ajaccio (Corsica), where most of the French fleet was stationed. The British felt that the French fleet in these ports would be open to a quick Axis takeover, similar to one they themselves were planning against the French ships in the English ports and at Alexandria.

As the battle of Britain began, Churchill and the British Admiralty decided they must deny the Germans the possibility of putting the French fleet back into the war. The British Royal

Hitler takes in the sights as he visits his most recent prize, Paris.

Navy went into action, executing Operation Catapult to deal with the bulk of the French fleet at Oran and Operation Grasp, the takeover of French naval units stationed in England and Alexandria.

Two older French battleships, the *Paris* and *Courbet*, four light cruisers, eight destroyers and some submarines, including the large *Surcouf* were berthed at Portsmouth and Plymouth. The old French battleship *Lorraine*, four cruisers and other vessels were at Alexandria, Egypt. On 3 July the British sent boarding parties to quickly seize the ships in England. The only serious opposition occurred on the *Surcouf* resulting in the death of a French sailor and a few participants wounded.

Churchill considered it a successful operation, especially since several hundred French sailors joined the Free French. At Alexandria Admiral Cunningham's negotiations with the French admiral resulted in the neutralization of his ships.

Force H, including the aircraft carrier *Ark Royal*, the battle-cruiser *Hood* and the battleships *Valiant* and *Resolution*, 2 cruisers and 11 destroyers, sailed from Gibralter for Oran under Admiral Sir James Somerville after receiving the warning order early on 1 July. Anchored at Mers-el-Kebir, near Oran, was the main French battle fleet with the battle cruiser *Strasbourg* and *Dunkerque* and the older battleships *Bretagne* and *Provence*.

Admiral Somerville dispatched a destroyer to the entrance of the French naval base to deliver the ultimatum: either French Admiral Gensoul and his men joined the British in the war effort and sailed to British ports or French ports in the West Indies for demilitarization, or they must scuttle their ships. The French were granted six hours to reply. The Germans had allowed the French to keep their fleet in African Mediterranean ports on the condition that no attempt would be made to leave the Mediterranean. Before the British arrived, Admiral Darlan authorized Gensoul to sail to the West Indies in the event of future problems. In response to the British ultimatum, Gensoul chose to stay put. According to historian John Costello, the British intercepted a message from the French government that naval reinforcements were on the way, forcing the Admiralty to order Somerville to settle the matter quickly.

When the deadline expired late in the afternoon of 3 July, it appeared the French chose to fight, so the British opened fire while aircraft from the *Ark Royal* soon engaged the French ships. By the time the action ended, the *Strasbourg* and six destroyers escaped, but the *Bretagne* had blown up, the *Provence* had run aground and the *Dunkerque* and other ships were damaged, and over 1,200 French sailors, former allies, were dead. Two days later the British carrier *Hermes* launched a strike against the battleship *Richelieu* at Dakar causing enough damage to keep her out of action. Pétain's government broke all diplomatic ties with the British after the incident on 4 July. On 5 July the French took their revenge by sending aircraft flying out of North Africa to bomb Gibraltar, a mission capable of achieving little, save to satisfy their tarnished honor.

Victorious German officers take a tour of the famous Maginot Line.

The news of the operation against the French fleet was released early on the morning of 4 July. Harold Nicholson, member of Parliament, wrote in his diary that Britain now faced the danger of finding herself at war with France and that "The House is at first saddened by this odious attack but is fortified by Winston's speech." He also commented that the speech ended in an "...ovation, with Winston sitting there with tears pouring down his cheeks."

Although it did not bubble with pride, the British public received the news with a sense of relief on 5 July in the *London Times* which announced "French Fleet Denied To Germany; British Action At Oran." The next day the same paper reported the status of the French fleet: the *Dunkerque* was reported badly damaged and ashore at Oran, while the *Strasbourg* was reported to have reached Toulon after being torpedoed. Finally,

The graves of British soldiers who fell during the blitzkrieg campaign of 1940 lie beside those who died in the War to End All Wars, World War I.

the aircraft transport *Commandant Teste* was sunk at Oran together with two torpedo boats. No mention was made of other ships damaged in these operations.

General de Gaulle, disapproving of the action, clearly stated in his speech that the French navy had been relatively helpless and that the British should consider it a tragedy, not a naval victory. He also added that:

> There could not be the slightest doubt that on principle and out of necessity the enemy would have used them either against Great Britain or against the French Empire, and I say without hesitation that it was better they should have been destroyed....

The alliance was not only over, but all ties were severed and no peaceful relationship could exist between the Vichy French government and Great Britain. The British felt no compulsion to honor France's neutral stance, and allowed de Gaulle and the Free French to begin winning over the colonies. Still, Britain stood for another year alone in her struggle.

Appendix

British Tanks of the 1940 Campaign:

Tanks	Total	Weight(Tons)	Speed	Armor	Main Gun	Crew
Vickers A-10	126	14	26 kph	30mm	40mm	4-5
Vickers A-13	30	14	48 kph	14mm	40mm	4
Infantry A-11 (Matilda)	100?	11	12 kph	10-60mm	MG	2
Infantry A-12 (Matilda)	75	26.5	24 kph	20-78mm	40mm	4
Mark VI	402	5.2	55 kph	15mm	MG	3
Carden Loyd (Bren)	1300+	1.5	45 kph	6-9mm	MG	2

+Howitzer

Belgian Tanks of the 1940 Campaign:

Tank	Total	Weight(Tons)	Speed	Armor	Main Gun	Crew
T-13(Type I)+++	228	1.5	40 kph	6-9mm	47mm	2
T-13(Type II)+++		4	40 kph	9mm	47mm	2(7)
T-15(British M1934)	42	9	64 kph	4-9mm	MG	2
R-35(French)	?	9	20 kph	30mm	37mm&20mm	2
ACG(French AMC 35)	8	14.5	40 kph	20mm	47mm(rearmed)	3

+++ Type I was British Carden Lloyd carrier with gun mounted and Type III was built by British Vickers like T-15.

Netherlands Tanks of the 1940 Campaign:

Tank	Total	Weight(tons)	Speed	Armor	Main Gun	Crew
Vickers MK II (British)	40 Ordered but not delivered	3.5	48 kph	4-10mm	MG	2
Carden Loyd Mk VI** (British)	5	1.5	45kph	6-9 kph	MG	2

**Tankettes.

German Tanks of the 1940 Campaign:

Tanks	Total	Weight(tons)	Speed	Armor	Main Gun	Crew
PzKw I	1045	5.8	40 kph	7-13mm	MG	2
PzKw II	1095	9	26 kph	10-30mm	20mm	3
PzKw III	388	20	40 kph	10-30mm	50mm	5
PzKw 38t (Czech)	410	9.7	41 kph	25-50mm	37.2mm	4
PzKw 35t (Czech)	135?	10.5	40 kph	35mm	40mm	4
PzKw IV	278	17.3	29 kph	8-20mm	75mm	5

Italian Tank of the 1940 Campaign:

L3	?	4	50 kph	5-15mm	MG	2

French Tanks of the 1940 Campaign:

Tank	Total	Weight(Tons)	Speed	Armor	Main Gun	Crew
Renault AMR 35	380	6	50 kph	13mm	MG or 25mm	2
Renault FT	534	7	7 kph	22mm	MG or 37mm	2
Renault AMC 34	180	10.8	40 kph	25mm	25mm	3
Renault R35	855	9.8	20 kph	40mm	37mm*	2
Renault R40	90	12.5	20 kph	45mm	37mm	2
Hotchkis H35	545	11.5	28 kph	34mm	37mm	2
Hotchkis H39	276	12	36 kph	40-45mm	37mm	2
FCM 36	90	12	34 kph	40mm	37mm	2
D-1	150	13	20 kph	30-37mm	47mm	3
D-2	310	20	25 kph	20-40mm	47mm	3
Somua S35	260	20	40 kph	40-55mm	47mm	3
Char B1	?	28	28 kph	40mm	75mm+ & 47mm	4
Char B1 bis	321	32	28 kph	60mm	75mm+ & 47mm* +	4
Char 2C	6	68	12 kph	45mm	75mm+	12
UE 31**	?	2.6	30 kph	9mm		2

*Low velocity 1918 model gun   + Howitzer   *+ High velocity gun.

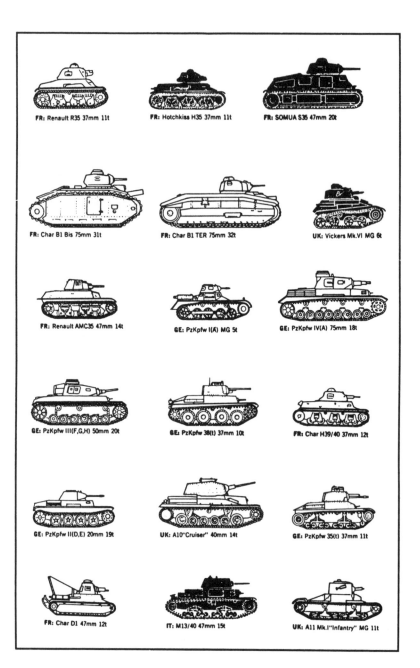

FR: Renault R35 37mm 11t

FR: Hotchkiss H35 37mm 11t

FR: SOMUA S35 47mm 20t

FR: Char B1 Bis 75mm 31t

FR: Char B1 TER 75mm 32t

UK: Vickers Mk.VI MG 6t

FR: Renault AMC35 47mm 14t

GE: PzKpfw I(A) MG 5t

GE: PzKpfw IV(A) 75mm 18t

GE: PzKpfw III(F,G,H) 50mm 20t

GE: PzKpfw 38(t) 37mm 10t

FR: Char H39/40 37mm 12t

GE: PzKpfw II(D,E) 20mm 19t

UK: A10"Cruiser" 40mm 14t

GE: PzKpfw 35(t) 37mm 11t

FR: Char D1 47mm 12t

IT: M13/40 47mm 15t

UK: A11 Mk.I"Infantry" MG 11t

Selected Aircraft of the French Air Force

Amiot 143, Bomber
* From early 1930s—obsolete by 1939.
* Phony War—used in leaflet raids.
* May 1940—approx. 60 still in use.
* Limited bombing missions over Germany.
* Unsuccessful daylight attack on bridges at Sedan.
Description: 1,984 lb. bomb load, 4 MG, speed 300 kph, and crew of 4-6.

Amiot 350 series, Bomber
* Amiot 354 and 357 moder: less than 100 delievered before May 1940.
* Used mainly in night operations.
* Most units delievered still being equipped in May.
Description: 1,760 to 2,645 lb. bomb load, 3 MG or 2 MG and one cannon, speed 450 kph, and crew of 4.

Bloch 200, Bomber
* From early 1939s—obsolete by 1939.
* Relegated to training units after war begins.
Description: 2,746 lb. bomb load, 3 MG, speed 210 kph, and crew of 4.

Bloch 210, Bomber
* Obsolete in 1939—equipped many squadrons.
* During June 1940 used in night operations against Germany.
Description: 3,527 lb. bomb load, 3 MG, speed 310 kph, and crew of 5.

Bloch 131, Recon, Bomber
* Too slow for intended mission: suffered heavy losses on recon missions.
* Restricted to night use.
* Replaced with Potez 63/11 by May 1940.
Description: 1,764 lb. bomb load, 3 MG, speed 330 kph, and crew of 4.

Bloch 151, 152 and 155, Fighter
* Early model from mid-1930s—relatively modern.
* B-151 underpowered and relegated to secondary duties.
* B-152 could sustain heavy damage—many stood idle for lack of propellers.
* B-155 not ready in time for campaign of 1940.
Description: B-151 4 MG, speed 450 kph (85 built). B-152 more powerful engine, same weapons or 2 MG and 2 cannons, speed 500 kph (614 built). B-155 6 MG, speed 550 kph.

Bloch 174 and 175, Recon, Light Bomber, Attack Bomber
* Modern aircraft—few produced by May 1940.
* B-174 used for long range recon.
Description: B-174 1,102 lb. bomb load, 7 MG, speed 500 kph. B-175 1,323 lb. bomb load, 7 MG, speed 510 kph. Both had crew of 3.

Breguet 693, Attack Bomber
* Modern aircraft—106 delivered by May 1940.
* Used in low level attacks in Belgium in May and later in the Battle of France taking heavy losses.
Description: 880 lb. bomb load, 1 cannon and 6 MG, speed 460 kph. Crew of 2.

Dewoitine 501 and 510, Fighter
* From early 1930s—becoming obsolete in 1939.
* All units withdrawn to North Africa in 1940.

Description: 1 cannon and 2 MG, speed 350 kph.

Dewoitine 520, Fighter
* Most modern French fighter—considered an equal to the Spitfire.
* In service by March 1940.
Description: 1 cannon and 4 MG, speed 530 kph

Farman 222 and 223, Heavy Bomber (4 Engine)
* Main bomber of air force from mid-1930's.
* F-222 was night bomber—used against Germany.
* F-223 entered service during war—used to bomb Berlin in June 1940.
Description: F-222 9,240 lb. bomb load, 3 MG, speed 360 kph, crew of 5.
F-223 same bomb load, 1 MG and 3 cannons, speed 400 kph, crew of 5-6.

Leo 451, Bomber
* Modern bomber—equipped many groups in 1940 (only 5 aircraft in Sept 1939 and 360 by May 1940)
* Used as attack bomber and in night bombing raids.
Description: 3,085 lb. bomb load, 2 MG and 1 cannon, speed 500 kph, crew of 4.

Morane-Saulnier 406, Fighter
* Relatively modern aircraft—no match for ME 109 and suffered heavy losses.
Description: 1 cannon and 2 MG, speed 485 kph.

Mureaux 115/117, Recon
* From early 1930s—obsolete.
* Suffered heavy losses in 1940.
* Used for recon and bombing missions.
Description: 660 lb. bomb load, 1 cannon and 2 MG, speed 330 kph, crew of 2.

Potez 631, 633, 63.11, Night Fighter, Bomber, Recon
* P-631 night fighter.
* P-633 light bomber—took heavy losses.
* P-63.11 recon and army support—equipped most observation groups by May 1940.
Description: P-631 2 cannon and 2 MG, speed 440 kph. P-633 880 lb. bomb load, 3 MG, speed 440 kph. P-63.11 660 lb. bomb load, 10 MG, speed 430 kph. Crew of 3.

Allied Aircraft from US

Curtiss Hawk 75, Fighter
* Ordered before war—equipped several groups in 1939.
* Modern aircraft—about 100 in service and more on order.
Description: 2 MG, speed 488 kph.

Martin 167 Maryland, Recon, Bomber
* Modern aircraft—only 75 arrived by June 1940.
* Suffered light losses.
Description: 1,250 lb. bomb load, 6 MG, speed 500 kph, crew of 3.

Selected Aircraft of the British Air Force

Boulton Defiant, Fighter
* Unsuccessful fighter because only guns were on rear turret.
* Used as a night fighter after Dunkirk

Description: 4 MG in turret, speed 490 kph, crew of 2.

Bristol Blenheim I, Bomber
• Medium bomber used in France.
• Description: 1,000 lb. bomb load, 2 MG, speed 459 kph, crew of 3.

Fairey Battle, Bomber
• Developed as a fast light bomber.
• Suffered heavy losses in French campaign and removed from front line service./
Description: 1,000 lb. bomb load, 2 MG, speed 414 kph, crew of 3.

Gloster Gladiator, Fighter
• Last biplane in British service.
Description: 4 MG, speed 407 kph, crew of 1.

Handley Page Hampden I, Bomber
• Developed as heavy bomber capable of defending itself.
• Proved a failure in 1940—later used for night operations.
Description: 4,000 lb. bomb load, 6 MG, speed 426 kph, crew of 4.

Hawker Hurricane, Fighter
• Main British fighter in early years of war.
Description: 8 MG, speed 511 kph, crew of 1.

Supermarine Spitfire, Fighter
• Equipped 10 squadrons at beginning of war—only recon machines sent over to France before May 1940.
• Best British fighter aircraft and superior to ME-109s.
Description: 8 MG, speed 582 kph, crew of 1.

Selected Aircraft of the German Air Force

Dornier 17, Bomber, Recon
• One type used for recon and the other was a medium bomber.
• Known as the "Flying Pencil" because of its shape.
Description: 2,205 lb. bomb load, 4-6 MG, speed 350 kph, crew of 3-5.

Heinkel 111, Bomber
• Multi purpose medium bomber.
Description: 7,165 lb. bomb load, 1 cannon and 6 MG, speed 405 kph, crew of 5.

Junkers 87, Dive Bomber
• Known as "Flying Artillery"—vulnerable to fighters.
Description: 1,102 lb. bomb load, 3 MG, speed 383 kph, crew of 2.

Junkers 88, Bomber, Recon
• Most important medium bomber of German air force.
Description: 7,935 lb. bomb load, 6 MG, speed 450 kph, crew of 4.

Messerschmitt 109, Fighter
• Most important fighter in first years of the war.
• Quantities of faster model Es arrived to replace the slower Ds before 1940 campaign began.
Description: D-1 cannon, 2 MG, E-3 cannons, 2 MG; D-speed 520 kph, E-speed 570 kph.

Messerschmitt 110, Fighter
• Twin-engined fighter—not very manueverable.
• After summer of 1940 relegated to night fighter role.
Description: 2 cannon, 5 MG, speed 525 kph, crew of 2-3.

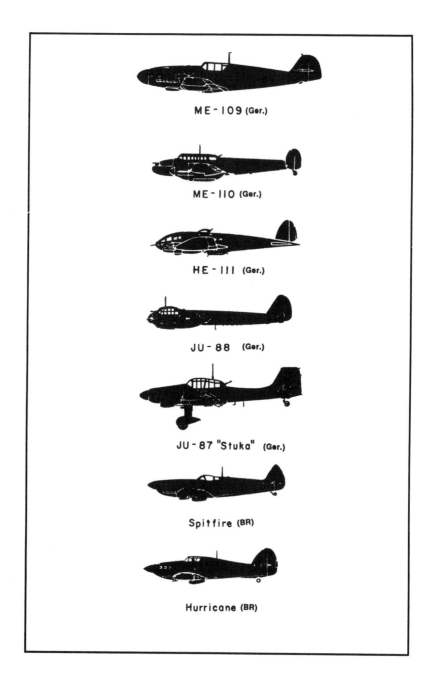

ME-109 (Ger.)

ME-110 (Ger.)

HE-111 (Ger.)

JU-88 (Ger.)

JU-87 "Stuka" (Ger.)

Spitfire (BR)

Hurricane (BR)

Appendix

Major Features of Maginot Line
Combat Units and Supporting Facilities:

1. *Gros Ouvrage* - primary combat unit and included some type of artillery weapons and garrisons from 200 to 1000 men.

Most *GOs* had:
>   Two entrance blocks
>   Several combat blocks (artillery, infantry & obsv.)
>   Subterranean galleries (approx. 30 meters deep)
>   *Caserne* (garrison area)
>   *Usine* (power plant)
>   *Metro* (underground railroad in main gallery)
>   Magazines
>   One or more emergency exits and secret escape exits

2. *Petit Ouvrage* - covered gaps which lacked *GOs* and varied in size from single monolithic block to several blocks.

Many were initially planned as *GOs*
Most *POs* had:
>   Entrance in combat block or single entrance block. Infantry weapons only (except for a few with 81mm mortar)
>   Subterranean galleries but deep only when possible
>   *Usine*
>   *Caserne*
>   Magazines

3. Smaller Works

   a. Casemates (*CORF* type only) - fill gaps between *ouvrages* and received support from them. All were self sufficient. Some were built in pairs and linked to each other.

   b. Observation Posts - provided observation for *ouvrages* from key terrain.

   c. *Abri* (shelters) - for use by interval troops. Usually located behind line of *ouvrages*. Two types: monolithic block and subterranean work with two small surface entrances.

   d. *Avant Postes* (advanced posts) - located in a forward line to give warning and delay enemy advance. In the Alps they consisted usually of several small blocks.

   e. Fortified Houses - located near border crossings to give early warning.

   f. Fortified Sub-Stations - to channel electricity from National Grid to *ouvrages*. Located in rear of main line.

4. Other Features:

  a. Each *ouvrage* was normally surrounded by barbed wire obstacles and anti-tank rails where needed. Some individual blocks also had these. Some booby traps and anti-tank mines were found in these but the French had no anti-personnel mines.

  b. Continuous line of anti-tanks rails in some regions.

  c. No *ouvrages* were linked to each other by underground galleries but some did have underground power cables.

  d. *Ouvrages* used the face of some casemate and entrance blocks for antennas for their short range radios.

  e. An extensive system of underground telephone lines between combat and support positions.

  f. Most *ouvrages* had a nearby surface *caserne* to be used in peacetime.

French Scheme of Defense

Purpose:

1. 1920s - main purpose was to delay enemy and give time for army to mobilize.

2. Mid-1930s - decision made to create an impassable obstacle to permanently prevent any type of enemy advance.

Fortified Regions:

1. Three Fortified Regions (*RFs*) planned:

  a. *RF of Haute Alsace* covering Belfort Gap never established because of expense and factors making terrain already easily defensible.

  b. *RFs of Metz* and *Lauter* covering Lux-German frontier.

2. Sarre (Saar) Gap:

  a. Separated *RFs of Metz* and *Lauter*

  b. The low terrain, with many ponds and marshes, made it difficult to build subterranean works.

  c. Intended as region through which army would launch its offensive against Germany using the two *RFs* to secure its flanks.

  d. After 1935 an attempt made to fortify the gap which previously had relied on water obstacles.

3. *Rhine Defenses*:

  a. Not truly part of *Maginot Line* and had no *ouvrages*.

  b. Two main lines of casemates with river as main barrier.

Positions:
1. Forward Line - situated along or near border.
   a. Fortified Houses covering border crossings for advance warning.
   b. Advanced Posts (*Avant Postes*), usually strung out in a line slightly behind border, used to provide early warning, block and delay enemy.
2. Main Line - about 10 to 15 km behind border and, although not dense, heavily fortified with *ouvrages* and casemates. Where possible a continuous anti-tank barrier was created with anti-tank rails.
3. Stop Line - to rear of main line and only constructed at end of 1930s but never completed and lightly defended.
4. Supporting Facilities:
   a. Special military railroads serving several *ouvrages*.
   b. Special military roads serving most *ouvrages*.
   c. Depots for supplies, munitions, engineers, etc.
   d. Fortified sub-stations transmitting power from National Grid to *ouvrages*.
   e. Military camps including small *casernes*.
   f. Old German forts from World War I era mainly around Metz and Thionville used for fire support or headquarters.

Other Fortified Sectors:
1. *Maginot Extension*:
   a. Added in mid-1930s to cover more of border with Southern Belgium.
   b. With Sarre region became part of New Fronts and *ouvrages* were of modified designs.
   c. *Ouvrages* partially supported by each other and positions not as strong as in *Maginot Line Proper*.
2. Maubeuge and vicinity:
   a. A number of casemates and five *POs* were created out of old forts.
   b. Covered area between "impassable Ardennes" and industrial region of Lille (the latter not practical to defend).
3. Alpine Regions:
   a. *Ouvrages* modified to suit needs of mountain terrain.
   b. Many *POs* never completed and had almost no combat function.
   c. *Avant Postes* larger and stronger than in NE Front.
   d. Some old forts incorporated in defenses.

e. Distance between main line and forward lines varied greatly in some places adding much depth.

f. Fortified Sectors:

1) Alps Maritime - resembled a fortified line like either *RF* of *Maginot Line Proper.*

2) Other sectors - covered major towns and passes and most heavily defended at Modane and Briançon.

OUVRAGES

Components:

1. Entrance Blocks

a. Three types

1) Munitions Entrance (*EM*) - could house trucks or rail cars for unloading.

2) Men's Entrance (*EH*)

3) Mixed Entrance - served same function as other two entrances when only one entrance used.

b. Number and Location

1) Most *GOs* had an *EM* and an *EH* in *Maginot Line Proper.* (*Hochwald* major exception with 2 *EH* and 1 *EM*).

2) In Alps more mixed entrances used.

3) Usually located about 1 km. behind combat blocks in *Maginot Line Proper.*

4) In Alps usually close to combat blocks because of terrain.

c. Characteristics of Blocks

1) Entrance way closed by heavy gate

a. In *EM* an armored door at end of entrance corridor of about 10 meters with:

- Weapons embrasure in corridor.
- rolling bridge in corridor which uncovered a deep tank trap in most *ouvrages* (except in Alps).
- on Alps a drawbridge replaced heavy gate leading into entrance corridor.

b. In *EH* an armored door at end of a small 'L' shaped corridor with weapons embrasure in corridor.

c. Mixed Entrance same characteristics as other two except in Alps a few had entrance for aerial cable.

2) Defense and Observation

a. Embrasures which mounted some or all of the following:

- 37mm or 47mm AT gun.
- *JM* (twin machine guns).

- *FM* (automatic rifle).
  b. One or more *cloches* (non-movable steel turrets)
  c. *Fosse* (ditch or moat) in front of crenels and entrance:
    - prevented accumulation of debris from fragmenting concrete blocking firing crenels and entrance.
    - contained grenade launcher which dropped grenades into it to keep attackers away from crenels.
    - *EM* used concrete bridge to cross it and *EH* used small removable metal bridge (in Alps drawbridge on truck entrance)
  d. Inside the entrances where trucks or rail cars could be unloaded were:
    - interior blockhouses.
    - an armored door at end of block led into subterranean gallery
3) Most were of two levels.
4) Types of access to subterranean galleries of *ouvrage*.
  a. Level - possible when block could be placed in side of hill (considered ideal for *EM* or Mixed Entrances).
  b. Lifts - used when galleries too deep to reach by other means (considered ideal for *EH*).
  c. Inclined - used for same reason as lift but galleries not too far below. Also required special transport cars (not used in *EH's*).

2. Combat Blocks
  a. Four types
    1) Artillery - mounted any of the following:
      a. 75mm guns or mortars (latter in Alps).
      b. 135mm *Lance Bombe* (similar to howitzer).
      c. 81mm mortar (breech loaded).
      d. 95mm naval guns (*ouvrage* of *Janus* only).
    2) Infantry - mounted any of the following:
      a. 37mm or 47mm AT gun.
      b. 25mm cannon.
      c. 50mm mortar (breech loaded).
      d. *JM* (heavy twin machine guns).
      e. *FM* (automatic rifle).
    3) Observation - equipped with any of the following:
      a. Observation crenel in casemate.
      b. Observation *cloches*.
      c. *GFM cloches*.
    4) Combination of the above types.
  b. 3 designs:

1) Casemate

2) Turret (also *cloches* only included).

3) Combination of above two types.

   c. Description of various blocks:

      1) Artillery Casemate - embrasures for artillery weapons usually in the following combinations:

         a. 3 x 75mm guns or

         b. 1 x 135mm *Lance Bombe* or

         c. 2 x 81mm mortars (found in lower level of block).

         d. In Alps mixtures of these weapons more common.

      2) Artillery Turret - no more than one turret and it mounted one of the following:

         a. 2 x 75mm guns or

         b. 2 x 135mm *Lance Bombe* or

         c. 2 x 81mm mortars.

      3) Infantry Casemate - usually mounted:

         a. 37mm or 47mm AT gun.

         b. *JMs*.

         c. *FMs*.

      4) Infantry Turret - no more than one turret mounting either:

         a. *JM* (planned to add a 25mm gun) or

         b. 2 x 25mm guns and each with a set of JM.

         c. 25mm gun and JM with 50mm mortar.

      5) Observation Block - included observation cloches.

      6) Combination - any mixture of the above.

   d. Characteristics

      1) Two levels with firing positions normally on upper level. Some exceptions with one level or more than two levels.

      2) Fosse used like in entrance blocks:

         a. Some included an exit on upper or lower level of block. @LISTF = b. When mortars used they were in lower level and fired out of the fosse.

      3) Few turret blocks had exits.

      4) Most blocks had one or more *cloches*.

      5) Each block had air vents leading to filter system:

         a. Casemates had them on exposed wall covered by large armor plate.

         b. Turret blocks had one or more small armored air vents.

3. *Caserne, Usine,* and other subterranean facilities:

   a. *Caserne*

      1) Usually located near entrance blocks.

      2) Normally 30 meters below the surface - in some *POs*

special metal sheeting had to be used to prevent
fragmenting of ceiling since it was not possible to place
these facilities deep enough into the ground.

   3) Included:

      a. Triple bunks in large chambers for the men.

      b. Double and single bunks in smaller, but Spartan like
chambers for officers and NCOs.

      c. Medical facilities (*GOs*) - size varied from small with
operating room to large with dental offices based on
size of garrison.

      d. Kitchen - no mess hall - soldiers ate off of folding
tables along corridors or food was brought up to the
blocks.

      e. Storage - for food & wine and other supplies.

 b. Well and water storage tanks - one or more wells in each
fort.

 c. *Usine* (power plant):

   1) Diesel engines for producing power(the capacity of each
depended on the size of the *ouvrage*):

      a. Four in most *GOs* (two for normal operations).

      b. Three in most Alpine *GOs*.

      c. Two in most *POs*.

      d. In the Alps some *POs* did not have any or only one
installed.

   2) Transformers for using current from the National Grid in
most *GOs*.

   3) Sub-stations in *GOs* to receive, convert and redistribute
current sent from *usine*.

   4) Fuel storage facilities - approx. two month supply.

 d. *Metro* - underground railroad in *GOs* used except when
distance from entrances to combat blocks not great.

 e. Interior blockhouses for small arms, armored doors, air
tight armored doors, and emergency demolition points.

 g. Defenses against poison gas:

   1) Decontamination facilities.

   2) Air filters in all blocks and *caserne*.

   3) Maintenance of a higher internal air pressure to keep gas
out.

 h. Magazines - *GOs*

   1) *M-1* - main magazine found in many *GOs* and located
near *EM*.

2) *M-2* - large magazines, but not even 1/2 the size of the *M-1*, located near combat blocks.

3) *M-3* - not a subterranean facility - these were the magazines located in the artillery blocks.

i. Command Post - usually located near the combat blocks.

j. Main gallery - *GOs*

1) Led from entrance block to combat blocks.

2) Small access galleries branch off from it in combat block and rear areas.

a. Air tight doors used in these smaller galleries.

b. Included *M-2*, equipment for lifts, storage for expended shell casings for artillery blocks above .

Armor, Armament and Equipment

1. Communications

a. Telephone primary source:

1) Underground telephone lines linked all the *ouvrages* and most interval positions with higher HQ.

2) Telephone lines linked blocks of *ouvrages*.

b. Radio *(TSF)*:

1) Short ranged and of limited value.

2) Usually found in casemate blocks with antenna strung over face of block.

c. Order transmitter:

1) Similar to those on ships.

2) Used for sending firing commands from command post of *ouvrage* to blocks and from block commander to gun positions.

d. Signal equipment - used in some *ouvrages* in Alps where line of sight possible.

2. Armor

a. Reinforced concrete was the main form of protection.

1) Four thicknesses used (Protection #1, #2, #3 & #4):

a. Maximum of 3.5 meters would resist 420mm caliber weapons and used on sections of blocks facing enemy and roof in *GOs*. - Protection #4.

b. #3 type protection was the most used on *POs* and could resist 300mm caliber weapons.

c. #1 type of protection, 1.7 meters, used on rearward facing casemates and could only resist light artillery to make recapture of position easier.

2) Earth and rock work gave extra protection to roofs and walls without casemate positions.

b. *Cloches* (bell shaped non-movable turrets).

1) They were the most recognizable feature of a *Maginot* fort.

2) Made of special steel and varying in thickness from 200mm to 300mm and much of it sunk into ground and concrete roof of block.

3) The number and position of the crenels depended on the terrain.

4) Most blocks had one or more.

5) Crenel equipped with armored covers and all weapons mounted in special armored plates that kept crenel sealed.

6) Linked to block below by ladder and movable floor.

7) Voice tubes normally used to communicate with block.

8) Types:

    a. *GFM* (Observation and *FM* - automatic rifle).

    i. mounted *FM* and 50mm breech loading mortar.

    ii. some included small roof periscope.

    iii. came in different styles.

    iv. special episcopes and binoculars.

    b. *JM* (twin machine-gun):

    i. had two small openings for observation adjacent to *JM* crenel.

    ii. exposed a lower profile than *GFM* on surface.

    c. Mixed Arms

    i. had two weapons crenels covering 45° each.

    ii. mounted a single 25mm gun with a *JM* - only one firing embrasure used at a time.

    d. Observation

    i. small observations slits and usually a periscope or

    ii. large periscope with *cloche* almost flush with the surface.

    e. *Lance Grenade*

    i. mounted a 60mm mortar which was to shower area around the block with bombs.

    ii. the weapons system was never perfected.

c. Turrets (all eclipsable)

1) The steel roofs and walls were 300mm thick in most types.

2) The turret column was protected by large plates of

frontal armor which surrounded it projecting outward like a skirt.

  3) Types turrets:

    a. 75mm Gun Turret (two basic types not including one refurbished from older fortifications) two 75mm guns and position for direct observation in one type.

    b. 135mm *Lance Bombe* Turret - two 135mm *lance bombes* and no position for observation of any type.

    c. 81mm Mortar Turret - two 81mm mortars in fixed positions and no position for observation of any type

    d. MG Turret - two machine guns with observation position and plans to add a 25mm gun later.

    e. Mixed Arms Turret - two types:

      i. MG and 25mm gun and observation position with 50mm mortar fired through roof.

      ii. Two pairs of *JM* and each with a 25mm gun and a single observation position between them.

3. Weapons

  a. Turret weapons (artillery):

    1) 75mm gun-howitzer - two basic types (with one exception):

      a. 1932 model - range of 9,500 meters.

      b. 1933 model - range of 12,000 meters and 30 rounds a minute.

    2) 135mm *lance bombe* - 1932 model - range of 8,200 meters and 8 rounds a minute.

    3) 81mm mortar - 1932 model

      a. Breech loaded.

      b. Range of 3,500 meters and 15 rounds a minute.

  b. Casemate weapons (artillery):

    1) 75mm gun-howitzer -

      a. 1929 model - range of 12,000 meters and 30 rounds a minute.

      b. 1932 model - range of 12,000 meters and 12 to 24 rounds a minute.

      c. 1932 R model - range of 9,500 meters.

      d. 1933 model - range of 12,000 meters and 12 to 24 rounds a minute.

    2) 135mm *lance bombe* - same as turret weapon.

    3) 81mm mortar - same as turret weapon.

    4) 75mm mortar (Alps only) - 1931 model range of 6,000 meters.

c. Infantry weapons:
    1) Anti-tank guns:
        a. 47mm 1934 model - replaced 37mm weapon.
        b. 37mm 1934 model.
        c. 25mm 1934 model - mainly an anti-personnel weapon.
    2) 50mm mortar 1935 model.
        a. Breech loaded.
        b. Range of 800 meters and 12 to 18 rounds per minute.
    3) Machine guns:
        a. *Jumelages de Mitrailleuses Reibel* (JM - twin MGs).
            i. 7.5mm and fired maximum of 750 rounds a minute.
            ii. Effective range 1,500 meters.
        b. *Fusils Mitraileurs* FM or automatic rifle Model 1924/29.
            i. 7.5mm and fired maximum of 500 rounds a minute.
            ii. Effective range 600 meters.

4. Crews of Turret blocks:

  a. 75mm gun turret.
    1) Turret crew of 4 (gunner, 2 loaders and chief).
    2) Upper level of block 6 men (2 on monte-charge, 2 on ammo, 1 on controls and chief).
    3) Lower level of block 2 men on controls.
  b. 135mm *lance bombe* turret.
    1) Turret crew of 2 loaders.
    2) Upper level of block 9 men (2 on monte-charge, 2 powder men, 2 on fuses and charges, and chief).
    3) Lower level of block 4 men on controls.
  c. 81mm mortar turret.
    1) Turret crew of 2 loaders.
    2) Upper level of block 5 men (2 on monte-charge and ammo, 2 on controls and chief).
    3) Lower level of block 3 men on controls.
  d. Mixed Arms turret (2 sets of JM and 2 x 25mm guns).
    1) Turret crew of 6 (1 gunner, 4 loaders and chief).
    2) Upper level of block 5 men (2 on monte-charge, 1 ammo, 2 on controls and chief).
    3) Lower level of block 6 men on controls.
  e. MG turret.
    1) Turret crew of 2 (gunner and chief).
    2) Upper level of block 3 men (1 ammo, 2 on controls).
    3) Lower level of block 2 men on controls.

Glossary

AA: anti-aicraft or Flak.

AAA: anti-aircraft artillery

abris: shelter. This was usually an infantry position which could be used for shelter or a headquarters.

Abwehr: German Military Intelligence

alpin: French mountain troops.

alpini: Italian mountain troops.

Armée de l'Air: French Air Force

armes mixtes: mixed arms. Refers to a combination of weapons which were usually a 25 mm gun and machine guns.

AT: anti-tank.

avant postes - advanced posts: These were positions which might consist of one or several block houses and obstacles layed out in front of the Maginot Line. They did not form a continuous line.

blitzkrieg: lightning war.

casemate: a position which includes one or more firing chambers for weapons.

caserne: barracks. The garrison area. It should be noted that there were also normal surface garrison areas that were part of the Maginot Line as well as those that were part of the underground works of a fort.

char: French tank.

chausser: light, fast, specialized infantry and cavalry units of the French and Belgian armies.

chicane: a defensive feature which denies direct access. Usually it was two or more walls covering an entrance or inside a gallery to form a maze. This was also a standard method for block roads:

_____ _____   or   _____
_____   _____

cloche: a bell shaped feature. This was a non-moveable or fixed turret type of position used in the fortifications. The steel dome's armor extended a below the level of the surface.

CORF - Commission d'Organisation des Régions Fortifiés: This commission was created in the late 1920s to set up the fortified areas and prepare the plans and designs.

DCR: French Heavy Armored Division, although designated as reserve.

DLC: French Mechanized Cavalry Division.

DLM: French Light Mechanized Division.

Entrée des Hommes (EH): The entrance for troops or the mens entrance.

Entrée Mixte: single entrance of a fort for which had to be used for both troops and munitions.

Entrée des Munitions (EM): the entrance for munitions. This was the larger type entrance and designed to take trucks or small rail cars.

feste: fortress. Term usually referring to German type of fortifications built between 1870 and World War I.

flak: anti-aircraft.

fosse: ditch, trench or moat. Term used to describe the trench running along casemate walls of individual ouvrages and the anti-tank ditches built or planned to partial defend or completely surround ouvrages.

Fusil Mitrailleur (FM): an automatic rifle or light machine gun. In the Maginot Line the 7.5mm FM 24/29 was the weapon used.

Génie: French army engineers.

Guet Fusil Mitrailleur (GFM): observation and light machine gun.

Jumelages de Mitrailleuses (JM): twin machine guns. It consisted of two FM MAC 31 which was a modification of the FM 24/29. This weapons had a greater range and rate of fire than the FM 24/29.

Lance Bombe: a bomb thrower. This is a weapon that lies falls between a mortar and a howitzer. The Maginot forts used a 135 mm weapon but it did not have the range or effectiveness against hard targets that the 75 mm gun had.

Lehr: refers to a German training or demonstration unit.

Luftflotten: German Air Fleet.

Luftwaffe: German Air Force.

M-1, M-2, M-3: The three types of magazines used for artillery munitions in an ouvrage. The M-1 was the largest and main collecting point but not found in all forts. The M-2 was located in the subterranean gallery below artillery blocks. The M-3 was the smaller magazine situated in the artillery block.

monte charge: Lift or elevator for materiel. In the forts this was the small lift in the combat blocks which was used to send up ammunition. It is also the term use for the large elevators but in an ouvrage these were used for carrying large loads and not normally men.

OKH: German Army High Command.

OKW: German Armed Forces High Command.

ouvrage: works. Refers in text to a type of fortified work or more commonly a fort.

panzer: armor, tank.

Panzergruppe: An armored grouping of panzer divisions which was larger than a corps and smaller than an army.

pioneer: term for German army engineers.

Région Fortifiée (RF): Fortified Region. These were the large areas that were fortified as part of the Maginot Line and they were subdivided into several Secteur Fortifiée (SF) or Fortified Sectors.

sapper: term for British and French army engineers.

Sitzkrieg: the sitting war or what the Allies called the Phony War.

Spahi: Algerian cavalry created by the French in 1834 from native forces.

Stuka: Sturzkampf or dive bomber.

usine: works. Refers to the power plant of a fort in text.

Code Names

AERIAL: British operation to remove their troops and allies from the Channel and Atlantic coasts of France in June 1940.

AUGSBURG: German code name for offensive in the West in 1939.

AVONMOUTH: British Code name for initial plan to occupy Narvik in 1940.

BAR (BEAR): Early plan for an Italian army to join the Germans in attacking Alsace.A second plan in June 1940 for Army Group C's 7th Army to cross the Rhine and attack Alsace.

BLAU (BLUE): *Luftwaffe* plan for operations against Great Britain during the proposed Czech Campaign of 1938.

CATAPULT: British plan to attack or neutralize French Navy in North Africa in July 1940.

CATHERINE: British naval plan to interdict iron ore shipments from Sweden in April 1940. Canceled because of German air superiority.

DYNAMO: British operation to evacuate British and allied troops from Dunkirk at the end of May 1940.

GELB (YELLOW): New name, replacing AUGSBURG, for German offensive in the West.

GRASP: British operation to seize French ships in British ports in July 1940.

GRUN (GREEN): German plan for the conquest of Czechoslovakia in 1938.

JUNO: German naval raid by *Scharnhorst, Gneisenau* and *Hipper* off Norwegian coast in early June 1940.

MAURICE: Allied plan to land at Andalsnes to outflank Trondheim in April 1940.

NICKEL: British bombing of Germany with leaflets during Phony War.

NORDMARK: Unsuccessful raid against Allied shipping between British Isles and Norway by *Scharnhorst, Gneisenau* and *Hipper*.

ORANGE: Dutch plan to linke their front with that of the Belgians, but the latter would not cooperate making it impossible to form a continuous line of defenses along the German frontier.

OTTO: German plan for occupation of Austria in 1938.

PAULA: German air offensive to destroy French Armée de l'Air on 3 July 1940.

R-4: British plan to seize key Norwegian west coast ports if Germans should react to mining operations.

ROT (RED): German plan to attack France if that country became involved in a war with Czechoslovakia.

German plan for final Battle of France beginning on 5 June 1940.

ROYAL MARINE - British plan to use aerial mining against German waterways such as the Rhine.

RUPERT: Allied plan recapture Narvik.

SEELOWE (SEALION): German invasion plan for Great Britain.

STRATFORD: British plan to land five battalions of 49th Division

in Southern Norway and to hold for reinforcements of several
divisions to operate against Sweden. Canceled in late February.

TANNENBAUM: German plan for invasion of Switzerland in
1940.

TIGER: Plan for German Army Group C's 1st Army to
breakthrough the Maginot Line in June 1940.

UTOPIA: Plan for British forces to occupy Andalsnes and
outflank Germans at Trondheim. Name changed to MAURICE.

WEISS (WHITE): German plan for the invasion of Poland.

WESERUEBURG NORTH: German plan for conquest of Norway.

WESERUEBURG SOUTH: German plan for conquest of Denmark.

WILFRED: British plan to mine Norwegian waters to stop iron
ore shipments to Germany.

Z: The final Polish plan for a war with Germany. They intended
to hold their frontier and withdraw fighting a war of
manuever during he first two weeks, while awaiting the
Allied offensive in the West.

Abbreviations for Aircraft

French Aircraft:

Reconnaissance

A-351 Amiot 351 +
B-131 Bloch 131
B-174 Bloch 174 *
P-39Potez 39 +
P-540 Potez 540 +
P-637 Potez 637 *
P-63.11 Potez 63-11*

Observation

B-27Breguet 27 +
L-C-30 or C-40 LeO C-30 or C-40 (autogyros) +
M-115 Mureaux 115 +
M-117 Mureaux 117 +
P-25Potez 25 +
P-39Potez 39 +
P-540 Potez 540 +

Fighter

B-151 or 152 Bloch 151-152 **
Curtis H-75 (American)
D-510 Dewoitine 510 +
D-520 Dewoitine 520 *

M-406 Morane-Saulnier 406
P-631 Potez 631 (multi-seat night fighter)
P-671 Potez 671 (multi-seat)*
(Other obsolete types used in rear support echelons and North
  Africa including: Dewoitine 501, Nieuport 62, Spad 510).

Bomber

A-143 Amoit 143 +
B-175 Bloch 175 +
B-200 Bloch 200 +
B-210 Bloch 210
B-691 or 693 Breguet 691/693 *
F-222 Farman 222 +
L-45LeO 45 *
M-115 Mureaux 115 +
M-167 Glen Martin 167 (American) *
P-633 Potez 633

+ Obsolete aircraft

* Most modern and advanced aircraft

German Aircraft:

Reconnaissance

Do 17 Dornier Do 17
Do 215 Dornier Do 215 * (assigned to OKL)
He 126 Henschel Hs 126 +

Fighter

Me 109 Messerchmitt Bf 109 *
Me 110 Messerchmitt Bf 110 *

Bomber

He 111 Heinkel He 111 *
Ju 88 Junkers Ju 88 *

Dive Bomber and Ground Support

He 123 Henschel Hs. 123 +
Ju 87 Junkers Ju 87

Transport

Ju 52 Junkers Ju 52/3

Seaplane

Do 18 Dornier Do 18 +
BV 138 Blohm & Voss Bv 138 *
He 115 Heinkel He 115 *

Orders of Battle

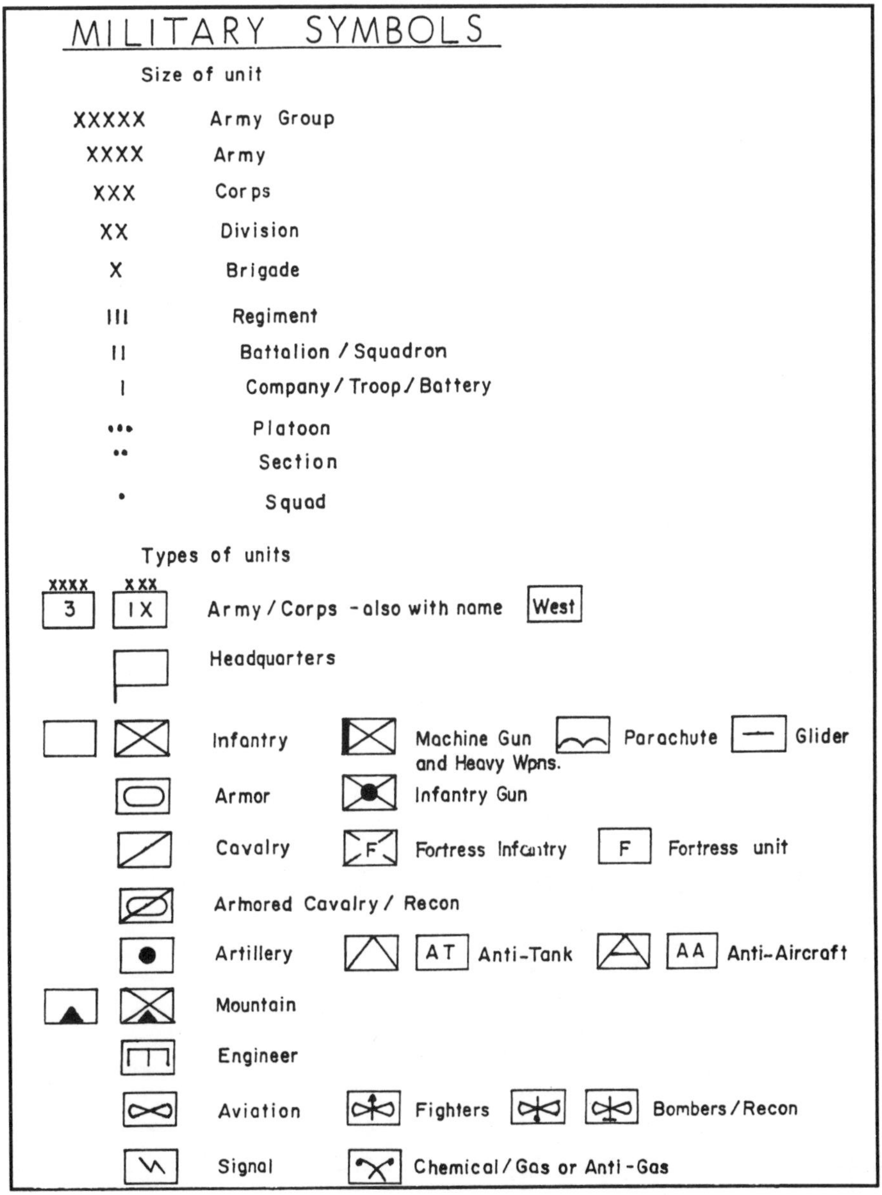
MILITARY SYMBOLS
Size of unit
XXXXX Army Group
XXXX Army
XXX Corps
XX Division
X Brigade
III Regiment
II Battalion / Squadron
I Company / Troop / Battery
••• Platoon
•• Section
• Squad
Types of units
XXXX
3
XXX
IX
Army / Corps - also with name
West
Headquarters
Infantry
Machine Gun and Heavy Wpns.
Parachute
Glider
Armor
Infantry Gun
Cavalry
F
Fortress Infantry
F
Fortress unit
Armored Cavalry / Recon
Artillery
AT
Anti-Tank
AA
Anti-Aircraft
Mountain
Engineer
Aviation
Fighters
Bombers / Recon
Signal
Chemical / Gas or Anti-Gas

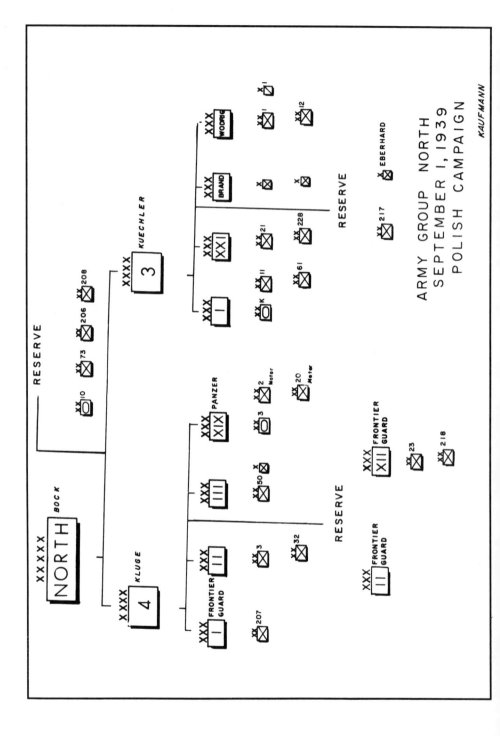

ARMY GROUP NORTH
SEPTEMBER 1, 1939
POLISH CAMPAIGN

KAUFMANN

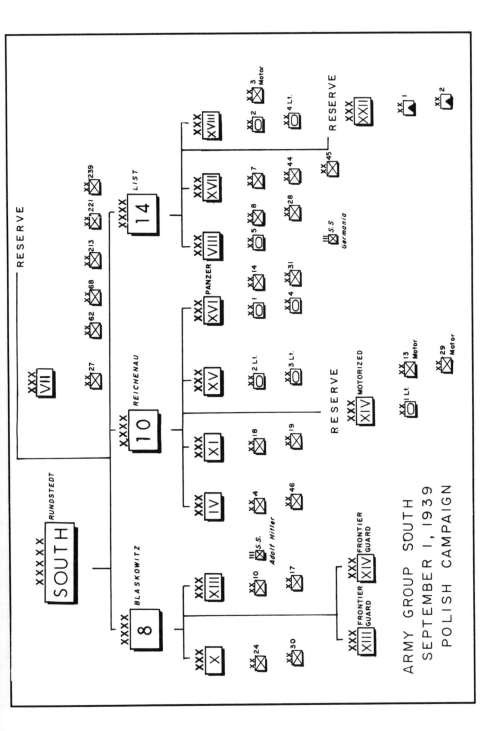

ARMY GROUP SOUTH
SEPTEMBER 1, 1939
POLISH CAMPAIGN

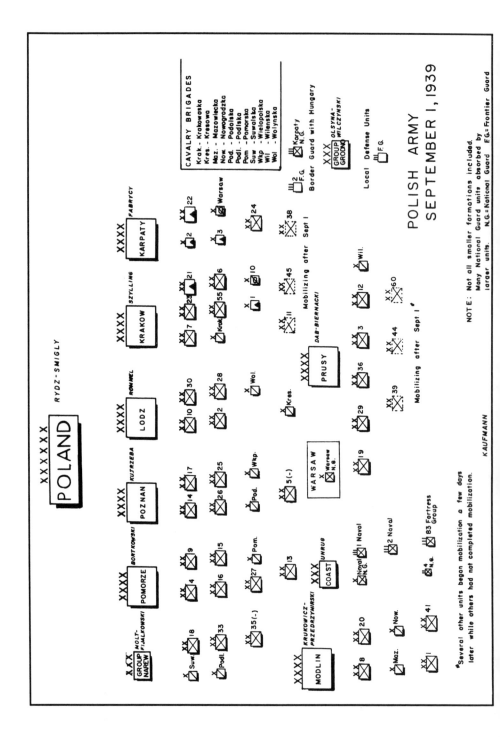

POLISH ARMY
SEPTEMBER 1, 1939

KAUFMANN

NOTE: Not all smaller formations included.
Many National Guard units absorbed by
larger units.   N.G.=National Guard   F.G.=Frontier Guard

*Several other units began mobilization a few days
later while others had not completed mobilization.

Orders of Battle

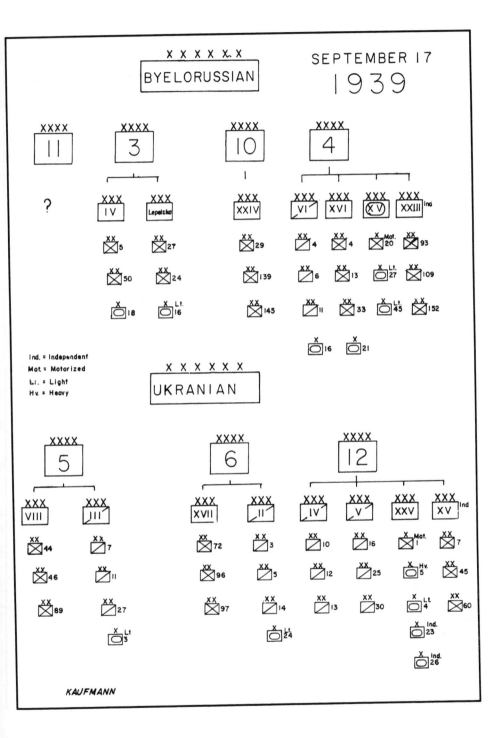

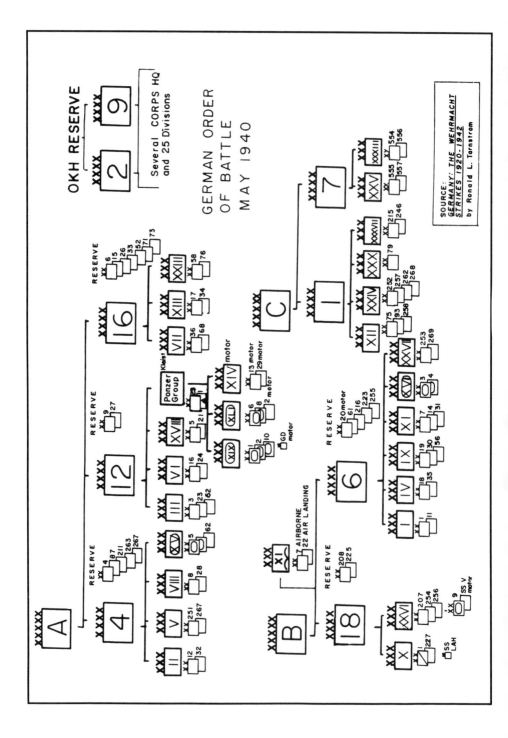

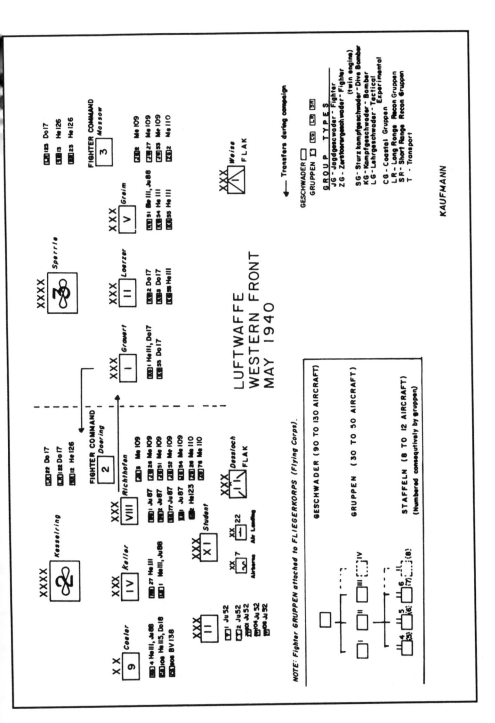

LUFTWAFFE
WESTERN FRONT
MAY 1940

KAUFMANN

NOTE: Fighter GRUPPEN attached to FLIEGERKORPS (Flying Corps).

GESCHWADER (90 TO 130 AIRCRAFT)

GRUPPEN (30 TO 50 AIRCRAFT)

STAFFELN (8 TO 12 AIRCRAFT)
(Numbered consecutively by gruppen)

→ Transfers during campaign

GROUP TYPES

GESCHWADER ☐
GRUPPEN ☐

JG - Jagdgeschwader - Fighter
ZG - Zerstoerergeschwader - Fighter
        (twin engine)

SG - Sturzkampfgeschwader - Dive Bomber
KG - Kampfgeschwader - Bomber
LG - Lehrgeschwader - Tactical
        Experimental

CG - Coastal Gruppen
LR - Long Range   Recon Gruppen
SR - Short Range Recon Gruppen
T - Transport

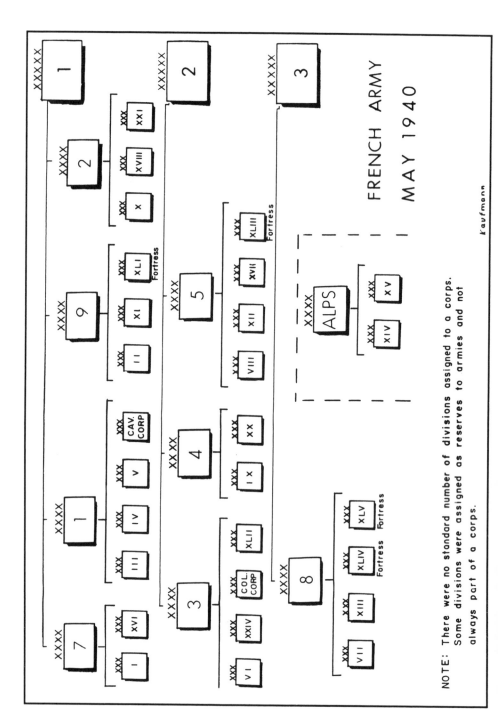

FRENCH ARMY
MAY 1940

Kaufmann

NOTE: There were no standard number of divisions assigned to a corps.
Some divisions were assigned as reserves to armies and not
always part of a corps.

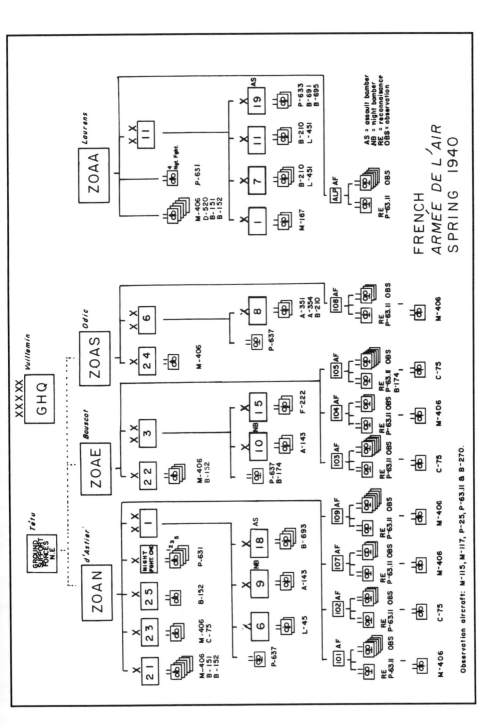

FRENCH
ARMÉE DE L'AIR
SPRING 1940

AS = assault bomber
NB = night bomber
RE = reconnaissance
OBS = observation

Observation aircraft: M-115, M-117, P-25, P-63.11 & B-270.

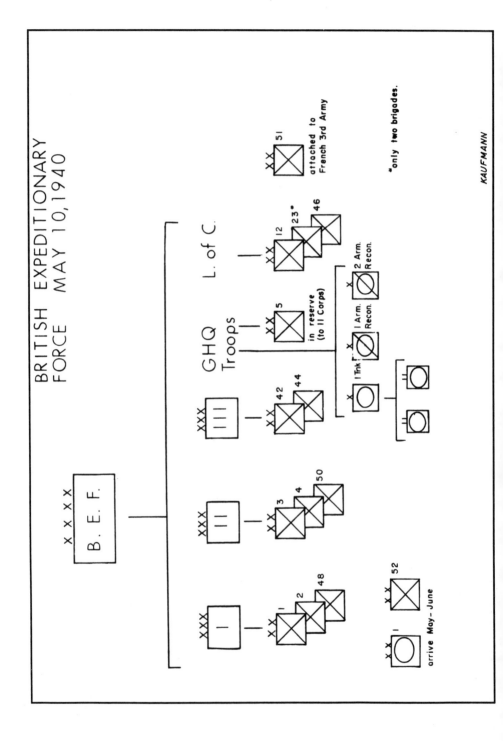

BRITISH EXPEDITIONARY
FORCE   MAY 10, 1940

B. E. F.

GHQ
Troops

L. of C.

51   attached to
French 3rd Army

*only two brigades.

12   23*   46

5   in reserve
(to II Corps)

2 Arm.
Recon.

1 Arm.
Recon.

1 Tnk.

42   44

3   4   50

1   2   48

52   arrive May-June

1

KAUFMANN

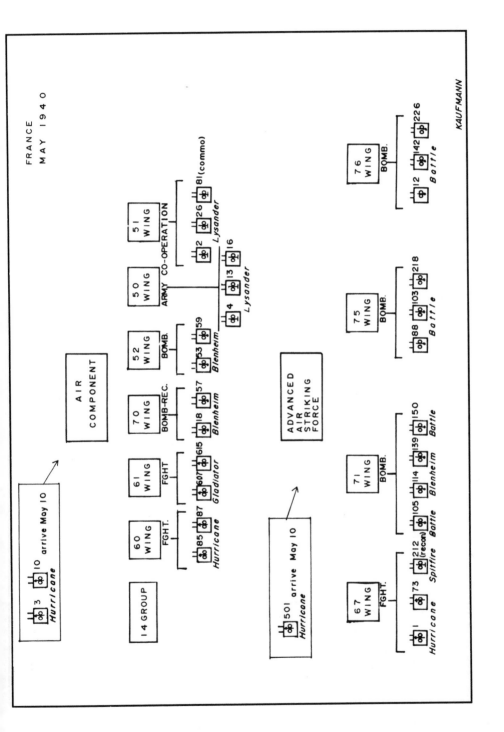

FRANCE
MAY 1940

KAUFMANN

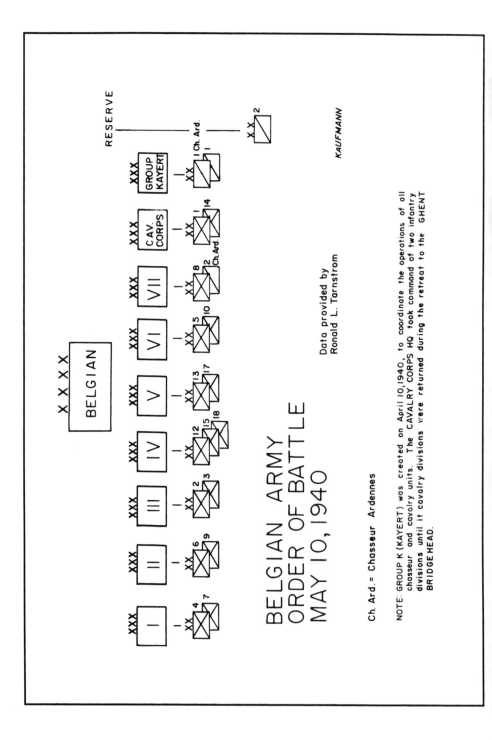

BELGIAN ARMY
ORDER OF BATTLE
MAY 10, 1940

Ch. Ard. = Chasseur Ardennes

Data provided by
Ronald L. Tarnstrom

NOTE: GROUP K (KAYERT) was created on April 10, 1940, to coordinate the operations of all chasseur and cavalry units. The CAVALRY CORPS HQ took command of two infantry divisions until it cavalry divisions were returned during the retreat to the GHENT BRIDGEHEAD.

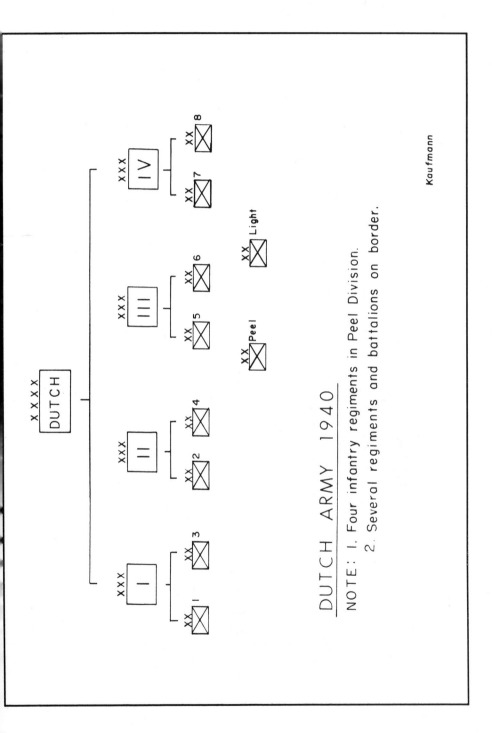

DUTCH ARMY 1940

NOTE: 1. Four infantry regiments in Peel Division.
2. Several regiments and battalions on border.

Kaufmann

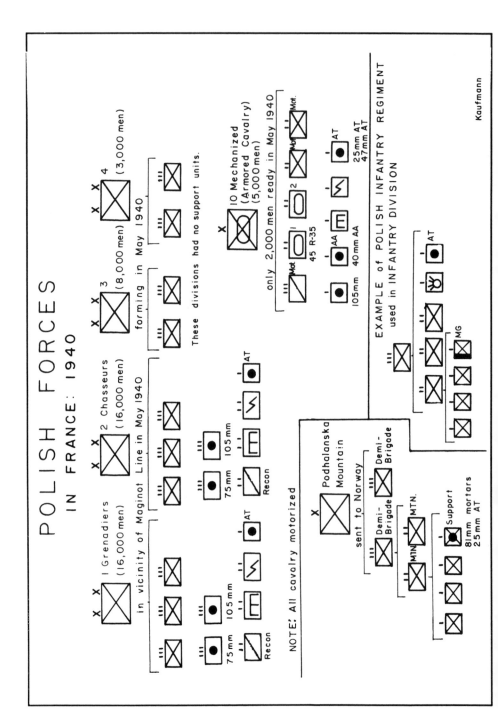

POLISH FORCES
IN FRANCE: 1940

1 Grenadiers (16,000 men)
in vicinity of Maginot Line in May 1940

2 Chasseurs (16,000 men)

3 (8,000 men)

4 (3,000 men)

forming in May 1940

These divisions had no support units.

75mm   105mm   Recon   AT

75mm   105mm   Recon   AT

NOTE: All cavalry motorized

10 Mechanized (Armored Cavalry) (5,000 men)

only 2,000 men ready in May 1940

Mot.   Mot.   Mot.   Mot.
45 R-35
AA   AA
105mm   40mm AA   25mm AT   47mm AT

Podhalanska Mountain
sent to Norway

Demi-Brigade   Demi-Brigade

MTN.   MTN.

Support
81mm mortars
25mm AT

EXAMPLE of POLISH INFANTRY REGIMENT
used in INFANTRY DIVISION

AT
MG

Kaufmann

354

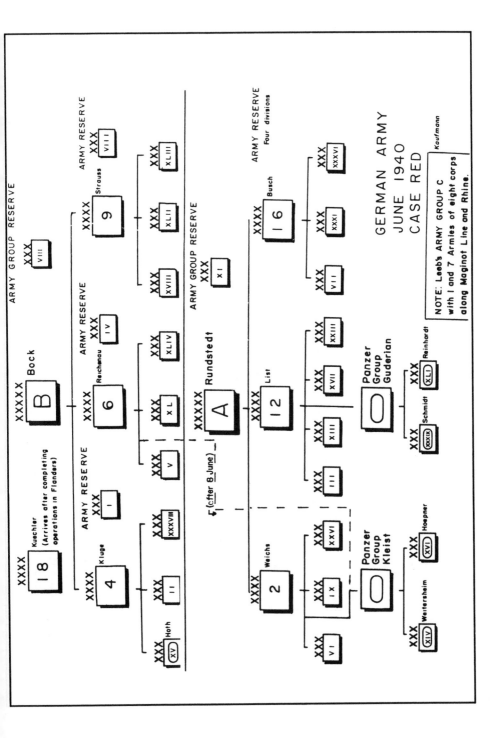

GERMAN ARMY
JUNE 1940
CASE RED

NOTE: Leeb's ARMY GROUP C with I and 7 Armies of eight corps along Maginot Line and Rhine.

Kaufmann

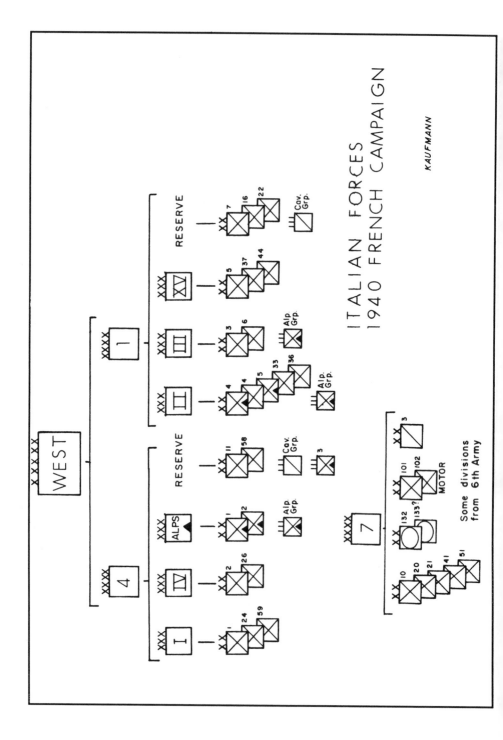

ITALIAN FORCES
1940 FRENCH CAMPAIGN

KAUFMANN

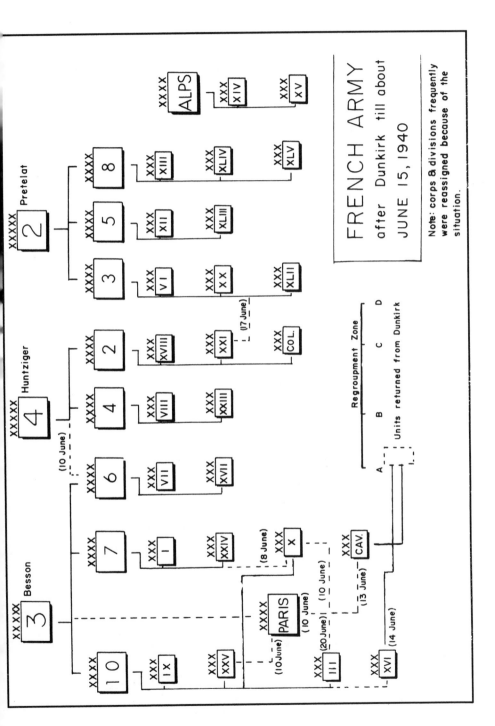

FRENCH ARMY
after Dunkirk till about
JUNE 15, 1940

Note: corps & divisions frequently were reassigned because of the situation.

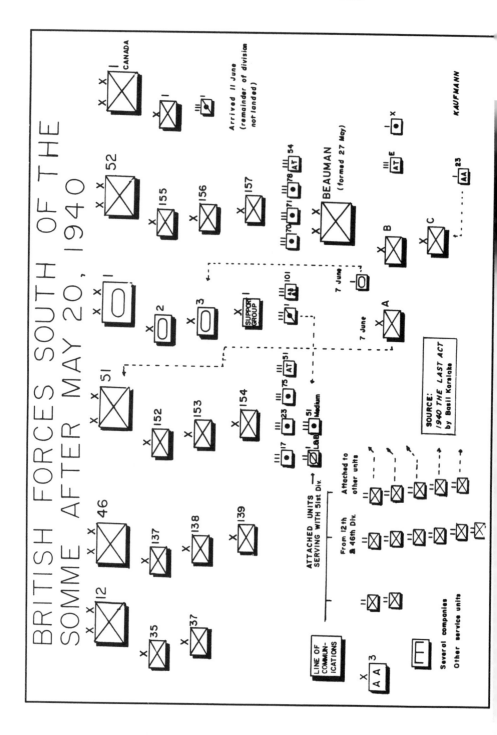

BRITISH FORCES SOUTH OF THE SOMME AFTER MAY 20, 1940

KAUFMANN

SOURCE:
1940 THE LAST ACT
by Basil Karslake

Unit Organizations

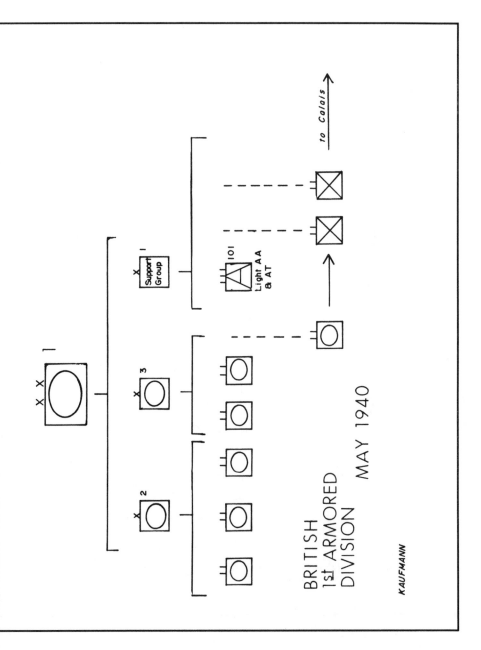

BRITISH
1st ARMORED
DIVISION   MAY 1940

KAUFMANN

to Calais

X
Support
Group

101
Light AA
& AT

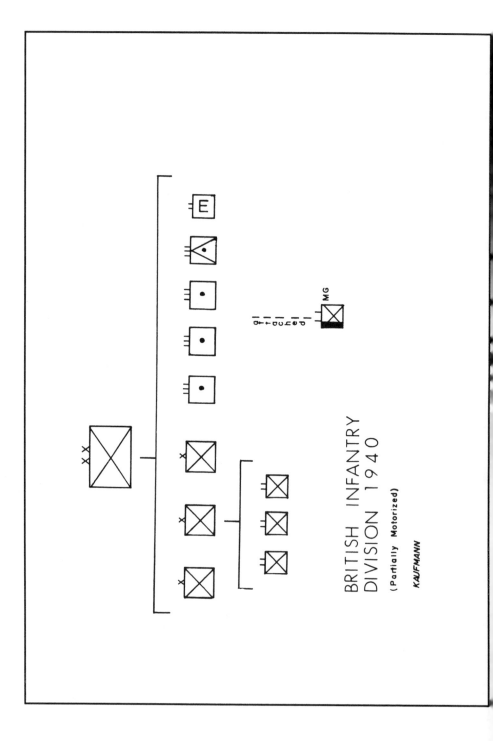

BRITISH INFANTRY
DIVISION 1940
(Partially Motorized)

KAUFMANN

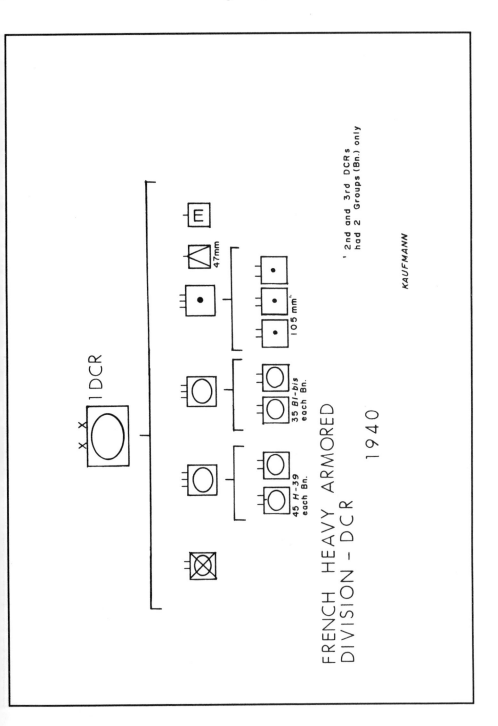

FRENCH HEAVY ARMORED
DIVISION – DCR

1940

1 DCR

45 H-39 each Bn.

35 B1-bis each Bn.

47mm

105 mm"

" 2nd and 3rd DCRs had 2 Groups (Bn.) only

KAUFMANN

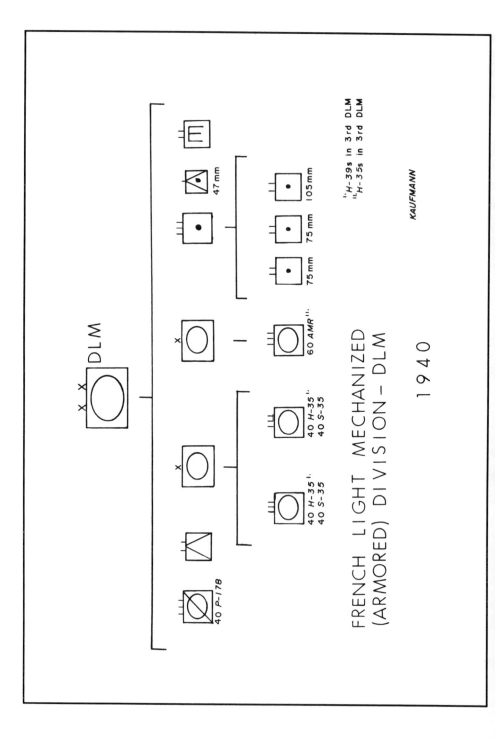

FRENCH LIGHT MECHANIZED
(ARMORED) DIVISION – DLM

1940

KAUFMANN

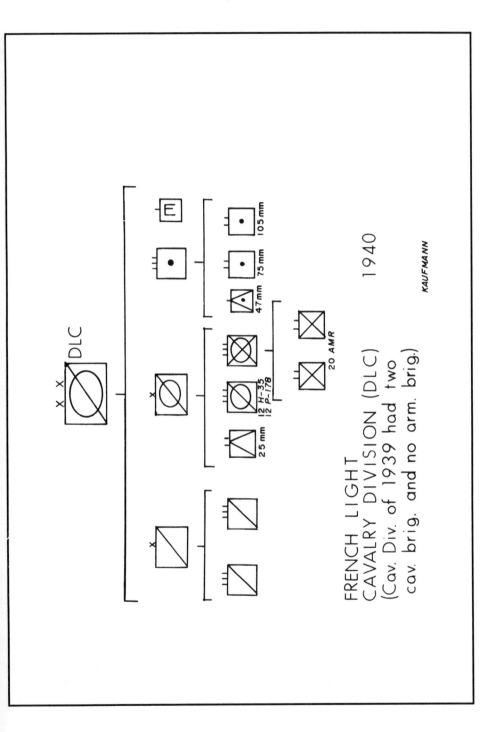

FRENCH LIGHT
CAVALRY DIVISION (DLC)
(Cav. Div. of 1939 had two
cav. brig. and no arm. brig.)

1940

KAUFMANN

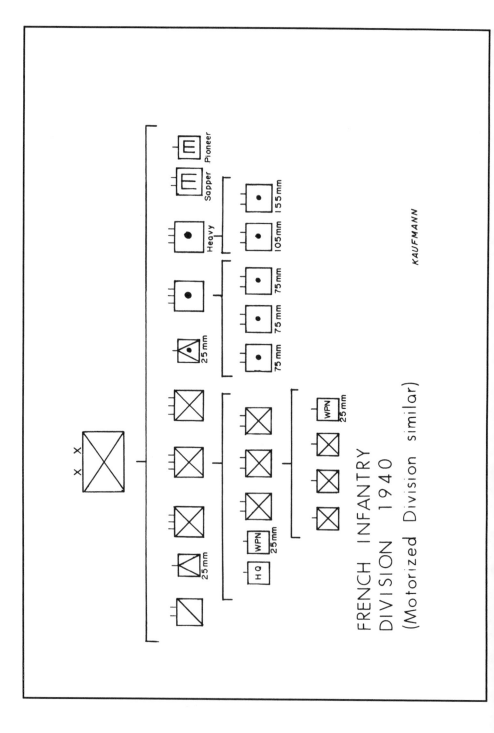

FRENCH INFANTRY
DIVISION 1940
(Motorized Division similar)

KAUFMANN

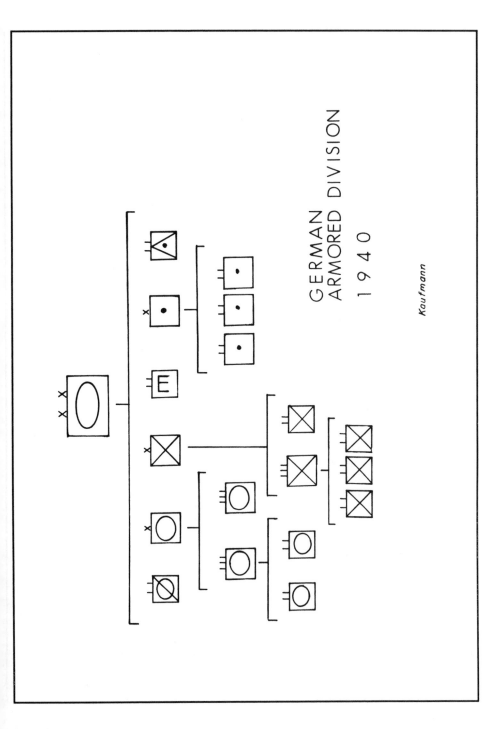

GERMAN
ARMORED DIVISION
1 9 4 0

Kaufmann

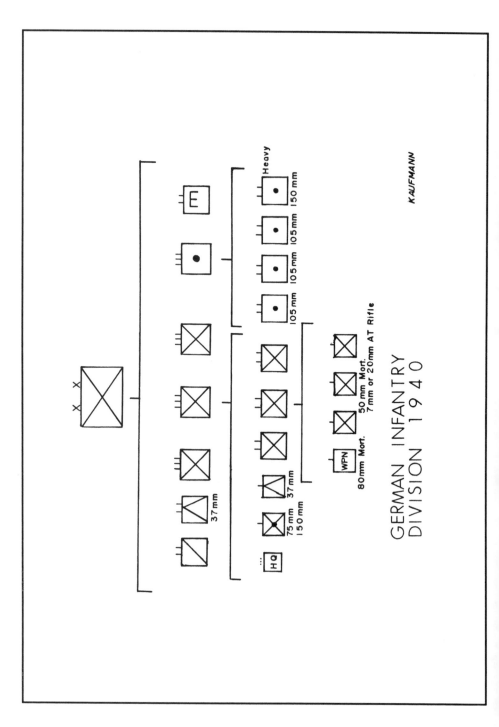

Bibliography

Newspapers:

Chicago Daily Tribune
Christian Science Monitor (Boston)
Daily Telegraph (London)
London Times
Los Angles Times
New York Times
San Antonio Express
Washington Post

Documents and Reports:

Denkschrift: uber die belgische, Landesbefestigung, German Army High Command, Berlin, 1941.

Denkschrift: uber die franzoische, Landebestigung, German Army High Command, Berlin, 1941.

Denkschrift: uber die niederlandesche, Landebefestigung, German Army High Command, Berlin, 1941.

Denkschrift: uber die tschecho=slowakische, Landesbestigung, German Army High Command, Berlin, 1941.

Grosses Orientergungsheft, German Army High Command, Berlin, 1936.

Grosses Orientergungsheft, German Army High Command, Berlin, 1937.

Military Attache Reports from Berlin and Paris for 1939 and 1940 (National Archives of the U.S.)

Numerous plans and diagrams from the French Army Engineers of Grenoble, Metz, Nice and Strasbourg.

Books:

Air Ministry (Great Britain), *The Rise and Fall of the German Air Force* (reprint), St. Martin's Press, New York, 1983.

Aron, Lubomir, *Ceskoslovenské Openvenëni 1935-1938*, Okresni Muzeum Náchod, Czechoslovakia, 1990. First significant account of Czech defenses since the German denkshrift of 1941.

*Ausems, Andre, "The Netherlands Military Intelligence Summaries 1939-1940 and the Defeat in the Blitzkrieg of May 1940, *Military Affairs*, Vol 50, No 4, October 1986. An interesting evaluation of the military situation during the Phony War.

Barber, Noel, *The Week France Fell*, Stein & Day, New York, 1976.

*Barker, A.J., *Dunkirk, The Great Escape*, David McKay Company, Inc., New York, 1977. A good account of the events which includes a number of first hand accounts.

Bauer, Eddy, *World War II Encyclopedia*, H.S. Stuttman, 1978.

*Bekker, Cajus, *The Luftwaffe War Diaries*, Ballantine Books, New York, 1964. Good account of German air activities and special operations.

——*The German Navy: 1939-1945*, The Dial Press, New York, 1974.

Bingham, James, *French Infantry Tanks: Part 1*, Profile Publications, Windsor, England, 1973.

——*French Infantry Tanks: Part 2*, Profile Publications, Windsor, England, 1973.

——*Chars Hotchkiss, H35,H39, and Somua S-35*, Profile Publications, Winsdor, England, 1971.

*Bond, Brian, *France and Belgium 1939-1940*, University of Delaware Press, Newark, 1975. Good description of political and military relations between the two countries during the Phony War.

Briggs, Susan, *The Home Front: War Years in Britain 1939-1945*, American Heritage Publishing Co., 1975.

Brongers, E.H., *Grebbe Linie 1940*, Holandia N.V., 1971.

*Bruge, Roger, *Faites Sauter la Ligne Maginot!*, Fayard, France, 1973.

*——*On a Livre la Ligne Maginot*, Fayard, France, 1973. Both are excellent accounts of operations against Maginot Line and positions in front of it (in French). Only a brief summary of campaign in Luxembourg and activites on Maginot Line used, but Bruge's books have more detail.

Bryant, Arthur, *The Turn of the Tide 1939-1943*, Collins, London, 1957.

*Buchner, Alex, *The German Infantry Handbook 1939-1945*, Schiffer Military History, West Chester (PA), 1991. Detailed breakdown on organization and functions of components of a German infantry division.

*Buffetaut, Yves, *De Gaulle chef de guerre: 15 Mai-6 Juin 40*, Hemidal, France, 1990. Well illustrated account.

Bullock, Alan, *Hitler, A Study in Tyranny*, Harper Torchbooks, New York, 1964.

*Burdick, Charles and Hans-Adolf Jacobsen, *Halder War Diary 1939-1942*, Presidio, Novato, 1988. Excellent account of daily activities as recorded by Army Chief of Staff. Reader should be well aquainted with events before using this book.

Butler, J.R.M., ed, *History of the Second World War: United Kingdom Military Services*, HMSO, London, 1953.

Campbell, John, *Naval Weapons of World War Two*, Conway, London, 1985.

Cannadine, David (ed), *Blood, Toil, Tears, and Sweat: The Speeches of Winston Churchill*, Houghton Mifflin Co., Boston, 1989.

Carver, Field Marshal Lord, *The Seven Ages of the British Army*, Beaufort Books Inc., New York, 1984.

*Castellano, Edoardo, *Distruggete lo Chaberton*, il capitello, Torino, 1984. Excellent description of one of Italy's most important Alpine forts (in Italian).

*Chamberlain, Peter and Ellis, Chris, *Tanks of the World 1915-45*, Galahad Books, Harrisburg, Pa, 1972. One of the best standard references.

——*British and American Tanks of World War II*, Arco Publishing Company, Inc., New York, 1975.

*Chant, Christoper, et.al. *Airborne Operations*, Crescent Books,New York, 1978. Good accounts of individual operations.

*Christienne, Charles and Pierre Lissarage, *A History of French Military Aviation*, Smithsonian Institution Press, Washington D.C., 1986. Probably the best, if not the only account in English of the *Armée de l'Air* in 1940.

*Churchill, Winston, S. *The Gathering Storm*, Houghton Mifflin Co.,Boston, 1949.

*Cima, Bernard and Raymond, *Ouvrage de Sainte-Agnés: Cote d'Azur* Auto-Edition, Menton, France, 1990. Well illustrated book on a major Maginot Alpine ouvarge.

——*Their Finest Hour*, Houghton Mifflin Co., Boston, 1949.

Although some of the material written by Churchill after the war may be questionable, the correspondence is valuable reference.

Claudel, Louis, *La Ligne Maginot: Conception-Realisation*, Association Saint Maurice la Recherche de Documents Sur la Fortresse, Switzerland, 1974.

*Collier, Richard, *The Sands of Dunkirk*, Dell Publishing Co., New York, 1962. One of the more interesting accounts of the evacuation.

Condon, Richard W., *The Winter War: Russia Against Finland*, Ballantine, New York, 1972.

Cooper, Bryan, *The Story of the Bomber 1914-1945*, Octopus Books, London, 1974.

Cooper, Matthew, *The German Army 1933-1945*, Bonanza Books, New York, 1984.

*Costello, John, *Ten Days to Destiny*, William Morrow and Co. Inc., New York, 1991. Excellent account of events of 1939 through 1941 based on newly released documents. Although the book covers the events of the 1940 Campaign on an almost day to day basis, the main emphasis is on attempts to negotiate a peace.

Cross, Robin, *The Bombers*, Macmillan Publishing Co., New York, 1987.

*Davies, W.J.K., *German Army Handbook*, Arco Publishing, New York, 1973. Good reference.

*Davis, Brian L., *The British Army in World War II*, Presido Press, Novato, 1990. A reprint of the U.S. Army manual put out during the war, this book is a major reference on the British Army.

Deighton, Len, *Blitzkrieg*, Alfred A. Knopf, New York, 1980.

——-*Battle of Britain*, Coward, McCann & Geogrhegan, London, 1980.

De La Gorce, Paul-Maries, *The French Army: A Military-Political History*, George Braziller, New York, 1963.

*Doumenc, A., *Dunkerque et la Campagne de Flandre*, Arthaud, Paris, 1947. This book is an important post war account of the campaign (in French).

Draper, Theodore, *The Six Weeks War: France May 10-June 25 1940* Viking Press, New York, 1944.

Edwards, Roger, *German Airborne Troops*, Doubleday, New York, 1974.

Eis, Egon, *The Forts of Folly*, Oswald Wolff Ltd., London, 1959.

*Ellis, L.F., *The War in France and Flanders*, HMSO, London, 1953.

This is the official history of the British part in the campaign and is an excellent reference with much detail on the operations.

Elstob, Peter, *Condor Legion*, Ballantine Books, New York, 1973.

Elting, John R., *Battles for Scandinavia*, Time-Life Inc., Alexandria, 1981.

Engelmann, Joachim, *German Railroad Guns in Action*, Squadron/Signal Publications, Warren, Michigan, 1976.

Farrar-Hockley, A.H., *Student*, Ballantine Books, New York, 1973.

Franks, Norman, *Aircraft vs. Aircraft*, Macmillan, New York, 1986.

*Gamelin, Maurice Gustave, *Servir*, Librairie Plon, Paris, 1946-7. Excellent book for French point of view through eyes of their commander.

Gamelin, Paul, *La Ligne Maginot: Hackenberg-Ouvrage A-19*, Maisonnevue Imprimeur, France, 1982.

*Gander, Terry and Chamberlain, Peter, *Weapons of the Third Reich*, Doubleday and Co., New York, 1978. Excellent reference.

*Garlinski, Jozef, *Poland in The Second World War*, Hippocrene Books, New York, 1985. One of the best books in English on Polish political and military activities during the war.

Gelb, Norman, *Dunkirk*, William Morrow and Company, Inc. New York, 1989.

*Gibbons, Tony, *Battleships*, Crescent, New York, 1982. Excellent reference.

*Gibson, Hugh (ed.), *The Ciano Diaries 1939-1943*, Doubleday & Company Inc, New York, 1946. Ciano's diary gives much insight on the attitude and plans of the Italians.

*Goralski, Robert, *World War II Almanac 1931-1945*, Putnam's Sons, New York, 1981. Although there are many books that cover the war and are claimed to be major references, this is probably the best and most complete although there are a few errors.

*Goutard, A., *The Battle of France 1940*, Washburn Inc., New York, 1959. Excellent reevaulation of the campaign, although many of the statistics may not be accurate (which is true with most books on the subject).

Gunston, Bill, *Fighting Aircraft of World War II*, ARCO, New York, 1988.

*Guderian, Heinz, *Achtung-Panzer!* translated by Christopher Duffy, Arms and Armor Press, London, 1992. First English translation of this important 1937 work of Guderian which cover development of armor tactics before 1937 and expounds his pre-war theories.

*Guderian, Heinz, *Panzer Leader*, Ballantine Books, New York, 1961. Excellent first hand account of operations.

*Gunsburg, Jeffery A., *Divided and Conquered*, Greenwood Press, Westport, Ct., 1979. Excellent book detailing all events just before the Allies were trapped at Dunkirk. Possibly the best single reference on the period covered.

*Hambro, C.J., *I Saw It Happen In Norway*, D. Appleton-Century Co., New York, 1941. Good first hand account by leader of government.

Hamilton, Nigel, *Monty: The Making of a General 1887-1942*, McGraw Hill, New York, 1981.

Harman, Nicholas, *Dunkirk: The Patriotic Myth*, Simon and Schuster, New York, 1980.

Haupt, Werner, *A History of the Panzer Troops: 1916-1945*, Schiffer Publishing, West Chester (Pa), 1990.

*Herzstein, Robert E., *The War That Hitler Won*, Putnam's Sons, New York, 1978. Good description of propaganda war.

*Hicks, James E., *French Military Weapons*, N. Flayderman and Co., New Milford, 1973. One of the few English references on the subject.

Hiegel, Henri, *Drôle de guerre*, Edition Pierròn, Paris.

Hoffmann, Peter, *Hitler's Personal Security*, The MIT Press, Cambridge, Mass., 1979.

Hogg, Ian V., *Fortress*, St. Martin's Press, New York, 1977.

Hogg, Ian V. and Brian L. Davis, *German Order of Battle 1944*, Hippocrene, New York, 1975.

Hohnadel, Alain and Michel Truttmann, *Guide de la Ligne Maginot*, Editions Heimdal, France, 1988.

Hohnadel, Alain and R. Varoqui, *Le Fort De Hackenberg*, AMIFORT, France, 1986.

*Horne, Alistair, *To Lose a Battle: France 1940*, Little, Brown, and Co., Boston, 1969. The book covers the political and military events leading to the campaign and has become a classic on the subject. It is the best single source in English on the campaign.

——*The Price of Glory: Verdun 1916*, Little, Brown and Co., Boston, 1969. The section on Forts Douamount and Vaux helps one understand their relationship, as well as the French attitude, toward the construction of the *Maginot Line*.

Hughes, Judith M., *To the Maginot Line*, Harvard U. Press, Cambridge, 1981.

*Ironside, Sir Edmund, *Time Unguarded, The Ironside Diaries 1937-1940*, Greenwood Press, Westport, 1974. Good first hand account from leader of the British Army.

Jacobsen, Hans-Adolf, *Dokumente zum Westfeldzug*, Musterschmidt-Verlag, Berlin, 1960. Excellent source material on 1940 campaign.

*Johnson, Brian, *The Secret War*, Methuen Inc., New York, 1978. This book covers some of the more interesting aspects of the war including the development of radar.

*Johnson, Douglas W., *Topography and Strategy in the War*, Henry Holt and Company, New York, 1917. Excellent description of influences of military geography relating to World War I and still applicable to the next war.

*Karslake, Basil, *1940 The Last Act*, Archon Books, 1979, London. Excellent description of activities of British forces in France after Dunkirk. The best book on the subject.

Kaufmann, J.E., "Unusual Aspects of A Unique Fortification: The Maginot Line", *Military Affairs*, Vol 52, No 2, April 1988.

_____"The Dutch and Belgian Defences in 1940", *Fort*, Vol 17, 1989.

Kaufmann, J.E. and H.W., *The Fortifications of Western Europe: 1940*, privately published, San Antonio, 1984.

Keegan, John (ed), *Churchill's Generals*, Grove Weidenfeld, New York, 1991.

_____*The Second World War*, Viking, New York, 1989.

*Kennedy, Robert M. *The German Campaign in Poland (1939)*, Department of the Army, Washington DC, 1956. Good account of Polish campaign and German army.

Kesselring, Albert, *The Memoirs of Field-Marshal Kesselring*, Presidio, Novato, 1989.

**La Battaglia Delle Alpi Occidentali: Giugno 1940*, Ministero Della Difesa, Roma, 1947. Excellent description of the Battle for the Alps from Italian point of view. (in Italian)

La Ligne Maginot en Basse Alsace, Association des Amis de la Ligne Maginot d'Alsace, France, 1981.

Leach, Barry, *German General Staff*, Ballantine Books, New York, 1973.

Le Comite de l'Amicale, ed., *Ceux du Fort d'Eben-Emael*, Centre Liegeois de'Histoire et d'Archeologie Militares, Liege, 1981. One of the best descriptions of the fort and accounts of the action (in French).

Le Catalogue du Musee des Blindes, Centre de Documentations sur les Engins Blindes, Saumur, France.

*Liddell Hart, Basil, *The Defence of Britain*, Faber and Faber Ltd., London, 1939. Excellent book for pre-war estimate of the situation.

——*The German Generals Talk*, William Morrow Company, New York, 1948.

*——*The Rommel Papers*, Da Capo, New York, 1953. Excellent first hand account.

Loewenheim, Francis L., Harold D. Langley and Manfred Jonas (editors), *Roosevelt and Churchill: Their Secret Wartime Correspondence*, Da Capo Press, New York, 1990.

*Lyet, Pierre Commandant, *La Bataille De France (Mai-Juin 1940)*, Payot, Paris, 1947. A significant post-war account of the campaign (in French)

Liege 1000 Ans de Fortifications Militaires, Centre Liegeois d'Histoire et d'Archeologie Militaires, Liege, 1981.

Linklater, Eric, *The Highland Division*, HMSO, London, 1942.

Lucas, James, *Kommando: German Special Forces of World War II*, St. Martin's Press, New York, 1985.

——*Das Reich: The Military Role of the 2nd SS Division*, Arms and Armour Press, London, 1991. Good description of activites of the 2nd SS Division although Lucas intentionally neglects some of the more brutal aspects of this SS unit and attempts to put these men on a par with other elite units.

Luck, Hans von, *Panzer Commander: The Memoirs of Colonel Hans von Luck*, Praeger, New York, 1989.

Macksey, Kenneth, *Tank Force: Allied Armor in World War II*, Ballantine Books, New York, 1970.

——*Tank: Facts and Feats*, Two Continents Publishing Group, New York, 1970.

——*Tank vs. Tank*, Salem House Publishers, Topsfield, 1988.

Macksey, Kenneth and John Batchelor, *Tank*, Charles Scribner's Sons, New York, 1970.

*Madej, Victor W., *Italian Army Handbook, 1940-1943*, Game Publishing Co, Allentown, 1984. Summary of primary U.S. government source.

*Madej, Victor W., *Italian Army Order of Battle 1939-1943*, Game

Marketing Co., Allentown, 1981. Taken from U.S. Army sources, this is one of the only books on the subject available and thus a significant reference.

*Maistret, Georges, *Le Gros Ouvrage A-2 Fermont de la Ligne Maginot*, Association des Amis de l'Ouvrage de Fermont et de la Ligne Maginot, France, 1979. A detailed account of the fort and its history (in French).

Mallory, Keith and Ottar, Arvid, *The Architecture of War*, Pantheon Books, New York, 1973.

Manstein, Erich von, *Lost Victories*, Presidio Press, Novato, Calif., 1982.

Marshall,Cornwall, James, "Defending Great Britain", *War Monthly*, Vol 7, Number 68, September 1979.

*Mary, Y.V., *La Ligne Maginot*, Sercap, Italy, 1980. Details and sketches of all the forts.

May, Ernest R., *Knowing One's Enemies*, Princeton U. Press, 1986.

*Mayer, S.L. ed., *Signal: Years of Triumph 1940-42*, Prentice-Hall, Englewood Cliffs, 1978. The book contains a collection of pages from various issues of *Signal* but fails to point out which issue they come from making it difficult to use as a reference. Some individual copies of *Signal* are available at the U.S. Archives.

*MCNair, Ronald, *Mai-Juin 1940 Les blindés francais*, Hemidal, France, 1990. Excellent descrpition of French armor and units and well illustrated.

Memorial of the Maginot Line, Marckolsheim (Bas-Rhin), SEAP Colmar-Ingersheim, France, 1973.

*Murray, Williamson, *Strategy For Defeat, The Luftwaffe 1933-1945*, Chartwell Books, Secaucus, 1986. Good statistical reference.

*Middlebrook, Martin and Chris Everitt, *The Bomber Command War Diaries*, Penguin, London, 1990. Important reference which lists all bomber missions and aircraft dispatched.

Nazi Europe, Marshall Cavendish Books Ltd., London, 1984. Excellent collection of articles describing all events from 1939 to late 1940. This is the best single book on the period and covers activities in all parts of the world.

Mellenthin, F.W., *Panzer Battles*, U. of Oklahoma Press, Norman, 1964.

Mearsheimer, John J., *Liddell Hart and the Weight of History*, Cornell University Press, Ithaca, 1988.

*Ministry of the Army, Historical Service, *Les armées francaises dans* *la 2éme guerre mondiale campagne 1939-1940: atlas des situations quotidiennes des armées Alliées*, Impression Nationale, Paris, 1964. Most important reference to detail information on location of French Army units in 1940.

*Ministry of the Army, Historical Service, *Les Grandes Francaises*, Imprimerie Nationale, Paris, 1967. French military reference on all major French military formations during World War II.

*Mitcham, Samuel W. Jr., *Hitler's Legions: The German Order of Battle, World War II*, Stein and Day, New York, 1985. The best book in English for basic identifcation of major German formations.

*Mollo, Andrew, *The Armed Forces of World War II*, Crown Publishers, New York, 1981. Excellent description of not just uniforms, but also some of the military formations.

Montgomery, Bernard L., *The Memoirs of Field Marshal Montgomery*, Da Capo, New York, 1958.

*Mrazek, James E., *The Fall of Eben Emael*, Presidio, Novato, 1991. Good account of capture of the fort and background.

*Mueller-Hillebrand, Burkhart, *Das Heer 1933-1945*, Mittler, Darmstadt, Vol 1-3, 1954-6. This is one of the best descriptions given of the German Army (in German).

*Nicolson, Nigel, ed., *Harold Nicolson, The War Years 1939-1945*, Atheneum, New York, 1967. Good first hand account of a politican's view of the events.

Nofi, Albert A., "The Fall of France", *Strategy and Tactics Magazine*, Simulations Publications, New York, 1971.

Nowarra, Heinz, *Heinkel He 111: A Documentary History*, Jane's Publishing Inc, New York, 1979.

*Packard, Jerrold M, *Neither Friend Nor Foe*, Charles Scribner's Sons, New York, 1992.

*Parkinson, Roger, *Peace For Our Time*, McKay Company, New York, 1972. Excellent description of events from material not available until 25 years after war.

*Perrett, Bryan, *Knights of the Black Cross*, St. Martin's Press,New York, 1986. Good account of development of German armor before and during the war.

*Piekalkiewicz, Janusz, *The Cavalry of World War II*, Stein & Day, New York,1980. Good coverage of a little known topic.

*Plan, E., General and Lefevre, Eric, *La Bataille Des Alpes 10-25 Juin 1940*, Charles-Lavauzelle, Paris, 1982. Excellent description of Battle of Alps from French point of view. (in French)

Porten, Edward P. van der, *The German Navy in World War II*, Thomas Crowell Company, New York, 1969.

Preston, Antony, *Navies of World War II*, Bison Books Ltd, London, 1976.

*Reiss, Günther, "Die Entwicklung der Schweizerischen Landesbefestigung zwischen 1840 und 1940", *Deutschen Gesellschaft Fuer Festungsforschung*, vol 7: Wesel 1988. Good description of the Swiss fortifications (in German).

Rhodes, Anthony, *Propaganda, The Art of Persuasion: World War II*, Chelsea House Publishers, New York, 1976.

*Rodolpne, R., *Combats dans la Ligne Maginot*, Klaufeldas SA, Switzerland, 1975. Good account of the subject.

Rothbrust, Florian K., *Guderian's XIXth Panzer Corps and the Battle of France*, Praegar, New York.

*Roton, G., *Années Cruciales: La Course Aux Armements 1933-1939: La Campagne 1939-1940*, Charles-Lavauzelle & Co, Paris, 1947. A significant post-war account of the campaign (in French).

*Rowe, Vivian, *The Great Wall of France*, Putman's Sons, New York, 1961. The first book in English on the *Maginot Line*.

Rumpf, Hans, *The Bombing of Germany*, Holt, Reinhardt, & Winston, New York, 1962.

Salmond, J.B., *The History of the 51st Highland Division*, William Blackwood and Sons Ltd., London, 1953.

Sawodny, Wolfgang, *German Armored Trains in World War II*, Schiffer Publishing, West Chester (Penn.), 1989.

Shachtman, Tom, *The Phony War 1939-1940*, Harper and Row, Cambridge, 1981.

*Schulman, Milton, *Defeat in the West*, Ballantine Books, New York, 1967. This book presents some interesting information obtained by Schulman when he interviewed prisoners during the war.

*Schwartz, Urs, *The Eye of the Hurricane*, Westview Press, Colorado, 1980. Good description of the strategic role of Switzerland in relation to the belligerents of 1939-1940.

Senger und Etterlin, F.M. von, *German Tanks of World War II* Galahad Books, New York, 1969.

*Showell, Jak P. Mallman, *Fuehrer Conferences on Naval Affairs 1939-1945*, Naval Institute Press, Annapolis, 1990. Important reference in relation to naval planning and operations.

*Shirer, William L., *Berlin Diary, The Journal of a Foreign*

Correspondent 1934-1941, Alfred A. Knopf, New York, 1941. Excellent first hand account of events taking place from German side of the front, but still a pro-Allied account.

*———*The Collapse of the Third Republic*, Simon and Schuster, New York, 1969. Excellent account of the rather confused political situation in France.

*Steenbeek, Wilheminia, *Rotterdam: Invasion of Holland*, Ballantine Books, New York, 1973. Good description of events in Netherlands.

*Stichting Kornwerderzand, *Kornwerderzand*, Amsterdam, 1986. The only work available on the history of the fort (in Dutch).

*Sydnor, Charles W. Jr., *Soldiers of Destruction: The SS Death's Head Division, 1933-1945*, Princeton University Press, Princeton, 1977. Excellent description of creation and operations of Totenkopf Division and how its soldiers were distinctly different and more brutal than other SS troops.

*Tarnstrom, Ronald L., *Germany: The Wehrmacht Strikes 1940-1942*, Trogen Books, Lindsborg (Kansas), 1989.

———*Poland and the Baltic Republics*, Trogen Books, Lindsborg, 1990. Both books provide hard to find orders of battle for German and Polish forces as well as details on weapons used. Excellent references.

*Taylor, James and Warren Shaw, *The Third Reich Almanac*, World Almanac, New York, 1987. Excellent quick reference.

*Taylor, John W.R., *Combat Aircraft of the World*, Putnam's Sons, New York, 1969. Excellent reference.

*Taylor, Telford, *The March of Conquest*, Simon & Schuster, New York, 1958. Classic account of the campaign with emphasis on German point of view.

*———*Munich: The Price of Peace*, Doubleday & Company, New York, 1979. Excellent and very detailed account of the events surrounding Munich.

The Small Fortification of Immerhof, Township of Hettange Grande, France, 1979.

Thomas, Hugh, *The Spanish Civil War*, Harper & Row Inc., New York, 1963. Includes details on operations of Condor Legion.

Thompson, Laurence, *1940*, Fontana Books, London, 1968.

*Trevor-Roper, H.R. (ed), *Blitzkrieg to Defeat*, Holt, Reinhardt, and Winston, New York, 1964. Compilation of Hitler's Directives. A key reference.

Bibliography

Truttmann, Michel, *Le Fort de Guentrange*, Imprimerie Henz, France, 1977.

*Truttmann, LTC Philippe, *La Fortification Francaise de 1940*. University of Metz: Doctorial Thesis, 1979. (published in book form in 1984) The best single work on the French fortifications by the leading authority (in French).

Turnbull, Patrick, *Dunkirk, Anatomy of Disaster*, Holmes and Meier Publishers, New York, 1978.

Warlimont, Walter, *Inside Hitler's Headquarters 1939-45*, Presidio, Novato, 1964.

Watt, Donald Cameron, *How War Came*, Pantheon Books, New York, 1989.

Weal, Elke E., Weal, John A., and Barker, Richard F., *Combat Aircraft of World War Two*, Bracken Books, London, 1977.

*Wetter, Ernst, *Duell der Flieger und Diplomaten*, Frauenfeld, 1987. An excellent account of the undeclared air war between the Swiss and the Germans during World War II.

White, B.T., *Tanks and Other Armored Fighting Vehicles of World War II*, Peerage Books, London, 1975.

Weisbecker, A., *Ouvrage du Four á Chaux*, Syndicat d' Initiative de Lembach, France, 1985.

*Wieringen, J.S. Van, "The Grebbe Line: a long defence line with a long history", *Fort*, Volume 19, 1991. Probably the best article in English available on the Grebbe Line and Dutch strategy in 1939-1940.

*Williams, John, *France: Summer 1940*, Ballantine Books, New York, 1970. Good account of the campaign.

Wills, Henry, *Pillboxes: A Study of U.K. Defences 1940*, Leo Cooper, London, 1985.

World Almanac and Book of Facts 1929 (also the years 1930-39), American Heritage Press, New York. Excellent reference.

Zaloga, Steven J., *Blitzkrieg, Armour Camouflage and Markings, 1939-1940*, Arms & Armour Press, London, 1980.

——*The Polish Army 1939-45*, Osprey Publishing Ltd, London, 1982.

*Zaloga, Steven J, and Victor Madej, *The Polish Campaign 1939*, Hippocrene Books Inc., New York, 1985. Excellent English account of the campaign.

*Ziemke, Earl F., *The German Northern Theater of*

Operations,1940-1945, Dept. of Army Pamphlet No. 20-271, 1959. Good account of opertions in Norway.

*Zorach, Jonathan, "Czechoslovakia's Fortifications", *Militärgeschichtliche Mitteilungen*, January 1976. One of the few works on the subject.

*Indicates recommended books covering various aspects of the 1939-1940 campaigns and are of special interest.

Index